# SOMALI FOREIGN POLICY
## 1969-1990

# SOMALI FOREIGN POLICY
## 1969-1990

*An Analysis of Thirty Years of Diplomatic History*

**IBRAHIM FARAH**

2024

**LOOH PRESS LTD.**
Copyright © Ibrahim Farah 2024
Second Edition, First Print March 2024

All rights reserved.
No part of this publication may be reproduced, stored in any retrieval system, or transmitted in any form or by any means, including photocopying, recording, or other electronic or mechanical methods, without the prior written permission of the publisher, except in the case of brief quotations embodied in critical reviews and certain other non-commercial uses permitted by copyright law.

For permission and requests, write to the publisher or the author, at the address below.

**PRINTED & DISTRIBUTED BY**
Looh Press Ltd.
56 Lethbridge Close
Leicester, LE1 2EB
England. UK
www.LoohPress.com
LoohPress@gmail.com

A catalogue record for this book is available from the British Library.
British Library Cataloguing-in-Publication Data

**COVER DESIGN & TYPESET**
Kusmin (Looh Press)

**ISBN**
978-1-912411-06-1    (Paperback)

**Dedication**

In memory of the late Abdulkadir Yahya,
a man who for over five (5) years taught me all about the Somali Republic, Somali cultural values and, through hands-on mentorship, the importance of Somali history, politics and society.
To my family and to the Somali people in the Horn of Africa region and beyond ...with the hope that they will one day enjoy the benefit of peaceful, constructive, and cooperative foreign policies.

# Acknowledgements

First of all, I thank Allah (SWT) for everything! This work would have not been completed without the guidance and assistance of Prof. Makumi Mwagiru and the late Prof. J. D. Olewe Nyunya whose timely support and academic guidance and attention to detail helped me to develop the best of my potential as a scholar of international studies, particularly foreign policy and conflict; I salute them and thank them so much. In particular, I owe the greatest intellectual debt for this book, and other similar works, to Prof. Makumi Mwagiru.

I am also very grateful to the German Academic Exchange Service (DAAD), representing the German establishment, for the scholarship opportunities both for my Master's and Ph.D. degrees. In particular, I am deeply indebted to Ms. Katarina Burr. Also, Dr. Mustafa Hassouna, Dr. Cirino Hiteng, Dr. Nyinguro have all contributed to this work in one way or the other.

A number of Somali diplomats deserve my thanks more than anybody else: Ambassador Hussein Ali Duale, the late Abdulkadir Yahya and Mohammed Haji. Similarly, special thanks go to Jibril Warsame, Abdulfatah Nero, Ken Menkhaus, Pat Johnson, and Miles Henderson for their support, insights and discussions on Somalia, the region and beyond; especially more on the global political context within which we had to locate Somalia. Special thanks go to Dr. Baadiyow, Prof. Mohamed Eno and Ali Hersi for their constructive review and comments; especially Prof. Eno's policy-oriented academic debate and discourse. Also, a million thanks to MM Dirir (and Dansom Consultancy) for all his support. With humility, I also thank my students from the University of Nairobi and from SIMAD University; especially those who underwent the unit: Foreign Policy Analysis (FPA), for being the testing ground for my policy-oriented, academic discussions. I assure them all -- and others in this field -- that this will, however, go a long way.

And, most important of all, my family, and the many others who are very central to my life: Delta, Ramla, Shukriya, Aisha, Bahja, Mohammed-Amin, Adnan, Yahya, Sadiya, Ishraaq, Faduma-Ilwad, Ahmed-nur, Ikram, Ilyaas and Safiya have all contributed to the successful completion of this work. In addition to their unwavering support, my family was indeed an inspiration and my greatest source of motivation. I thank them for everything. Special thanks also go to Xalwo and Delta for everything since the late 1980s!

## Preface

Somalia is one of the most homogenous countries in Africa, yet it is the only one that has been without a functional government for over twenty one (21) years. The causes of the Somali civil war which broke out in early 1991 are also wide and varied. These range from the country's colonial legacy, Somali nationalism, clan politics, and Cold War politics and rivalry, to structural conflict. Over the first 30 years after independence, the country experienced effective central governance and functional administrations despite regional tensions. Since the war broke out, there have been numerous peace and reconciliation attempts, both official and non-official. However, the country is yet to enjoy peace or a return to normalcy and an opportunity to reclaim its place in the international community of nations. It is only from the year 2012 that the country held its first, post-war 'indirect elections' on Somali soil.

The Somali conflict is also one of the protracted conflicts in the Horn of Africa that has had severe consequences, not only for the country itself but also for the stability and development of the entire region. Makinda observes that since the 1960s, the Horn of Africa has been a microcosm of the tensions that beset the world.[1] As a result of the Cold War, "domestic, regional and global forces have impinged on the Horn's international politics"[2] and Somalia was no exception, especially since the conflict has to do with the structure of the country's past; and even more so with its 1960 – 1990 conflict-oriented foreign policy in the still turbulent Horn of Africa region.

Moreover, the Somali conflict can be traced back to pre-civil war Somali foreign policy (and that of other countries in the region and other major players) both at the regional and international levels.[3] For example, all past Somali governments' pan-Somalism tendency and the whole idea of "Greater Somalia" was not received well in the Horn of Africa region and beyond, for various reasons.[4]

---

[1] S. M. Makinda, *Superpower Diplomacy in the Horn of Africa* (London & Sydney: Croom Helm, 1987), p.1.
[2] Ibid.
[3] More of this shall be dealt with in detail in Chapter Four and Five.
[4] Interview with Ambassador Abdullahi Ahmed Addou, former Somali ambassador to the United States, Nairobi, August 7, 2004.

The fact that issues like foreign policy behaviour have generally been given less systematic attention -- than other factors often cited as underlying causes of conflict in the region and particularly in Somalia -- calls for such a policy-oriented academic research and therefore justifies the contribution of this book both on academic and policy grounds. A study on Somali foreign policy and conflict poses a unique academic and policy opportunity not only for the future of Somalia but also for the long term stability and development of the Horn of Africa region. This book academically contributes to research on the causes of war in the Horn of Africa by focusing on conflicts involving one country, Somalia, by exploring the role of one potential driver of conflict. It therefore delves into the foreign policies of both Somalia and key external actors; making it an essential reference for Somali scholarship, policy-makers in Somalia, the region and beyond.

This book provides an overview of pre-1991 Somali foreign policy and conflict; mainly during the 1960 – 1990 period. It examines the extent to which the foreign policies of Somalia, regional states and other key external actors were a contributory factor to armed conflict in Somalia. By doing this, the book explores the theoretical linkages between foreign policy and conflict as it examines the role of foreign policy as a potential driver of conflict in Somalia and in the Horn of Africa. It answers the question of the extent to which the international and internal conflicts involving Somalia from 1960 to 1990 are a function of foreign policy choices, behaviour, and orientation on the part of Somalia, regional states, and major powers.

The theoretical framework is derived from the works of Graham Allison, which provide a deeper insight into pre-1991 Somali foreign policy and conflict. The analysis of Allison's framework suggests three different and complementary ways of understanding decision-making in times of crisis: a 'rational actor' model, an 'organisational process' model, and a 'bureaucratic politics' model. The book relies on both primary and secondary sources of data wherein the primary data was collected through unstructured interviews.

This book argues that Somali foreign policy, and the foreign policy of regional states and other key external actors, during the period under study, promoted armed conflict in Somalia either inadvertently or by design. The book contends that while Somali foreign policy was a manifestation of its orientation towards a 'Greater Somalia,' other external factors like colonial legacy, Somali nationalism, Cold War politics and rivalry also contributed to the escalation of armed conflict. The book also finds that Somali irredentism had a selective impact, producing both warfare and subsequent skirmishes with Ethiopia but relatively stable relations with Kenya and Djibouti.

In terms of originality, the idea for this book project derives from providing a deeper understanding of insights into the Somali conflict from a foreign policy perspective both in Somalia and in the Horn of Africa regional context. This book project was motivated by the works of Korwa Adar whose thesis discussed Kenya's foreign policy behaviour towards Somalia, 1963 - 1983.[5] The fact that Somalia was the epicentre of the foreign policy crisis in the Horn of Africa, the resultant regional tension between Somalia and its neighbours, has created a need to study the problem further and broaden the focus by including other external actors: mainly other neighbouring countries like Ethiopia and Djibouti. This book, therefore, extends the focus and brings in issues of foreign policy and conflict in Somalia during the early years of the country's independence and the period of the Cold War. In addition to broadening the focus, it also provides a detailed analysis of thirty years of diplomatic history; and from a Somali, regional, and global perspective.

In a nutshell, this PhD thesis-tuned book "*Somali Foreign Policy, 1960 – 1990: An Analysis of Thirty Years of Diplomatic History*" is concerned with applying theories of state behaviour to Somali foreign policy during the years between independence in 1960 and state collapse in early 1991. It addresses an important issue in Somali history, and at the outset indicates the aspiration of connecting this issue to the dynamics of the civil war and the conflicts that have followed state collapse. This is an important topic, made more so by the growing interest in inter-state conflicts in Africa and the ways in which armed conflicts on the continent arise from a combination of internal and external factors. It is also potentially an important contribution to the neglected topic of African diplomatic history.

As the author points out, Somalia is chiefly a topic of interest among scholars and policymakers because it is the most protracted case of state collapse in the modern world. Prior to that, it had a fascinating foreign policy history, as the sole state to oppose the OAU Charter in 1963, as a bold state in the most ambitious territorial war in post-colonial Africa, as

---

[5] See K. G. Adar, *Kenya's Foreign Policy Behaviour towards Somalia, 1963 – 1983* (Lanham, New York and London: University Press of America, 1994).

the instigator of a dramatic volte face by the superpowers that caused the collapse of détente (the greatest African-caused global crisis between the U.S. and USSR of the Cold War era), and as a state that managed simultaneously to receive military and financial assistance from the most diverse array of sponsors in the 1980s. A book that brought these issues into focus and connected them to the subsequent regional and international politics of the Horn of Africa wouldn't be more timely and more revealing than this volume.

# Foreword

For a little while, during the first fifteen years or so of the turn of this century, a group of new scholars entered the Institute of Diplomacy and International Studies at the University of Nairobi. They undertook postgraduate studies, beginning with the MA in International Studies, followed by PhDs in the same theme from the Institute. Dr. Ibrahim Farah was one of the pioneers of this group. They took the study of conflict and diplomacy to new levels. Prof. Robert Mudida's constitutional conflicts and their negotiation in Kenya, Dr. Farah's foreign policy and conflict in Somalia, Dr. Ochieng Kamudhayi's study of the Somalia National Reconciliation Process, Dr. Anita Kiamba's study of negotiation leaders in the IGAD region, and Dr. Rosemary Anyona's conflict and mediation in Mozambique and Angola opened up new insights into the processes of regional conflict and diplomacy. They also lent a new impetus of the detailed study of the strategic perspectives of foreign policy, conflict and diplomacy in the region, and from Dr. Farah's perspective, a little beyond. That was a golden age of new scholarship. The publication of their respective doctoral theses has also contributed immeasurably to the study of conflict and diplomacy in the region.

The theme emerging from Dr. Ibrahim Farah's outstanding *"Somali Foreign Policy, 1960 – 1990: An Analysis of Thirty Years of Diplomatic History"* is that in the Horn of Africa, in the period he studied, the foreign policy – of Somalia and other Horn of Africa regional states - was often the cause of conflict. This is not a startling revelation. Given that diplomacy is one of the sources of national power of states, it has always been the case. Indeed, it is agreed that diplomacy creates wars: and also, its processes bring them to an end. The importance of Dr. Farah's assertion however is that: it calls for an altogether new study of Somalia's foreign policy, the foreign policies of states in the region, and a re-examination of the institutions for conflict management like the IGAD. Dr. Farah's hedging that the foreign policies of other regional states – by accident or design - promote armed conflict does not hide the intellectual depth of the assertion.

Dr. Farah focuses his theme on the thirty-year period of state stability in Somalia from its independence to the unseating of Siyad Barre. This allows him to project the theme of the book that foreign policies in the region can promote and have promoted armed conflict. It also allows him to locate the three major conflicts that the stable Somalia engaged in on the foreign policies of the comparatively stable Somalia state until 1991. It also makes it possible to examine the interplay of foreign policies of regional states in comparative stability, and their effect on the foreign and conflict relations of the region.

But there is yet another important basis for this: that the "reformation" of IGAD (from IGADD to IGAD) in 1996 was prompted *inter alia* by the instability of post-Barre Somalia, and in turn the engagement of other regional countries foreign policies in addressing the problem of instability in the IGAD region and especially in Somalia. This is responsible for the tendency of "presuming [foreign policy] to be a force for conflict management and resolution…and ignoring that foreign policy orientation can as well promote…armed conflict." The question – that is understandably beyond the remit of the book – is then what shall happen to IGAD when Somalia returns to relative state stability.

The theme of foreign policy orientation and its relationship with regional conflict is much easier to appreciate when seen in the larger cold war context. The theme of those relations being based on relative state stability is also easy to appreciate. But the enduring problem in the Horn of Africa and its conflict relations has since 1991 been pegged on the failure of the state of Somalia. The failed Somalia state, and its neighbours, have not predisposed themselves to avoid using some form of foreign policy orientation, to act in ways that might generate region-wide conflict. That is the context of Ethiopia's incursion into Somalia, and Kenya's later one in 2011. It is also at the heart of the trend that the maritime conflict between Somalia and Kenya is taking.

So, there is clearly an important research agenda that Dr. Farah's book generates – by accident or design: whether the same framework of the role of foreign policy of states in conflict generation does not also apply to the foreign policy of unstable states. And in the Horn of Africa that provides room for more serious contemplation about the other Somalia-like states like South Sudan and Eritrea, and their effect on shaping the larger foreign policies of the Horn of Africa region.

The book *"Somali Foreign Policy, 1960 – 1990: An Analysis of Thirty Years of Diplomatic History"* is a useful contextual contribution to the analysis of the relationship between foreign policy and conflict in the Horn of Africa region. It frames the framework of that relationship lucidly. But it also creates a yearning for its logical development in the different state context – especially of Somalia – that has happened since 1991. And ultimately, the book provides the intellectual bedrock for a re-examination of foreign policy and conflict in the wider Horn of Africa region – aka the Greater Horn of Africa region. That is the greatest service that this timely and exciting book has performed.

**Prof. Makumi Mwagiru**
Three Legs Consortium, Nairobi &
Adjunct Professor of Diplomacy (Strathmore University-Nairobi)

# Table of Contents

*Dedication*..................................................................................vii
*Acknowledgment* ........................................................................ix
*Preface*........................................................................................xi
*Forward*.....................................................................................xv
*List of Acronyms*.......................................................................xiv

1 An Introductory Overview............................................17
2 Foreign Policy and Conflict: Somalia & the Region...............43
3 Conflict in Somalia: The History....................................69
4 Somali Foreign Policy, 1960 – 1969................................91
5 Somali Foreign Policy, 1969 – 1990................................123
6 Somali Foreign Policy: Emerging Issues........................153
7 Conclusions................................................................. 179

*Bibliography*............................................................................187

# List of Acronyms

| | |
|---|---|
| AU | African Union |
| DAAD | German Academic Exchange Service |
| EAC | East African Community |
| EAF | Ethiopian Air Force |
| EC | European Commission |
| EU | European Union |
| ELF | Eritrean Liberation Front |
| FLCS | *Front de Libération de la Conte des Somalis* |
| HDM | Hisbia Digil Mirifle |
| ICG | International Crisis Group |
| IGAD | Inter-Governmental Authority on Development |
| IGADD | Inter-Governmental Authority on Drought and Development |
| KADU | Kenya African Democratic Union |
| KANU | Kenya African National Union |
| NAM | Non-Aligned Movement |
| NFD | Northern Frontier District |
| NFDLF | NFD Liberation Front |
| NIEO | New International Economic Order |
| NRC | National Refugee Council |
| NSS | National Security Service |
| OAU | Organisation of African Unity |
| RDF | Rapid Deployment Force |
| SAF | Somali Air Force |
| SDA | Somali Democratic Action |
| SDM | Somali Democratic Movement |
| SDR | Somali Democratic Republic |
| SNA | Somali National Alliance |
| SNC | Somali National Congress |
| SNL | Somali National League |
| SNM | Somali National Movement |
| SNRC | Somali National Reconciliation Conference |
| SPM | Somali Patriotic Movement |
| SRSP | Somali Revolutionary Socialist Party |
| SSDF | Somali Salvation Democratic Front |
| SSF | Somali Salvation Front |

| | |
|---|---|
| SRRC | Somali Reconciliation and Restoration Council |
| SYC | Somali Youth Club |
| SYL | Somali Youth League |
| TNA | Transitional National Assembly |
| TFG | Transitional Federal Government |
| TNG | Transitional National Government |
| TFIs | Transitional Federal Institutions |
| TFP | Transitional Federal Parliament |
| UN | United Nations |
| UNDP | United Nations Development Programme |
| UNHCR | United Nations High Commissioner for Refugees |
| UNITAF | Unified Task Force |
| UNPOS | UN Political Office for Somalia |
| USA | United States of America |
| USAID | US Agency for International Development |
| USC | United Somali Congress |
| USMAAG | US Military Assistance Advisory Group |
| USSR | Union of Soviet Socialist Republics |
| WSLF | Western Somali Liberation Front |
| WSLG | Western Somali Liberation Group |

# CHAPTER ONE

## An Introductory Overview

### Introduction

The colonial partition of Africa divided the greater Somali community into five countries: French Somaliland (now Djibouti), British Somaliland (now the secessionist "Republic of Somaliland"), the Northern Frontier District (NFD) which was part of British colony of Kenya (currently the Northeastern province of Kenya), Italian Somaliland (southern Somalia), and the *Ogaden* (Somali territories annexed by Ethiopia, currently named 'Somali state of Ethiopia').[6] Upon independence in 1960, the French, Ethiopian and Kenyan-British Somali populations remained outside the new state, which was created by the union of Italian and British Somali colonies [UN Trust Territories under Italian and British Protectorate]: code-named the Somali Republic.[7] This colonial legacy of division of the Somali people gave rise to a central pillar of Somali foreign policy, its reclamation of Somali-inhabited portions in what are now Ethiopia and Kenya; and the whole of Djibouti. This pan-Somali, or Greater Somalia policy, helped, among other things, to give rise to the Somali-Kenyan insurgency in north-eastern Kenya known as the *Shifta*[8] wars in the mid -1960s.

Somalia's first decade of independence was characterized by a vibrant but increasingly dysfunctional and corrupt multi-party democracy.[9] Between 1960 and 1969, for example, the country underwent two civilian administrations led first, from 1960 to 1967, by President Adan Abdulle Osman "Aden Adde," and then, between 1967 and 1969, by President

---

[6] Jos van Buerden, "Somalia in a State of Permanent Conflict" in Mekenkamp, M. et al, *Searching Peace in Africa: An Overview of Conflict Prevention and Management Activities* (Utrecht: European Platform for Conflict Prevention, 1999), p.157.

[7] Ibid.

[8] Although the use of the term '*Shifta*' in Somali is itself derogatory, since it literally means 'a thief,' for the Somali people in the Northern Frontier District (NFD) it carries far reaching political connotation: a very difficult and complicated liberation struggle.

[9] Interview with Ambassador Hussein Ali Dualeh, former Somali ambassador to Kenya and Uganda, Nairobi, September 11, 2001.

Abdirashid Ali Sharma'arke.[10] In 1969, a bloodless military coup led by General Mohammed Siyad Barre toppled Somalia's parliamentary democracy, banned all political parties, dismantled the national assembly and placed the country under military rule.

Barre's coming to power, for example, was preceded by intense criticism launched against the previous civilian governments resulting from widespread dissatisfaction with the policies and conduct of these regimes.[11] Barre introduced a new and totally different type of political system in Somalia known as *"Scientific Socialism,"* a combination of various ideas borrowed from the Islamic *Sharia* law, Somali customary law and the concept of communism; some form of community development, based on the principle of self-reliance and mainly deriving from Marxist ideology; in other words called as the perfect and main ideology of *Kacaanka*). In practice, this ideology was applied as a political principle and served mainly to justify state repression and monopoly of access to national resources.

Throughout history, the pre-1991 Somali governments, and the colonial administrations before them, have been characterized by the practice of nepotism, corruption and general political and administrative inefficiencies. In addition, they concentrated much of Somalia's economic activity, development work and political control in the Somali capital, Mogadishu, ignoring the rest of the country. This imbalance, coupled with the effects of the Cold War and government repression of political opponents, eventually gave rise to several clan-based liberation movements in the late 1970s and throughout the 1980s, including the Somali Salvation Democratic Front (SSDF), a Majeerteen sub-clan movement led by Abdullahi Yusuf, the Somali National Movement (SNM), a front by mainly Isaq sub-clans in northern Somalia and the United Somali Congress (USC), a Hawiye clan-based movement. These insurgencies used Somalia's neighbour and archrival Ethiopia as the base of their operations, enjoying abundant support from the Ethiopian government.

---

[10] Some of the most comprehensive accounts of politics and development in independent Somalia include the works of D. Laitin and S. Samatar, *Somalia: Nation in Search of a State* (Boulder: Westview, 1987); A. Metz, (ed.), *Somalia: A Country Study* (Washington: Library of Congress, 1992); I. Lewis, *Modern History of Somalia* (London: Zed, 1988); and A. I. Samatar, *Socialist Somalia: Rhetoric and Reality* (London: Zed, 1988).

[11] A. J. Ahmed, *Daybreak is Near: Literature, Clans and the Nation-State in Somalia* (Lawrenceville, NJ: The Red Sea Press, Inc., 1996), p.154.

Out of several armed engagements, three notable armed rebellions define the legacy of the past regimes in Somalia. These are the *Shifta* war with Kenya in the 1960s, the 1977-78 *Ogaden* war with Ethiopia, and armed conflict between the Somali military and the SNM insurgency in northwest, Somalia. Other than local rebellion, and the UK-backed Kenyan military response, there was little progress in the *Shifta* war. In the *Ogaden* war of 1976 - 1977, the Somali forces intervened in Ethiopia, in 'support' of Somali rebel fighters, in a bid to liberate the Somali-inhabited region of the *Ogaden*. Somalia suffered around 25,000 casualties at the hands of Soviet-backed Ethiopia,[12] a military regime that had become the USSR's new ally in the Horn of Africa region.

Another major armed conflict in Somalia, especially during the military regime, was the war between the Somali military and the Somali National Movement (SNM)– known as the SNM insurgency -- for control over northwest Somalia. The SNM grievances were initially fuelled by the conduct of the *Ogaden* War, but was exacerbated over the course of the 1980s when the military regime placed the northwest under extensively repressive military control, used the military administration to crackdown on dissidents and introduced large numbers of mainly *Ogaden* clan refugees into north-western Somalia;[13] with the possible implantation of these refugees in the north for purposes of future political support.

Whatever the political, economic, and military complications at the time, the plain historical fact remains that the civil war mounted by the SNM insurgency, which began in May 1988, had a devastating impact and in multiple aspects—geographically, politically, socially, economically as well as diplomatically at the international fore. In Northwest, for example, government forces allegedly committed atrocities against civilians: approximately 50,000 to 60,000 Somalis died; an estimated influx of 400,000 Somali refugees crossed into Ethiopia; and a similar number of internal displacement occurred.[14] These atrocities were later framed as the main ethno-political ideology behind the Isaq's bid for secession in May 1991 and led to the formation of the Republic of Somaliland, although it is yet to receive international recognition.

---

[12] Ahmed, I. Samatar, *Socialist Somalia: Rhetoric and Reality*, op cit., p. 137.
[13] World Bank, *Somalia Conflict Analysis: Synthesis Report*, (Nairobi: World Bank, 2004), p. 9.
[14] Africa Watch, *Somalia: A Government at War with its Own People* (New York: Africa Watch, 1990), p. 10.

In early 1991, another devastating civil war, which had been looming in parts of the country for some time, finally erupted in Somalia. This time around, it led to the total collapse of state institutions, disrupting all aspects of national and social development. Since then, the country was first divided into three parts: 'Somaliland,' in the northwest, 'Puntland,' in the northeast and South-central. As recent as 2019, other than 'Somaliland,' there are over five clan-based 'federal' entities autonomously working with the Somali government in Mogadishu and the Benadir Regional Administration (BRA); which is under the effective control of the central government. Since 2007, an African Union peace-keeping mission (codenamed AMISOM) is helping with the provision of security in Somalia. In the north, despite attempts to reunify with the South, the successive 'Somaliland' administrations have independently maintained peace and some remarkably functional institutions; based mainly on civic responsibility.

## Somalia: The Problem and Context

Somalia, located in the Horn of Africa along the Gulf of Aden and the Indian Ocean and bordering on Djibouti, Ethiopia and Kenya, is largely a culturally homogenous society. Unlike any of its neighbours, its people share a common language (Somali), Muslim religion, ethnic origin and a pastoral nomadic tradition. Once one of the strongest countries in the Horn of Africa with the third largest military force in sub-Saharan Africa during the 1977/78 Ogaden War, the need for a balance of power among the countries in the Horn of Africa was of paramount importance.[15]

Also, foreign policy has always been a major factor for Somalia and its neighbours in the achievement of peaceful co-existence. Despite this, Somalia had territorial disputes with some of its neighbours and the country was at war with Kenya and Ethiopia in the early 1960s and again with Ethiopia over the Ogaden in the late 1970s. This changed the attitude not only of Ethiopia, but also of Kenya towards Somalia. The hostility between Somalia and these two countries also endangered peace and security in the Horn of Africa.

Interestingly enough, in recent research on conflict drivers, foreign policy behaviour has generally been given less systematic attention than other factors often cited as underlying causes of conflict in the region.

---

[15] Interview with Ambassador Hussein Ali Dualeh, former Somali ambassador to Kenya and Uganda, Nairobi, September 11, 2001.

These include climate change, resource wars, ethno-politics, the struggle for political power, warlordism, land disputes, state collapse, and small arms and light weapons proliferation. However, due to the new 'conflict sensitivity' of foreign aid programmes, conflict analysis and the identification of conflict drivers has produced a plethora of new research on the issue.

A review of conflict assessment frameworks developed by different donors – the World Bank, the Department for International Development (DFID), Swedish International Development Agency (SIDA), the US Agency for International Development (USAID), and others – underscores the fact that foreign policy receives little attention as a potential conflict driver.[16] In various UN and other donor reports, an inventory of causes of conflict privileges internal drivers – environmental scarcity, political competition, greed and grievance. Only one section is devoted to "bad neighbourhoods" which can create conflict spill-over from adjacent countries.[17]

Another misunderstanding surrounds the fact that when foreign policy is cited, it is often presumed to be a force for conflict management and resolution; not as a cause in itself. This has especially been the case in the Horn of Africa since the reorientation of the Inter-Governmental Authority on Development (IGAD) into an agency for regional conflict resolution and prevention. The member states of IGAD have made laudable diplomatic efforts to mediate peace in Sudan and Somalia. That does not, however, preclude the possibility that, in other instances, the foreign policy orientation of regional states can also promote—by accident or design—armed conflict.

The case of Somalia is especially important, as the country has been embroiled in some of the worst inter-state conflicts and civil wars in the region since 1960, and because spill-over from Somalia's crises have had such profound negative effects on security in neighbouring states. Most studies of conflict in Somalia understandably focus on the extraordinary period of state collapse and war since 1991. Increasingly overlooked, however, is the fact that Somalia was involved in several wars in the pre-1990 period: the so-called '*Shifta* wars' in northeastern Kenya in the 1960s; the 1977-78 Ogaden War with Ethiopia; and the civil war, started by the SNM insurgency, in northern Somalia in 1988-90. These three

---

[16] See USAID *Conducting a Conflict Assessment: A Framework for Strategy and Program Development* (Nairobi: April 2005).
[17] Ibid.

cases—discussed throughout the chapters—are the focus of this book. The question to investigate at this point, therefore, is the consequences of Somalia's foreign policy choices in the Horn of Africa region, East Africa, Africa and the Arab world during the Cold War era.

It is essential to look back into this literature on foreign policy to establish trends in foreign policy formulation in states and its impact on external relations. This instance of the 30-year period is specifically noted as a time when Somalia had a functional government and foreign policy making structures in place. After 1990, the last Somali government was overthrown and there have since been no operational state (or foreign policy-making) structures in place; especially before the reformation of the Somali state and its structures at the *Arta* peace process in Djibouti in late 1999/early 2000. One must take note, however, that this book covers pre-1991 Somalia. In other words, its task focuses on Somalia's 30-year diplomatic history; notably Somali foreign policy and its impact on the Somali conflict.

The literature review will help to situate the linkage between foreign policy and conflict within the existing research on foreign policy, and help to show if, and how, the debate on foreign policy and conflict are correlated. The overview of the literature in the field of conflict will also be contextualised in relation to foreign policy and a coherent framework for analysis established for the book.

## (i) Foreign Policy: Definitions

The term "foreign policy" defies a clear-cut and widely agreed definition. There is nonetheless general agreement regarding some of its definitive attributes. Foreign policy refers to the actions and declarations that affect the external milieu, that is, the arena beyond a state's borders. It is goal-oriented and can be described as "a strategy or planned course of action ... aimed at achieving specific goals ..."[18] Also, foreign policy can be seen as an instrument through which a state seeks to "influence the activities of another country."[19] Like any other policy, it also consists of the means and methods chosen to pursue specific goals, which may be eco-

---

[18] See J. C. Plano and R. Olton, *The International Relations Dictionary* (New York: Holt, Rinehart and Winston, Inc., 1969), p.127.

[19] See Z. Mwamba, *Tanzania: Foreign Policy and International Politics* (Washington: University Press of America, 1978), p.iv.

nomic, cultural, social, political, military and psychological.[20] Taking all of these attributes into consideration, foreign policy may be comprehensively defined as "... a combination of aims and interests pursued and defined by the given state...in its relations with other states and the methods and means used by it for the achievement and defence of these purposes and interests."[21]

Various other definitions of foreign policy are used in the many other disciplines or sub-fields of international studies. For example, Reynolds argues that foreign policy consists of a range of actions taken by varying sections of a state's government.[22] The actions are taken with reference to other bodies acting on the international stage, of which usually the most important are other states, but which include international organisations, supranational and transnational groups, and, to some extent, individuals.

To Reynolds, foreign policy is not limited to the Westphalian state system and its relations with the outside world, but it encompasses other actors in the international system. Similarly, foreign policy has also been defined as a set of guides or choices being made about people, places and things beyond the boundaries of the state.[23] Modelski, on the other hand, views foreign policy as the process where a state adjusts its actions to those of other states so as to minimize adverse actions and maximize the favourable actions of foreign states.[24] Foreign policy is seen not as actions based on some grand design, but as a continuous process of pragmatic adjustments to the actions of others in the external environment.[25]

An important question, however, as far as foreign policy is concerned, is that of motivation. While, it has been highlighted that foreign policy could be formally conceptualized by a given state, it can also take place on an *ad hoc* basis and, therefore, be extremely flexible and dependent on the actions, actual or planned, of other actors in the international system. Reynolds also posits that states, primarily seek to advance their

---

[20] See R. B. Farrell (ed.), *Approaches to Comparative and International Politics* (Evanston: North Western University Press, 1966), p.213.
[21] Ibid.
[22] See P. A., Reynolds, *An Introduction to International Relations* 3rd Edition (London and New York: Longman, 1994), p.38.
[23] See B. Russet and H., Starr, *World Politics: The Menu for Choice* (New York: W. H. Freeman and Company, 1989), p.187.
[24] See G. Modelski, *A Theory of Foreign Policy* (London: Pall Mall, 1962), p.3.
[25] See C.M.B, Utete 'Foreign Policy and the Developing State,' in Olatunde Ojo et al., *African International Relations* (Lagos: Longman Group, 1985), pp. 43-51:43.

national interests.[26] This means that each state in the international system has certain goals that it aims to achieve and, since no state is self-sufficient, foreign policy is not conceived in a vacuum. According to the proponents of Realism, the chief aim of the state is security, which includes securing the country's sovereignty, its territorial integrity and political independence.

Utete argues that, in numerous circumstances, foreign policy reflects class interests of the ruling elite, which might be ideologically rationalized as the interests of the entire state.[27] This fact stems from the existence of middle range objectives, within countries' foreign policies, such as interstate economic, commercial and political relations including the attempts to influence the behaviour of other states.

Hillal et al observe that the study of foreign policies of developing countries has often been "underdeveloped" or "undeveloped;"[28] hence the absence of an agreed definition of the term 'foreign policy.' The authors analyze three dominant approaches to the study and understanding of developing countries' foreign policies including: the psychologistic approach; the great powers approach; and the reductionist or model builders approach. The psychologistic approach views foreign policy as a function of the impulse and idiosyncrasies of a single leader while the great powers approach views foreign policy as a function of East–West conflict, hence lacking autonomy. The reductionist or model builders approach, on the other hand, views the foreign policies of developing countries as determined by the same process and decisional calculi that shape the foreign policy of developed countries.

The authors also assert the emergence of a new body of literature on what can be called the foreign policy of development and the domestic social structure or domestic political process. Whatever the source of foreign policy and the range of national interests, the assumption is that these countries have a policy that they wish to pursue in their relations with other states in the international system whether it is formally articulated in their constitutions or not.

---

[26] See P. A. Reynolds, *An Introduction to International Relations* 3rd Edition, (London and New York: Longman, 1994), p.39.
[27] See C. M. B, Utete, "Foreign Policy and the Development State," in Ojo, O et al., African International Relations (Lagos: Longman Group, 1985), pp.43-51:43.
[28] See A. E. Hillal, and B. Korany, "A Literature Survey and a Framework for Analysis," in Korany, B. and Dessouki, A., The Foreign Policies of Arab States (London: Westview Press, 1984), pp.5-18:5.

## (ii) Approaches to Foreign Policy Analysis

The study of developing countries' foreign policies can be done based on various models whose respective values are argued by different authors. On the one hand, the behaviour of developing countries can be analysed through the lens of psychological worldview.[29] Here, foreign policy is viewed as a function of the impulses and idiosyncrasies of a single leader. Individual state or government leaders are, therefore, seen as a source of foreign policy in developing countries, who determine the issues of war and peace. The activities of a leader are, therefore, not designed to achieve societal goals, but are rather a function of public relations whose objectives are to improve the image of a state, enhance the popularity of a leader and divert attention from domestic upheavals through deceptive external victories.[30]

This view, however, is faulted on three levels. First, it makes foreign policy appear to be an erratic, irrational activity not subject to systematic analysis where a single leader is assumed to shoulder the making of external decisions. Secondly, the model ignores the domestic, regional and global contexts within which foreign policy is made and at the same time implemented. Indeed, there are constraints emanating from these contexts that a leader cannot ignore or surmount while making decisions that affect the state's external behaviour. Finally, it ignores the fact that because of their interest in political survival, most leaders downplay eccentricities that run counter to dominant attitudes, public mood, and political realities.

The realist approach of International Relations,[31] for its part, assumes that foreign policies of developing states are seen as lacking autonomy since they are weak and affected by external stimuli and are, therefore, reactive to initiatives and situations created by external forces. This approach links the foreign policy of developing countries to the former East-West rivalry that prevailed during the Cold War. There is, however, a weakness to this assertion. It overlooks the ability of weak states to

---

[29] See B. Korany, "Foreign Policy Models and their Empirical Relevance to Third World Actors: A Critique and Alternative, "*International Science Journal* No. 26, 19. 74, pp.70-94.

[30] See F. Weinstein, *Indonesian Foreign Policy and the Dilemma of Dependence*, (Ithaca: Cornell University Press, 1976), p.21.

[31] See H. Morgenthau, *Politics Among Nations: Struggle for Power and Peace*, (New York: Knopf, 1973), p.72.

bargain and manipulate stronger patrons in order to exercise constrained autonomy over their foreign policy;[32] as this was practically seen during the Cold War. Furthermore, it ignores domestic sources of foreign policy and implies that developing countries lack a purposeful foreign policy of their own making.

It also tends to presume that the foreign policies of developing countries are determined by the same processes and decisional calculi that inform the foreign policies of developed countries.[33] As such, the differences that emerge from their foreign policy behaviours are seen as founded on the resources and capabilities they possess. This view is predicated on the assumption by scholars that the behaviour of all states follows a rational actor model of decision making as they seek to enhance their power and advance their national interest.[34]

Therefore, the foreign policies of developing countries are perceived to be of the same nature as those of developed countries, taking place, however, at a lower level of conduct due to the lower level of material resources possessed by developing countries. The weakness emerging from this approach lies in its inability to account for specific features of developing countries, such as modernisation, low levels of political institutionalisation, dependency status in the global system, and political culture, that have an impact on the shaping of their foreign policies.

The above arguments aside, in addition to Graham Allison's models, there are over five key approaches to foreign policy analysis: the traditional approach; comparative foreign policy; cognitive processes and psychology; 'multilevel, multidimensional' and the constructivist turn approach.[35] More on Graham Allison's models – which are widely seen as the best framework for analysis in the study of foreign policy analysis – are discussed in the theoretical framework section.

*(iii) Levels of Analysis*

An enduring concern in research on foreign policy lies in the selection of the appropriate 'level of analysis.' In other words, levels of analysis at-

---

[32] See K. Menkhaus, and C. W. Kegley, Jr., "The Compliant Foreign Policy of the Dependent State Revisited: Empirical Linkages and Lessons from the Case of Somalia," *Comparative Political Studies*, Vol. 21, no. 3 (October 1988), pp. 315-46.

[33] See J. Rosenau, *The Scientific Study of Foreign Policy*, 2nd Ed., (London: Frances Printer, 1980).

[34] See M. Nicholson, *Rationality and Analysis of International Conflict*, (New York: Cambridge University Press, 1992).

[35] Jackson, R., and Sorensen, G., *Introduction to International Relations: Theories and Approaches* (Oxford: Oxford University Press, 2007), pp.222-224.

tempts to answer the question of the actors that shape a state's foreign policy. In his seminal work on a 'pre-theory' of foreign policy, James Rosenau identifies five different levels of analysis, each suggesting a different set of categories of actors making or shaping foreign policy, which are used to frame this section of the literature review.[36]

For political realists, the state is the appropriate unit of analysis and is seen as pursuing foreign policy to advance national interest. According to this view, a state's capacity or power is central to shaping its foreign policy strategies. For Rourke, the state's capability enables it to achieve its goals even when they clash with those of other states.[37] This observation can be applied to Somalia where the state's goal to unify the Somali population and the land they occupy in Ethiopia, Kenya, and the whole of Djibouti led to hostilities with these countries. Somali governments were willing to absorb the costs of this policy in the belief that they possessed a strong military capability, which would allow them to succeed.

Rourke's position begs the question of what precisely state capability is and how it is acquired. Goldstein, for example, observes that a state's capability to influence another is based on its possessions.[38] These include the size of the country, levels of income, armed forces and popula-

---

[36] Rosenau's "pre-theory" of foreign policy contends that the analysis of a nation's foreign policy must interpret the relationship among five sets of sources: i) **Individual** - variables concerning the attributes of a decision-maker that distinguish his/her particular behavior from those of all others who might have occupied the same position. His/her values, abilities, experience all act to structure his/her views and actions. ii) **Role** - variables related to the characteristics of an official that are derived from his/her policy-making responsibilities and which are expected to characterize any person who fills the same position. According to this formulation, individual and role variables can be behavioral attributes or frames of mind whose differentiation depends on whether they are "unique to the person or required by his/her position." iii) **Governmental** - variables that are conditions related to the structure of government that constrain or enable the choices made by government leaders. iv) **Societal** - sources of foreign policy behavior that consist of nongovernmental aspects that condition choices. The dominant value orientations of the nation, its internal cohesiveness, and the nature of its economic system all influence the contents of decisions and goals. v) **Systemic** - elements of the international environment that may shape the decisions made by a nation's leadership. See more in J. Rosenau, "Pre-Theories and Theories of Foreign Policy," in I. Barry Farrell (ed.), *Approaches to Comparative and International Politics* (Evanston, Ill: Northwestern University Press, 1966), pp. 27-93.

[37] See T. J. Rourke, *International Politics on the World Stage*, (Englewood, Cliffs, NJ.: Prentice Hall, 1996), p.230.

[38] See J. S. Goldstein, *International Relations*, 4th Ed., (New York: Priscilla McGeehan, 2001).

tion. However, the ability to use these possessions to influence another actor will depend on the sum total of the possessions vis-à-vis the national will. Somalia viewed itself as possessing adequate capability to influence its neighbours to surrender the Somali population and the territory they occupy. In practice, however, this was not the case. While the Somali state had a large territory and medium population levels, it did not have high enough levels of income to replenish its military needs in order to sustainably fight its neighbouring countries. As a result, its efforts to get Somali territories back were thwarted.

Rothgeb observes that despite a state's possession of power, this does not in itself always guarantee that it will prevail in conflicts.[39] This is based on the fact that power, if taken out of context, only provides a general understanding of typical outcomes. The relative power among states can indeed rise or decline depending on a state's ability to use it in order to achieve desired goals. Power is indeed not absolute and must be analysed in relation to others. In Somalia, for example, the quest for 'Greater Somalia' by its leaders was based on an estimate of the number of troops at their disposal at the time. Yet, despite the available manpower, the state did not realise any of its pan-Somali – or Greater Somalia -- ambitions.

An interesting sub-set of the realist theory of foreign policy is the mid-level theory of small or weak state foreign policy.[40] A number of researchers have sought to demonstrate that weak states seek to maximize their constrained autonomy by bargaining with stronger states, seeking principally to avoid total dependence or dominance by stronger states. Somalia's robust bargaining with the two superpowers during the Cold War is illustrative of this theory.[41]

The focus by realists on states as units of analysis leaves no room for the role of individuals. Indeed, states are seen as unitary, and individuals are only perceived to work towards attaining state goals. For realists, the only element that shows prominent impact on foreign policy apart from

---

[39] See J. M. Rothgeb, *Defining Power: Influence and Force in the Contemporary International System*, (New York, St. Martin's Press, 1992).

[40] See for instance R. L. Rothstein, *The Weak in the World of the Strong: The Developing Countries in the International System* (New York: Columbia University Press, 1977).

[41] See K. Menkhaus, K., and C. W. Kegley, Jr., "The Compliant Foreign Policy of the Dependent State Revisited: Empirical Linkages and Lessons from the Case of Somalia." *Comparative Political Studies*, Vol. 21, no. 3 (October 1988), pp.315-46.

state capability is the nature of leadership. At this level, one should evaluate the input of leadership in formulating foreign policy.

In contrast, Goldgeier demonstrates that individual leaders in states can be substituted as units of analysis without changing the way states behave.[42] States share common interests from time to time and their differences in behaviour are pegged to state resources, geography and national interests. Individual leaders are assumed to be rational when making decisions in the national interest and are thus expected to conform to state-rationality. In practice, however, states can at times filter irrational decisions taken by individual leaders to reach rational decisions, or vice versa. When such a situation occurs, it leads to a gap in harmonising individual and state rationality. The extrapolation of this gap is reflected in the three governments that dominated Somalia's post-independence period.

The leaders of these governments suffered from misperceptions and selective perceptions in their decision making processes.[43] Highly personalized explanations of foreign policy decisions, focusing on the inclinations and belief systems of top leaders, is of particular relevance to governments such as Somalia's during the 1969-1990 period when Siyad Barre dominated Somali politics and the country was characterized more by the politics of personal rule.

Alternatively, another school of thought focuses on bureaucratic politics as a driver of foreign policy decisions. Welch observes that apart from rational models of foreign policy formulation, bureaucratic politics can affect outcomes in state's decision-making.[44] From this perspective, foreign policy decisions result from bargaining exercises among various government agencies that have somewhat divergent interests and desired outcomes. This argument presents a challenge to the rational actor approach[45] since the decisions made by different state agencies are not reflective of what states desire, but rather what state departments aspire to achieve.

---

[42] See J. N. Goldgeier, *Leadership Style and Soviet Foreign Policy: Stalin, Khrushchev, Gorbachev*, (Baltimore, John Hopkins University Press, 1994), p.43.

[43] See R. Jervis, *Perception and Misperception in International Politics*, (Princeton: Princeton University Press, 1976), p.7.

[44] See D. A. Welch, "The Organisational Process and Bureaucratic Politics Paradigms: Retrospect and Prospect" *International Security* 17 (2), 1992, pp.112-146.

[45] This is made clear in the seminal work by G. Allison, *Essence of Decision: Explaining the Cuban Missile Crisis* (New York: HarperCollins, 1971).

Group decision-making dynamics can also be a decisive factor in the shaping of foreign policy decisions, and help to explain otherwise irrational, even disastrous decisions by states, such as going to war.[46] Groupthink, in this case, exerts influence on decision-making through emphasis on issues that would have been given a blind eye or bias by an individual leader. This concept serves to explain how individual leaders can be prevailed upon in decision-making, if a majority of the group members opposes or supports an idea. It also illustrates how the pressure to conform to group consensus works against careful consideration of policy choices. Groupthink is said to be especially common when the leadership is autocratic and dictatorial, as was the case in Somalia, resulting in subordinates fearing to raise objections to the leader's decisions.

## (vi) Somali Foreign Policy

The literature on Somali foreign policy focuses on several key features of the country. The most dominant ones are its status as a poor and weak third world state; its strategic position on the Horn of Africa, which gave it some bargaining leverage during the Cold War; and its dual membership and identity in both the OAU and the League of Arab States.[47] The history of Somalia itself can also provide a basis to analyse its foreign policy. As such, the Somali state is an amalgam of two different colonial entities: the former British protectorate, "Somaliland", and Italian Somalia.[48] Both territories joined in June 1960 to establish the Somali Republic; with the hope that the remaining three Somalia-claimed regions of the greater Somalia would join later. At independence, the Somali Republic was conscious of its colonial inheritance in terms of the frontier demarcations that placed some of its people and territories in Djibouti, Ethiopia and Kenya.[49] After the first two entities united, the Somali Republic sought to reunite the other three parts: this became a primary national goal and a key determinant of its foreign policy. It was also reflected in the initial refusal of the Somali Republic to sign the Organisation of Afri-

---

[46] See I. L. Janis, *Victims of Groupthink: A Psychological Study of Foreign-Policy Decisions and Fiascos*, (Boston: Houghton Mifflin, 1972), p.94.
[47] See B. Korany, B. and A. E. H., Dessouki, *The Foreign Policies of Arab States*, (Boulder & London: Westview Press, 1984), p.1.
[48] See for example K. Menkhaus, "Somali: Civil War, Intervention and Withdrawal 1990-1995," in Writenet Country Papers, UNHCR Writenet project.
[49] Ibid.

can Unity (OAU) Charter in 1963 because of a clause that stated that member states should respect the borders inherited at independence.[50]

Immediately after independence, the Somali Republic adopted the policy of irredentism,[51] setting an agenda to redeem the territories it felt rightfully belonging to it due to their pre-colonial claims in addition to the fact that those territories were wholly inhabited by members of the Somali ethnic group. This quest for territories in Somalia's neighbours bred interstate conflicts, pitting Somalia against Ethiopia and Kenya.

Jama observes that in defining Africa's borders, no specific criteria were used with regard to geographical, ethnic, religious or linguistic divisions.[52] The Somali Republic found this to be unreasonable as local circumstances were disregarded; splitting the Somali speaking people across four distinct states. As a result, the Somali Republic felt it had the responsibility to remedy the situation by acquiring those territories unjustifiably placed in Kenya's former Northern Frontier District (NFD), Ethiopia's Ogaden, and the whole of coastal Djibouti, then under France's authority. The question that arises in this context is: Why did the Somali Republic have these strong nationalist tendencies which no any other country in the Horn of Africa facing similar arbitrary demarcation of borders during the colonial period had?

In that respect, Touval argues that state policies can be attributed to a boundary's interference on economic activities and communication lines.[53] The location of borders, together with the combination of ecological factors of economic and human geography, represents a major factor in the formulation of national interest. In turn, nationalism is perceived as a strong basis for pursuing economic goals, and observing 'national' borders is pertinent to having peace or conflict. In Somalia, it was believed that the economic empowerment of the Somali people – locally and in the diaspora – would be achieved if they were united. In this case, it is clear that Somalia pegged its national interest on territory and population to acquire more power.

Somalia's external behaviour regarding borders is a reflection of the county's questioning of the legitimacy of the states occupying the Somali-

---

[50] Ibid.
[51] See J. S. Goldstein, *International Relations*, 4th Ed., (New York: Priscilla McGeehan, 2001), pp.203-204.
[52] See A. A. Jama, *Basis of the Conflict in the Horn of Africa*, (Mogadishu: NPA, 1978), p.35.
[53] See S. Touval, *The Boundary Politics of Independent Africa*, (Cambridge, Harvard University Press, 1972), p.25.

claimed areas.⁵⁴ The Somali Republic, for example, felt it was particularly wrong for Ethiopia to occupy the *Ogaden* region.⁵⁵ The disputed territory between Somalia and Ethiopia known as '*Ogaden* region' includes the *Haud* and *Reserve Area*, presently also under Ethiopian rule.⁵⁶ Somalia indeed perceived Ethiopia to have held an expansionist policy in the 1890s and, therefore, felt justified, during the study period, to help the Somalis in Ethiopia to secede. Somalia extended a similar struggle with regard to Djibouti that culminated the coastal region's independence from France in 1977. Although Djibouti decided to stand on its own after independence, the Somali Republic used this successful endeavour to examine how the principle of self-determination could be applied to other Somali territories in the Horn of Africa.⁵⁷

The desire by the Somali Republic to reunite all Somali people engendered an aggressive foreign policy towards Kenya, Ethiopia and France, which then colonised Djibouti.⁵⁸ During the 30-year independence period, the Somali Republic indeed spent a large proportion of its budget on military expenditure.⁵⁹ The agenda behind the purchase of this military equipment was to strengthen the Republic's position in fighting opponents who obstructed its perceived national interest.

In addition to the aspiration for unification, Cold War politics had a significant impact on Somalia's foreign policy. Having had neighbours whose tilt was either pro-east or pro-west, Somalia had no means of remaining neutral in conducting its foreign relations.⁶⁰ During this time, the superpowers sought to strengthen their positions in the Horn of Africa through military support of any regime that ascribed to their respective ideals. As a result, the Somali Republic attracted the USSR's attention and would not identify with any of its neighbours due to ideological differences and territorial perceptions. This relationship started in the 1960s when Prime Minister Abdirashid Ali Sharmarke signed a military cooperation with the USSR and during the absence of Aden Abdulle Osman who was on a trip outside Somalia. During that same period, Somali-

---

⁵⁴ Ibid.
⁵⁵ Ibid.
⁵⁶ Ibid.
⁵⁷ Ibid.
⁵⁸ See S. Touval, *The Boundary Politics of Independent Africa*, (Cambridge, Harvard University Press, 1972), p.25.
⁵⁹ See for example J. D. Singer, and M. Small, *Resort to Arms* (Beverly Hills, CA: Sage Publications, 1982).
⁶⁰ Ibid.

Ethiopian relations were volatile and the Somali support for insurgency in the *Ogaden* region led, among other things, to a large refugee influx into Somalia in 1978. The Somali Republic in turn used the presence of these refugees from the *Ogaden* region on its territory to solicit international support for their upkeep: the refugees hence became an economic asset to be exploited.

In the 1980s, the Somali government realised its inability to recapture any of the Somali territories from its neighbours as the then President Siyad Barre realised the limits of his government and its sponsors in fighting successful wars in the region. This led to a major shift in the clamour to acquire any territory in Kenya or Djibouti.[61] The foreign policy of Somalia towards Kenya and Djibouti, therefore, changed from confrontation to one of *rapprochement*. This shift was later extended to Ethiopia following the intervention of Kenyan and Djiboutian leaders. The literature on Somali foreign policy during the 1980s stresses that Barre's government became highly dependent, soliciting foreign aid[62] in whichever method it could manipulate, focusing on the acquisition of arms as a result of Cold War clientelism, which contributed to a climate of militarization in the Horn of Africa.[63]

Somalia's efforts to maximize its autonomy within the constraints of its status as a weak state have also been documented. It was, for example, no coincidence that Somalia sought membership in the Arab League in 1973 at precisely the moment when the OPEC cartel produced massive new wealth in the Gulf States. Somalia – at the time, a newly-declared Soviet ally and self-declared *'Scientific Socialist'* government – hoped to gain access to Saudi Arabia's foreign aid and thereby increase its leverage with the Soviet Union.[64] Another factor was that Egypt has also successfully lobbied for Somalia's inclusion for reasons related to the Arab country's long standing dispute with Ethiopia over the Nile waters. This, Egypt thought, would guarantee more of Somalia's commitment to stand

---

[61] Ibid.
[62] See P. Henze, *The Horn of Africa* (London: McMillan, 1991); David Rawson, *Somalia and Foreign Aid* (Washington: Foreign Service Institute, 1994); K. Menkhaus, "US Foreign Assistance to Somalia: Phoenix from the Ashes?" *Middle East Policy* vol. 5, no. 1 (January 1997), pp. 124-149.
[63] See J. Lefevre, *Arms for the Horn* (Philadelphia: University of Pennsylvania Press, 1986).
[64] See K. Menkhaus, and J. Creed, "The Rise of Saudi Regional Power and the Foreign Policies of Northeast African States," *Northeast African Studies*, vol. 8, nos. 2-3 (1987), pp. 1-22.

and support Egypt in the event that the water dispute escalated into military confrontation; Somalia's access of Saudi oil actually came after its diplomatic stand-off with USSR as Saudi Arabia was courting Somalia to join the USS bandwagon as a replacement for Ethiopia, which had switched camps to USSR.

Somalia's relations with Arab countries, however, are characterised by a strong dichotomy. First, Somalia is one of the only two non-Arab members of the Arab League. In addition, its dealing with Arab states has been marked by ambiguity. For example, Somalia was maintaining strong ties with Soviet-leaning members of the Arab League, such as Iraq, Algeria and Libya, who historically opposed US foreign policy in the Middle East. However, after its defeat in the *Ogaden* war in 1978, it aligned itself with Egypt and Saudi Arabia when the need arose for military aid. This indicates that Somalia did not have a specific approach in determining its external relations with the Arab world, but rather it weighed the issue at hand and chose allies that would help it achieve a particular goal. The dependence on Arab states for financial support, however, led to a weakening of its foreign policy in the Middle East.

Relations between Somalia and the superpowers during the Cold War period were not stable either.[65] At the onset of Barre's regime, the Somali government ascribed to the tenets of '*Scientific Socialism*' and, as a result, won the support of the Soviet Union, which it enjoyed until the outbreak of the *Ogaden* War in 1977. At that point, the Soviet Union changed its foreign policy, withdrew its support to Somalia and switched it to Ethiopia.

Somali-US relations warmed up at this time and Somalia became a recipient of US military and economic aid. The agenda for this shift of foreign relations from pro-Soviet to pro-US was necessitated by Somalia's national goals at the time. As the country and its leadership wanted to achieve victory in redeeming Somali-claimed territories from its neighbours, whoever supported this cause was accommodated as a friendly ally. For their part, the superpowers calculated the geo-strategic position of whoever they supported. For example, the US was ready to support Somalia in order to access its military bases and use these to launch US operations off the Somali coast along the Gulf.[66]

---

[65] See the US Department of State, *Background Notes: Somalia*, (Washington, D.C.: Office of East African Affairs, Bureau of African Affairs, July 1998).
[66] Ibid.

Ample literature exists documenting the extent to which Somali foreign policy degenerated over time into one driven mainly by regime survival. After the disastrous defeat in the *Ogaden* War, the Barre government was threatened by several domestically-organized armed insurgencies and serious unrest in its own ranks. Much of its subsequent foreign policy, argue analysts such as Abdi Samatar, Laitin and Samatar, and Hussein Adam, was guided by efforts to shore up the failing government and ward off internal opposition.[67]

## *(v) Inter and Intra-State Conflicts*

Because the Horn of Africa has been the site of multiple, protracted conflicts, a growing literature focusing on the regional dimensions of both conflict and foreign policy is available. The latter emphasises proxy wars waged by regional rivals; small arms and light weapons proliferation; and the cross-border nature of many regional conflicts.

Scholars and area analysts emphasise that inter-state conflicts in the Horn of Africa are driven mainly by border disputes and trans-boundary-shared resources.[68] To analyse the basis of conflicts between states, one therefore needs to contextualise colonial legacies, Cold War politics and the political and economic nature of governments functioning in states in the region. Apart from conflicts between states, internal conflicts in the Horn of Africa are also prevalent. For example, notable intra-state conflicts in the region include that of Somalia, Sudan, Ethiopia, and Uganda, while inter-state conflicts that have been discussed at length include those between Kenya and Somalia, Ethiopia and Somalia, and Ethiopia and Eritrea.

As mentioned earlier, the Horn of Africa, in the Cold War era, attracted attention from the superpowers that helped regimes to militarise.[69] Their agenda, as we can see from the proliferation of military

---

[67] See A. I. Samatar, *Socialist Somalia: Rhetoric and Reality* (London: Zed, 1986); David Laitin and Said Samatar, *Somalia: Nation in Search of a State* (Boulder: Westview, 1986); and Africa Watch, *Somalia: A Government at War with Its Own People* ( New York: Africa Watch, January 1990); See also H. M. Adam, "Somalia: Personal Rule, Military Rule and Militarism," in Eboe Hutchful and Abdoulaye Bathily, *Military and Militarism in Africa* (Dakar: CODESERIA, 1998), p.377.

[68] See G. P. Okoth, and B. A. Ogot, *Conflict in Cotemporary Africa*, (Nairobi: Jomo Kenyatta Foundation 2002), p.7.

[69] See C. H. Ofuho, "Security Concerns in the Horn of Africa," in Makumi Mwagiru, *African Regional Security in the Age of Globalisation* (Nairobi: HBF, 2004), pp.7-17:11.

equipment, protraction of wars, and direct or indirect meddling in the conflicts, was not to help states stabilise, but to carry forward their Cold War rivalries. This situation illustrates how conflicts in the Horn of Africa became globalised, for matters of either regional or global geopolitical, strategic interests, even when they were internal or interstate. Not surprisingly, some of these factors seem to borrow from each other and they are sometimes performed as interrelated occurrences, which are deliberately organized to function as such—and for the frustration of the rival party. However, in terms of isolating the factors that lead to conflict situations, case studies from the Horn of Africa delineate different causes that are uniquely linked to the governments in place. For example, the Ethiopia-Somalia conflict emerged from Somalia's ambition to establish a "Greater Somalia" in the Horn of Africa.[70]

A reflection of the political history of the region reveals how the issue of sovereignty and the sanctity of a state's territorial integrity formed the basis for other states harbouring Somali populations to put up resistance against Somali irredentism.[71] It is not, in any case, to suggest that these resistances and subsequent confrontations were waged in the same fashion. Rather, each of them can be viewed (despite the ideology of Greater Horn) as the development of a process that has been, in one way or another, driven by a current situation at the time of the resistance or confrontation. For instance, while the first two Somali civilian administrations chose to pursue diplomatic engagement in the international fora for their unification with these Somali people, Barre went further and chose the military mind of building up the country's military capability in order to achieve a complexity of goals 'adeptly' calculated to extend the survival of both the Republic and of his regime, domestically and internationally. In addition, he devised mechanisms to support insurgents within Ethiopian territory, intensifying conflict within that country besides engaging it in direct confrontation.

Nationalism, at its deepest sentiments and as a unifying factor among the Somalis, can be categorised as another key contributor to conflicts in the Horn of Africa.[72] In global terms, countries in the region are composed of communities of diverse cultures lumped up in the same territory. This diversity, if not maintained as a positive tool for unity and peace-

---

[70] See I. W. Zartman, *Ripe for Resolution: Conflict and Intervention in Africa*, (New York: Oxford University Press, 1989), p.124.
[71] Ibid., p.88.
[72] Ibid.

ful coexistence, can well be a disastrous recipe for communal/ethnic-based dysfunction and disruption. For, as we have witnessed in the Horn region, a misinterpretation of ethnic or cultural (including religious) diversity has been among the major contributors to ethnic or nationalist confrontations in both intra- and inter-state conflicts.

From another perspective, conflicts also emerge within a state due to bad political and economic governance.[73] Regimes that are in power often seek to perpetuate themselves and preserve elitist values at the expense of social development. According to the World Bank, for example, the regimes that ruled in Ethiopia and Somalia have demonstrated inadequacy in equitably propagating socio-political and economic values to their people while government structures imposed economic decisions on people without offering needed services in return. For example, Ethiopia's imperial regime taxed people heavily but, due to the existing weak government machinery, the regional government became too exploitative and Ethiopians sought an alternative centre of power, leading to the coming into power of Haile Selassie's overseer.

Clapham observes that the emergence of radical militarism also contributed to a rise of conflict in the Horn of Africa.[74] To that effect, both Somalia and Ethiopia can be demonstrated as states that suffered from the eventuality of militarism, particularly from 1969 in Somalia and from 1974 in Ethiopia. Apart from that, the regimes in the two countries during that time share the similarity that they both came into power through military *coups d'état*. Similarly, they were also both overthrown through the same means they came to power. This militarism mentality, which neglected the principles of peace and diplomatic approach to resolving sensitive matters, has encouraged civilians dissatisfied with the system of governance to seek justice by taking up arms against the regime. One can, therefore, argue that the military rulers' attitude of war mentality partly or mainly contributed to the situations that triggered civil wars. In the case of Somalia, it has taken a long time and, still remains to be a challenge to put up a government with effective control. The situations in Somalia and in Ethiopia are illustrative of the level of violence that emerges from poor state structures and repression of the people. They also, highlighted the impact of individual leader's failure to recognise the

---

[73] See World Bank, *World Development Report*, (Washington: World Bank, 1991), p.5.
[74] See C. Clapham, 'The Horn of Africa: Conflict Zone,' in Furley, O. (ed.), *Conflict in Africa*, (London: Tauris Academic Studies, 1992), pp.72-91.

shortcomings of their poor decisions in over-staying in power without delivering to the expectations and satisfaction of the ruled masses.

Henze remarks that the war and violence witnessed in the Horn of Africa is also a result of the exportation of arms to the region by major powers.[75] The Horn of Africa region does not possess the capacity to reduce the current stock, and the inflow of weapons that have served to sustain the magnitude of war experienced from the early 1960s onwards. During the Cold War, the superpowers provided weapons to states in the region to strengthen their governments, or individual leaders. These weapons later found their way into the hands of insurgents and their irresponsible leaders (warlords) who either captured them from the state or another faction; or who were supplied by governments which sought to destabilise their regional rivals. Somalia and Ethiopia represent such cases in that they were both supplied with arms by the US and USSR, with the deliberate intention of warding off each other's influence in the region.[76]

However, we also learn from here how the initial aim of the arms supplied to an ally changed the whole trend from that of national defence to the equipping of domestic insurgents and militias in a rival's territory. Thus, in line with Cold War rivalry, Ethiopia ended up supporting insurgency in Somalia which Somalia reciprocated in Ethiopia, eventually fuelling the toppling of both Siyad Barre and Mengistu Haile Mariam. Arms meant to strengthen Somalia and Ethiopia, in advancing the interests of 'eastern communism' or 'western democracy,' in effect ended up destroying their regimes when each of these military dictators facilitated explosion of armed fighting in the territory of his rival and as a consequence fuelled the fire that consumed their rule to a zero sum game.

Clapham also demonstrates the impact of ideology in the politics of the Horn of Africa.[77] In his analysis of new regimes in Ethiopia and Eritrea, he postulates that the Mengistu regime fought for all those objectives that made Marxism-Leninism attractive to third world countries. This Marxist-Leninist political thought espoused national unity, economic development and social transformation created through state power.

---

[75] P. Henze, *The Horn of Africa: From War to Peace*, (London: Macmillan, 1991), p.138.

[76] See for example J. G. Hershberg, "U.S.-Soviet Relations and the Turn toward Confrontation, 1977-1980: New Russian & East German Documents," *Cold War International History Project*, Bulletin 8/9, Winter 1996, p.130; See also See P. Woodward, *The Horn of Africa: State Politics and International Relations*, (London: Tauris, 1996), p.74.

[77] See C. Clapham, 'The Horn of Africa: Conflict Zone,' in O. Furley, (ed.), *Conflict in Africa*, (New York: Taurius Academic Studies, 1995), p.84.

Eritrea sought to separate from the central Ethiopian regime in 1991 as a result of economic decay and absence of meaningful political representation. The country sought allies to support its cause by renouncing Soviet ideology and thus attracting western sympathy. The Eritrean success shows the extent to which ideology can drive states into anarchy and secession.

From these observations, reality emerges that no single factor can be attributed to the causes of violence and conflict in the Horn of Africa. Instead, it is clear that a combination of multi-faceted factors subtly interplay in a dynamic process before leading to escalated violence. The views represented here also illustrate how domestic decision-making structures and the role played by individual leaders contribute to the failure of states to protect their people from violence and insecurity. Governments, therefore, often engineer and replenish violence in order to fulfil the will of external actors who offer free arms, development aid packages, and technical military assistance.

Experts on Somali studies have contributed notable works such as those of Lewis which give a deeper understanding of Somali politics;[78] Lee Cassanelli's works on Somali history;[79] David Latin, and Said Samatar's, which provide a good insight into Siyad Barre's political style, the formation of opposition movements and the conduct of foreign relations;[80] and those of Ahmed Samatar which cover the impact of the *Ogaden* war on the country's foreign relations.[81] Notwithstanding the contributions, they cannot cover the lack of any major academic work focusing on Somali foreign policy and conflict, particularly during the thirty years of the country's independence; in other words Somalia's thirty years of diplomatic history. Despite the paucity of literature on foreign relations, most studies of conflict in Somalia understandably focus on the extraordinary period since 1991 of state collapse and war. Increasingly overlooked, however, is the fact that Somalia was involved in three wars -- two inter-state wars and a local insurgency – in the pre-1991 period which was the result of its foreign policies and those of key external ac-

---

[78] See I. M. Lewis, *A Pastoral Democracy: A Study of Pastoralism and Politics among the Northern Somali of the Horn of Africa*, (London: James Curry, 1999).

[79] See L. V. Cassanelli, *The Shaping of Somali Society: Reconstructing the History of a Pastoral People, 1600-1900*, (Philadelphia: Pennsylvania University Press, 1982).

[80] See D. Laitin and S. S. Samatar, *Somalia: Nation in Search of a State*, (Boulder, Colorado: Westview Press, 1987).

[81] See A. I. Samatar, *Socialist Somalia: Rhetoric and Reality*, (London: Zed Books, 1988).

tors from 1960 to 1990. Similarly, when foreign policy is cited, it is often presumed to be a force for conflict management and resolution thus ignoring the fact that foreign policy orientation can as well promote – by accident or design – armed conflict. As an exploratory mission, this book aims to fill this gap by contributing to policy-oriented academic research on foreign policy and conflict in Somalia and the wider Horn of Africa region.

## A Framework for Analysis

The theoretical framework for this work is based on Graham Allison's models whose analysis suggests three different and complimentary ways of understanding decision-making during the times of crisis.[82] With a case study of the Cuban missile crisis, which pissed the United States against the Soviets, Allison came up with three approaches: a 'rational actor approach' that provides models for answering the question: with that information what would be the best decision to move towards one's goal? The assumption is that governments are unified and rational, wanting to achieve well-defined foreign policy goals; an 'organisational process' model, according to which concrete foreign policy emerges from clusters of governmental organisations that look after their own best interests and follow 'Standard Operating Procedures (SOPs); and a 'bureaucratic politics model' where individual decision-makers at different levels (each with their own particular goals in mind) bargain and compete for influence.[83]

This book develops the thesis that Somali foreign policy, and those of regional states and other key external actors, between 1960 and 1990, promoted armed conflict in Somalia by accident or design. This proposition is based on Graham Allison's models. In the models, which complement each other, Allison constructs three different ways or lenses through which analysts can examine events.[84] Under the rational actor model (RAM), Allison observes that governments are treated as the primary actor and it examines a set of goals, evaluates them according to their utility and then picks the one that has the highest 'payoff.' Under the organisational process, Allison argues that when faced with crisis,

---

[82] See G. Allison, *Essence of Decision: Explaining the Cuban Missile Crisis* (New York: HarperColins, 1971).

[83] R. Jackson and G. Sorensen, *Introduction to International Relations: Theories and Approaches* (Oxford: Oxford University Press, 2007), pp.222-224.

[84] See G. Allison, *Essence of Decision: Explaining the Cuban Missile Crisis*, op. cit.

government leaders do not look at it as a whole, but break it down and assign it according to pre-established organisational lines and that because of time and resource limitations, rather than evaluating all possible course of action to see which one is most likely to work, leaders settle on the first proposal that adequately addresses the issue.[85] In this case, Allison contends that leaders gravitate towards solutions that limit short-term uncertainty while organisations follow set "repertoires" and procedures when taking actions. Because of the large resources and time required to fully plan and mobilise actions within a government, leaders are, therefore, effectively limited to pre-existing plans.

Under the governmental politics model, Allison observes that a nation's actions are best understood as the result of politicking and negotiation by its top leaders. In this case, Allison adds that even if they share a goal, leaders differ in how to achieve it because of such factors as personal interests and background. If a leader holds absolute power (for example the President who is technically the commander-in-chief), the leader must gain a consensus with his underlings or risk having his order misunderstood, or in some cases, ignored. In this model, Allison observes that the makeup of a leader's entourage will have a large effect on the final decision (for example a group of advisors of 'yes men' vs. advisors who see things objectively and are at the same time willing to voice disagreement) and that leaders have different levels of power based on charisma, personality, skills of persuasion, and personal ties to decision-makers within the government.[86]

Allison further argues that in the governmental politics model, leaders who are certain enough will not seek input from their advisors, but rather, approval. That if a leader is already implicitly decided on a particular course of action, an advisor wishing to have influence must work within the framework of the decision the leader has already made, and that, if a leader fails to reach consensus with the inner circle, opponents may take advantage of these disagreements. Allison thus emphasizes the need for effective leaders to make consensus. Because of the possibilities of miscommunication, misunderstandings, and downright disagreements, different leaders may take actions that the group as a whole would not approve of.[87]

---

[85] Ibid.
[86] Ibid.
[87] Ibid.

Since the 1970s, Graham Allison's models became the founding study of foreign policy scholarship and in doing so revolutionised the field of international studies, and more so in foreign policy analysis. In explaining the actions of states -- as rational actors -- and the internal organisational processes and governmental politics, therefore, Allison's models best capture the link between foreign policy and conflict through his explanations of decision-making hence making the case for a multiple, overlapping competing conceptual models as the best that the current understanding of foreign policy provides. In this case, explaining the Somali crisis – and more so, foreign policy and conflict – can be best pursued by using Allison's models.

# CHAPTER TWO

## Foreign Policy and Conflict: Somalia & the Region

### The Global and Regional Environment

The foreign policy of states is shaped by domestic conditions, the values and perceptions of policy makers and by the global and regional environment in which they exist. National concerns influence what governments would like to do, while the environment in which they operate determines what they are able to do.[88] Here, the state as a social institution exists in two environments: the internal and the external. The former is influenced by all the institutions located in the territory of the state and their interactions with the state and with each other, while the latter is composed of all other states and organisations and their interactions with the state and with each other. Conventionally, the realist theory of international relations assumes that the state is constantly involved in attempts to intervene in both environments; that is, to engage in domestic and foreign policy.[89]

In the case of domestic policy, the state, in principle, is capable of getting its way once it has decided on an appropriately planned course of action; it possesses both the authority to act and the means to do so. As far as foreign policy is concerned, this is not generally the case. The final results of policy decisions – or the outcomes – are the product of interdependent decision-making. Since the state cannot expect that other states will always respect its authority, whether or not the state has the means to get its way is a contingent matter as no state has the ultimate authority.[90]

---

[88] See P. C. Noble, "The Arab System Opportunities Constraints and Pressures" in B. Korany, (ed.), *The Foreign Policies of Arab States* (Boulder and London: West View Press, 1984), pp.41-78:41.
[89] See C. Brown, *Understanding International Relations* (London: Macmillan Press, 1997), p.73.
[90] Ibid.

Consequently, systemic conditions have great influence in foreign policy formulation. This is the recognition and articulation of national interest in as far as it affects a particular issue. Noble, for example, asserts that there are two ways in which systemic conditions shape state behaviour.[91] In the first place, they either provide a set of opportunities, or more commonly serve as a set of constraints, permitting states a certain range of possible actions. Secondly, systemic conditions generate forces that push or pull states in certain directions. Furthermore, even if the system does not have a significant impact on the initial formation of a state's policies, it has a decisive say in whether those policies succeed or fail. These results are generally not lost on policy-makers, but instead they help shape their subsequent behaviour. Somali foreign policy from 1960-1990 is not an exception to this kind of foreign policy environment as it was shaped by these systemic forces, both in drawing its objectives and in the methods of implementation.

## The Global System

According to Korany, the global system refers to the pattern of interactions among international actors, which takes place according to an identifiable set of rules.[92] These actors include both state and non-state actors and the regular patterns of international conflict and cooperation are usually governed by international law. In the wake of World War II, major changes took place in the nature and operation of the world's political system. One of these was the collapse of the mostly European-based multipolar system which was replaced by a bi-polar system dominated by the US and the USSR.

In this bi-polar system, military power and diplomatic authority centred around two bloc leaders which dominated or led lesser units by combining rewards – such as providing security and economic assistance – with implicit or explicit threats of punishment against recalcitrant states. Interaction and communication, therefore, seemed to take place

---

[91] See P. C. Noble, "The Arab System Opportunities Constraints and Pressures," op. cit., pp.41-78:41.

[92] See B. Korany, et al., "The Global System and Arab Foreign Policies: The Primacy of Constraints," in B. Korany, et al., *The Foreign Policies of Arab States*, (Boulder and London: West View Press, 1984), pp.19-39:20.

between two antagonistic block leaders and their respective clients[93] were organised according to an east–west axis. Rourke observes that the causes of the confrontation are complex and controversial, but that varying economic and political interests and the collapse of the old balance of power structure created a system in which a great deal of world politics was centred on the confrontation between these two powers.[94]

This confrontation, commonly known as the Cold War, is normally taken to have begun in 1947 and concluded in 1989 with the collapse of the Soviet Union and its allies in Eastern Europe. The term 'Cold War,' at least in terms of international relations, has been used to describe the strained, uneasy and generally hostile relations between the two superpowers – the United States and the Soviet Union – in the post-World War II era and was thus a function of the fury and hostility that characterized American-Soviet relationships during that period.[95] It was composed of five different levels of reality: a strategic confrontation between the USSR and the US; an ideological standoff between communism and capitalism; a geographical and military confrontation that kept Europe and Germany divided for the best part of 40 years; an on-going struggle for the future control of the third world; and, finally a wider opposition between two material civilizations where each claimed and insisted that they alone were the ideal influencers of the wave of the future.[96]

The Cold War had a significant impact in different spheres of life in those two countries and in the international political, economic and diplomatic system as a whole. This is attributed to the foreign policies adopted by the antagonistic countries. For example, US foreign policy changed from that of pre-World War II isolationism, or politico-military non-engagement with other great powers, to one of containment.[97] This

---

[93] See T. A. Couloumbis and J. H. Wolf, *Introduction to International Relations: Power and Justice* 4th Edition (Englewood Cliffs.: Prentice Hall, 1988), p.87.

[94] See T. J. Rourke, *International Politics on the World Stage*, 4th Edition (Connecticut: Dushkin Publishing Group, 1993), p.43.

[95] See P. O. Nyinguro, "The Impact of the Cold War in Regional Security: The Case of Africa," in M. Munene et al., (eds.) *The United States and Africa: From Independence to the End of the Cold War*, (Nairobi: East African Educational Publishers, 1995), pp.65-83:66.

[96] See M. Cox, "From the Cold War to the War on Terror" in John Baylis and Steve Smith (eds.), *The Globalization of World Politics: An Introduction to International Relations* 3rd Edition (Oxford: Oxford University Press, 2005), p.133.

[97] See R. J. Art, "America's Foreign Policy" in C. M. Roy, *Foreign Policy in World Politics* 6th Edition (New Jersey: Prentice Hall Inc, 1985), p.11.

shift took place in reaction to the perceived Soviet threat and led to a policy of internationalism where the US opposed the Soviet Union (and later on China) both diplomatically and militarily. While this does not mean that every adverse situation was contained, each was scrutinized to determine whether or not acting would deteriorate the USA's general position in the world. In this case, containment, in terms of a conceptual approach to events and not in terms of omnipresent interventionism, was the essence of the global policy of the US.

Furthermore, the US policy led to involvement in Vietnam, bringing about significant changes in American attitudes about international relations. For example, there was increased resistance to the Cold War that urge the fight to communism everywhere, leading to *détente* with adversaries and retrenchment. This meant that instead of expanding its commitments, the US consolidated its positions and withdrew from areas where it was weaker as a new means of reaching an old goal. This was especially the case under Richard Nixon's administration. The US policy at the time was also informed by the rise of China and the subsequent fragmentation of alliances around the two poles. The scenario introduced new challenges of multivariate scales that affected not only the foreign policy of rival countries in the global environment but indeed also in the domestic arena, particularly at the state decision-making level, whose duties included the allocation of adequate resources to implement the policy.

The Soviet Union's foreign policy was, on the other hand, informed by the Leninist–Stalinist thesis that the destruction of capitalism, its dangers and related interventions are possible only through successful proletarian revolution, at least in several large states.[98] Although the Soviets never matched the US economically, they possessed a huge conventional armed force, a seemingly threatening ideology. And by 1949, the Soviet Union had acquired an undisputed capability in amassing voluminous stocks of lethal atomic weapons. Owning an atomic arsenal, sophisticated intelligence network, strong military technology and personnel, and authoritarian methods of rule, encouraged the Soviets to pursue an expansionist agenda. Therefore, the essence of the Soviet Union's national interest can, in one way or the other, be argued to have been one of world

---

[98] See C. M. Roy, *Foreign Policy in World Politics* 6th Ed., (New Jersey: Prentice-Hall, 1976), p.184.

revolution.[99] So, contrastively, these two strong states with each at the top rank of a coalition or ideological bloc, vied for expansion of its power, recruited allies in the developing countries and consequently supplied arms to governments and rebel groups in order to win their favour.

In Africa, the decade of the 1960s witnessed an era of superpower intrusion. For example, Somalia's geographic position on the Red Sea and the Indian Ocean was viewed as being of strategic importance,[100] hence inviting active involvement of the two superpowers. Although, Somalia followed a foreign policy of non-alignment for a brief period after independence, members of the top leadership were divided in their policy of superpower support. While the president and others in the cabinet were tilted to affiliation to the western bloc, the Prime Minister Abdirashid Ali Sharmarke and others close to him were attracted to cooperation with the Soviet Union which promised supply of military equipment to the Somali national army. Within a few years after Sharmarke's signing of a military agreement, the civilian administration was toppled by the army in a coup; allegedly with USSR support.[101] As a result of the leadership change, the country later allied to the east with Siyad Barre ultimately declaring a national ideology of *Hantiwadaagga Cilmiga ku Dhisan*, meaning '*Scientific Socialism.*' In the 1980s, and shortly after the 1977-78 Somalia-Ethiopia war, Somalia shifted its alignment to the west after its long-time ally, the Soviet Union, supported Ethiopia during the 1977-78 *Ogaden* war. Somalia, therefore, played a significant role in the Cold War rivalries and took advantage of its geographical location in order to secure arms and other benefits that led to the development of not solely a huge and sophisticated military[102] but indeed access to various categories of financial resources and funds for development.

The Cold War was, therefore, a cause of tension within the Horn of Africa. The policies pursued by the superpowers encouraged and sup-

---

[99] Ibid.

[100] See H. M. Adam, "Somalia: A Terrible Beauty Being Born" in I. W. Zartman (ed.) *Collapsed State: The Disintegration of Legitimate Authority* (Boulder and London: Lynne Rienner Publishers, 1994), p.75.

[101] See more in Gassim, Mariam Arif. *Somalia: Clan vs. Nation.* Printed in U.A.E. (2002).

[102] See A. J. Ahmed, *Daybreak is Near: Literature Clans and the Ethiopia Nation–State in Somalia* (Asmara Red Sea Press Inc, 1996), p.102; See also *Somalia: Background Note*, Bureau of African affairs; US Department of State, March, 2006.; See also N. A. Hashi, *Weapons and Clan Politics in Somalia* (Mogadishu: Horn of Africa Printing Press, 1999), p.63.

ported Somalia in its pursuit of its national interest; hence bringing about the 1963 and 1977-78 wars with Ethiopia and the 1963 *Shifta* proxy war with Kenya. During that time, it is likely that Somali leaders grew overconfident due to the huge military capabilities at their disposal. This is highlighted in the appeal made by Kenya's then Vice President Daniel arap Moi to US President Jimmy Carter, urging western countries not to sell arms to Somalia.[103] As a result, the superpowers precipitated an arms race between already hostile neighbours by supporting them against each other. They also supplied bigger quantity and better military equipment, hence infusing the potential for conflict already brewing in the region. The attitude as well as presence of the superpowers, no doubt, intensified the existing hostilities, raising the bar of the rivalry to what can be explained as the internationalisation of the conflicts in the Horn of Africa region.

## The Regional Environment

With a quick look at the Horn of Africa region, and even to some extent Africa in general, a large part of the population has been suffering under conditions created by poor governance, corruption, and politicians' individual interests. Historically viewing the continent's undesirable condition in the development sector, the observer encounters how there have been war, signs of war and widespread poverty, hunger and displacement and refugee influx. This has been the case throughout in the sense that the effects have in many cases crossed to neighbouring states and unavoidably also to the international community outside the continent. With each and every conflict having some kind of a relationship with others in the same region, it gives the analyst the notion that conflicts have become systems that operate under their own circumstance; sometimes predictable, sometimes unpredictable. The concept of 'conflict system' advances the understanding that every conflict not only has a regional dimension but, as a result, a reality that "what might at first appear as individualised conflicts in fact are parts of a wider pattern of conflict regionally."[104] This concept "rejects the idea that conflicts do not have

---

[103] See J. M. Ghalib, *The Cost of Dictatorship: The Somali Experience* (New York: Lilian Barber Press Inc, 1995), p.111.
[104] See M. Mwagiru, *The Greater Horn of Africa Conflict System: Conflict Patterns, Strategies and Management Practices* (Paper prepared for the USAID project on Conflict and Conflict

trans-border realities, and instead perceives individual conflicts as an integral part of a wider conflict system."[105] In terms of conflict management, what this entails is that systemic realities and other actors within the conflict system must be taken into account when addressing a specific conflict. This idea, however, negates theory-building as it concentrates only on one dimension of the conflict in the belief that each conflict is unique.

Traditionally, conflicts in the Horn of Africa were studied and managed individually and on an *ad hoc* basis.[106] There are five states that are often referred to as constituting the Horn namely: Ethiopia, Sudan, Somalia, Djibouti and Eritrea.[107] However, due to the spill-over of conflicts in Ethiopia, Sudan, and Somalia, and the workings of the IGAD leadership and its change of focus from general drought to issues of development and conflict management, the Horn of Africa has been extended to include Kenya and Uganda, which makes the name Greater Horn plausible for representing the seven neighbouring countries. The concept of conflict system is important in the analysis of systemic forces that either provide opportunities or constraints; hence influencing the foreign policies of individual states and impact on conflicts in the region as well as their management processes.

At the regional level, several systemic forces informed Somali foreign policy and led to hostile relations with its immediate neighbours, but also to friendly relations with others. Firstly, the creation of a non-aligned movement with Egypt under President Nasser and Yugoslavia under Tito, in the forefront of its leadership, institutionalized collaboration between Africa and other developing countries.[108] This was essentially the reflection of an awareness that these countries' foreign policy objectives could not be achieved through individual efforts,[109] hence the need to

---

Management in the Greater Horn of Africa, April 1997, Revised September 1997), p.4.
[105] Ibid.
[106] See M. Mwagiru, *Conflict: Theory, Processes and Institutions of Management* (Nairobi: Watermark Publishers, 2000), p.79.
[107] See C. H. Ofuho, Security Concerns in the Horn of Africa" in M. Mwagiru (ed.) *African Regional Security in the Age of Globalization* (Nairobi: Heinrich Boll Foundation, 2004), pp.7-17:11.
[108] See S. L. Spiegel, *World Politics in a New Era* (Los Angeles: Harcourt Brace College Publishers, 1994), p.155.
[109] See C. M. B. Utete, "Foreign Policy and The Developing State" in O. Ojo, et al., *African International Relations*, (Lagos: Longman Group, 1985), 43-51:48.

craft cooperative foreign policies among developing countries. Somalia pursued non-alignment as a core component of its foreign policy for a brief period after independence.[110]

Secondly, all newly-independent African countries joined the UN. The international organisation's development of international law, especially principles such as sovereign equality, territorial integrity, political independence, non-interference in the internal affairs of other states and the fundamental right to self-defence, have all impacted on the foreign policy of many African states.[111] Somalia's neighbours, Kenya and Ethiopia, aligned their foreign policies with these principles.

Thirdly, decolonization and the creation of the OAU was a significant milestone in Africa, in the early 1960s, when most countries were gaining independence from European colonizers.[112] Decolonization whetted Somalia's appetite for Kenya's Northern Frontier District (NFD) and France's coastal Djibouti; in effect, the Somali constitution explicitly challenged the borders with Ethiopia, Kenya and coastal Djibouti. Right after independence, these three territories indeed became the main target of Somali foreign policy. From the perspective of Somalia, however, this was not so much seen as a foreign policy but rather as a sacrosanct national duty, an irreversible territorial cause and a means to complete the independence of 'Greater Somalia.'[113] The philosophy had a strong ideological underpinning that the various Somalias, under British, Italian, French, Ethiopian and Kenyan leadership, be merged into one country with a strong central government.

Colonial powers partitioned Africa into territorial units, kingdoms, and states and, as some communities in Africa were arbitrarily divided, unrelated areas and people were also arbitrarily joined together.[114] In the 1960s, the newly-independent African states inherited those colonial boundaries together with the challenges this legacy posed to their territorial integrity and to their attempts to achieve national unity. Examples include Nigeria's Biafra State; Southern Sudan and the Moroccan Sahara.

---

[110] This will be discussed more in Chapter Four.
[111] See S. L. Spiegel, *World Politics in a New Era* (Los Angeles: Harcourt Brace College Publishers, 1994), p.155.
[112] Ibid.
[113] Interview with Amb. Hussein Ali Dualleh, March 7, 2004, Hargeisa.
[114] See K. Annan, "The Causes of Conflict and the Promotion of Durable Peace and Sustainable Development in Africa," Secretary General's Report to the UN Security Council, 16 April 1998, p.107.

In a 1998 UN report, the UN Secretary General, Kofi Annan, posits a strong link between colonial boundaries and the legacy they pose to the territorial integrity of states.[115] The challenge Annan posits is compounded by the fact that the framework of colonial laws and institutions, which some new states inherited, had been designed to exploit them and not to overcome them.[116]

Due to these colonially designed annexations and disruptions of lives and livelihoods of peoples, territorial or boundary disputes became the most explosive conflicts in African states.[117] Broadly speaking, Africa's colonial legacy regarding territorial disputes applies to claims involving large areas of a neighbouring state's territory. Beyond territory, however, Somali foreign policy was motivated by irredentism, which emerged when boundaries were drawn, because historical relationships were ignored and the outcome did not reflect the existing ethnic divisions. The Somali people were effectively divided among four countries even though the people residing in the disputed areas share the same culture, language and religion with those in Somalia.

Based on this argument, Somali leaders believed that while it was much easier to govern them under one administration, the attainment of a united Somalia would be better off compared to other African countries. This, not only motivated Somali leaders to take action both politically and militarily, but it also promoted the expansion of the idea of Somali nationalism into that of *pan-Somalism*. In this regard, and under the *pan-Somali* banner, Somalia encouraged Djibouti's decolonization, to Ethiopia's discontent. The country's leadership under Barre also sought to use force, rather than international diplomacy, to try and recapture *Ogaden* and the NFD from Ethiopia and Kenya respectively.[118] Although Barre fought Ethiopia militarily, he, however, did not encounter Kenya despite the fact that the military option was never off the table.[119]

---

[115] Ibid.
[116] Ibid.
[117] See D. K. Orwa, "Causes of Conflict in the Relations of African States," in O. Ojo, et al., *African International Relations*, (London: Longman, 1985), pp.129-141:135.
[118] Interview with Amb. Hussein Ali Dualleh, March 7, 2004, Hargeisa.
[119] Ibid.

## Kenya's Foreign Policy

In contrast to Somalia, its neighbours pursued policies that were an antithesis to its own. For example, Kenya's foreign policy, as guided by the election manifestos of the Kenya African National Union (KANU) in 1961 and 1963, stated that it would vigilantly safeguard national interests, including the protection of the security of its people by maintaining necessary military forces and by seeking cooperation and defence agreements. Under this policy and the perception of possible Somali attempt to use military force to regain NFD and Ogaden, Kenya and Ethiopia concluded a defence pact.[120] Kenya's foreign policy focused on the preservation of its national integrity while joining democratic movements in Africa to eradicate imperialism, racism and all forms of oppression.[121]

The KANU manifestos indeed called for collaboration with African countries to foster and promote African 'unity of action.' The manifestos also stated the need for Kenya to work for international peace and peaceful settlement of international disputes through the framework of the UN. Among other objectives, the manifestos entailed respect for existing boundaries, a call for the observance of the status quo as the only sure way to maintain the pre-independence equilibrium.[122]

The two documents largely informed Kenya's foreign policy behaviour, that is the concrete actions, positions and decisions that the state adopted in the conduct of its foreign policy. As a result, Kenya resisted and defended itself against Somali irredentism, in spite of the wishes of the Kenyan-Somalis to secede.[123] Despite the fact that the existing Northern Frontier District Liberation Front NFDLF secessionist movement –also widely known in Kenya as the *Shifta* -- was a crucial factor in Kenya's foreign policy, during Kenyatta's time, the country was largely indifferent and unconcerned with painting it in large strategic strokes. Instead, its image was one of a reactionary state. As the Moi regime

---

[120] See for example, K. G. Adar, *Kenya's Foreign Policy Behaviour towards Somalia, 1963 – 1983* (Lanham, New York and London: University Press of America, 1994), p.131.

[121] See P. K. Kurgat, "Kenya's Foreign Policy and African Conflict Management," in G. P. Okoth and B. A. Ogot, *Conflict in Contemporary Africa* (Nairobi: Jomo Kenyatta Foundation, 2000), pp.117-126:118.

[122] See for example M. Mwagiru, "The Elusive Quest: Conflict, Diplomacy and Foreign Policy in Kenya," in Okoth, G. P., and Ogot, B. A., (eds.), *Conflict in Contemporary Africa*, (Nairobi: Jomo Kenyatta Foundation, 2000), pp.117-140.

[123] See W. I. Zartman, *Ripe for Resolution: Conflict and Intervention in Africa* (Oxford: Oxford University Press, 1989), p.91.

changed this state of affairs and started to articulate a clean and conceptually complex foreign policy founded on concerns for regional peace and security, the country started to play a regional leadership role.¹²⁴

## Ethiopia's Foreign Policy

The tone of Ethiopia's international relations was set by Emperor Haile Selassie who was involved in foreign policy making as early as 1923 when the country joined the League of Nations. The country pursued foreign policy objectives that had numerous implications for its relationship with Somalia in particular and its other neighbours in general. For a time, Ethiopia was significantly allied to the west from which it received both military and economic assistance. Several factors have been highlighted to account for the close relationship between Ethiopia and the US, including the decline of the UK with which Ethiopia had a long-standing historical link. For example, the UK had conditioned Ethiopia's international relations in the 1940s after the liberation campaign that drove the Italians out of Ethiopia.¹²⁵

In the early 1940s, the heavy-handed British military administration in Ethiopia and the British diplomatic stand concerning the future of *Ogaden* and that of Eritrea served to heighten the emperor's suspicions about British motives in his country. In turn, the US was sympathetic to the Ethiopian plight under the British and revealed interest in preserving the country's independence. Haile Selassie played a central role in the country's foreign affairs due to his position as the leader of one of the oldest independent nations in the world. Ethiopia sought to play the role of strategic partner for the US [as it still does today] while at the same time back-tracking from the Anglo-Ethiopia Agreement of 1942, which virtually placed it under British military administration.¹²⁶

---

[124] Interview with Ambassador Bethwell Kiplagat, April 22, 2008, Nairobi.
[125] See M. Wubneh and Y. Abate, *Ethiopia: Transition and Development in the Horn of Africa*(Colorado: Westview Press, 1988), p.162.; See also A. Jalata, *Oromia and Ethiopia: State Formation and Ethnonational Conflict, 1868-1992* (Boulder and London: Lynne Rienner Publishers, 1993), p.88.; See also A. Jalata, *Fighting Against the Injustice of the State and Globalization: Comparing the Africa America and Oromo Movements* (New York: Palgrave, 2001), p.90.
[126] See B. Zewde, *A History of Modern Ethiopia 1855–1974*(Addis Ababa: Addis Ababa University Press, 1991), p.179.

Being a landlocked country with a fast-growing population, due to its majority Muslim Oromo and other Muslim communities, the other concern for Ethiopia was to gain direct access to the sea by preventing foreign control of coastal areas. It therefore made claims to both Eritrea and Somaliland based on historical, ethnic and geopolitical grounds.[127] In addition, and to consolidate its relationship with the west as a loyal pro-western country, and achieve its national interest of keeping the annexed Ogaden region, it locally supported the continued French presence, and control of coastal Djibouti and made a territorial claim on it, perhaps in fear of it being claimed by Somalia.[128] Ethiopia's third foreign policy objective was to minimize the impact of Arab nationalism on Ethiopian foreign and domestic affairs. As a non-Arab and non-Islamic nation in the region, Ethiopia has often been the target of *pan-Arab* movements. For example, the 1952 Egyptian revolution under Nasser, the 1956 Sudan independence, the 1962 Yemeni revolution, and Somali claims to the *Ogaden* all revived Ethiopian anxiety of Muslim radicalism. Its fear of Muslim 'encirclement' led the emperor's principal policy of maintaining friendly contacts with Arab leaders, perhaps to mute Arab propaganda for the secession of Eritrea and for a 'Greater Somalia.'[129]

Ethiopia's last foreign policy objective was to be active in African affairs and, as a result, the emperor championed African independence and the creation of the OAU (later transformed to the AU), the headquarters of which Ethiopia still hosts. As the host of the OAU, Ethiopia gained a lot of influence and hence received strong support from sub-Saharan African countries in order to contain Somali irredentism and Eritrean secession.[130] After the September 12, 1974 revolution, and the coming of Mengistu Haile Mariam to power, the new regime proclaimed its intention to pursue a non-aligned foreign policy, respect Ethiopia's international obligations and strengthen its ties with all African countries. From 1977 until its fall in 1990, Mengistu's Ethiopia conducted its international

---

[127] See M. Wubneh, and Y. Abate, *Ethiopia: Transition and Development in the Horn of Africa*, op. cit., p.164.

[128] See J. M. Ghalib, *The Cost of Dictatorship: The Somali Experience*, (New York: Lilian Barber Press Inc., 1995), p.91.

[129] See M. Wubneh and Y. Abate, *Ethiopia: Transition and Development in the Horn of Africa* (Colorado: Westview Press, 1988), p.164.

[130] Ibid.

relations in close cooperation with the Soviet Union, Cuba and Eastern Europe, while respecting the principle of 'territorial integrity.'[131]

## Djibouti's Foreign Policy

Due to clan cleavages, Djibouti's 1977 independence had to be guaranteed by Ethiopia and Somalia and by the French military presence. Indeed, the Issa, who constituted about 60 per cent of the Djiboutian population, have had ties to Somalia while the 40 per cent Afar members favoured political association with the Afar in Ethiopia, where the majority of this clan lives. At the same time, Djibouti's foreign policy was constrained by its domestic environment, especially its small size, population, economy and its military-strategic situation. Its first president, Hassan Guled Abtidon, wished to maintain stability in the midst of the political turmoil that surrounded the country.[132] In addition, President Abtidon harboured no ambition for the 'Greater Somalia' project, hence avoiding the possible provocation of enmity towards Ethiopia. Instead, Abtidon sought to avoid confrontation in Djibouti's dealing with all other states in its vicinity.[133]

Over the period under study, Djibouti maintained neutrality by diplomatically playing off claims by Ethiopia and Somalia to its territory, thus fostering friendly relations with both countries. Djibouti benefited from its strategic location and deep-water port, which made the country France's key, and with the biggest military base in Africa along the Indian Ocean. It was also an important port of call for US warships, ensuring it of enormous military support as well as other economic and development related ties. Djibouti also provided important trade links in the Horn of Africa region. Combined, these elements resulted in a strengthening of the country's position in its relations with its neighbours and allowed it to play an effective role as a mediator in situations requiring resolutions to daunting conflicts. For example, Djibouti's Abtidon facilitated a meeting between the Somali and Ethiopian leaders after the bitter 1977-78 Ogaden war between their two countries,[134] while its role in Somalia's internal conflict was, and still is, remarkably visible within

---

[131] Interview with Ambassador Bethwell Kiplagat, April 22, 2008, Nairobi.
[132] Interview with Ambassador Mohamed Siyad Dualeh, November 9, 2007, Djibouti.
[133] See P. Woodward, *The Horn of Africa: Politics and International Relations* (London and New York: Tauris Academic Studies, 1996), p.135.
[134] Interview with Ambassador Mohamed Siyad Dualeh, November 9, 2007, Djibouti.

IGAD's initiative of promoting peace and stability in Somalia and the entire region as well as its efforts as an individual nation.

In addition to the aforementioned factors of individual national foreign policy matters, the OAU principles had an underlying influence on the foreign policy of countries in the Horn of Africa. For example, article 3(3) of the OAU Charter and the 1964 OAU Cairo Resolution conferred legality, legitimacy and sanctity on existing inter-state boundaries. In effect, this hampered Somalia's irredentist efforts as it guaranteed respect for other states' sovereignty and non-interference in their internal affairs. In 1981, the OAU Summit adopted a ministerial report reaffirming Ethiopia's sovereignty over *Ogaden*. However, due to the fact that this was an issue of contention between the two states, it led to serious exchanges in multilateral forums at the level of the OAU and at that of the UN.[135]

Another dynamic important to state in the context of foreign policy discussion on the Horn of Africa is that of regional integration and the creation of regional economic communities, for example the East African Community (EAC). In the idealist and liberalist framework, the initiative can be characterised as an important highlight at this time. The presence of such organisations may have influenced Somalia's Prime Minister at the time, Mohammed Ibrahim Egal, to soften his stance on the issue of a 'Greater Somalia' in the hope of achieving favourable concessions within the regional community. IGAD's formation in 1986 under Djibouti's leadership in turn provided opportunities for conciliation and led to a reorientation of foreign policy on the part of Somalia and Ethiopia.

A historicization of the foreign policy approaches in the Horn of Africa can, in certain perspectives, contextualized within the framework of the wider international system, particularly when considering the fact that there was an increased appeal for Arab nationalism and calls for Arab unity. These dynamics of Arabism and Arab nationalism have brought about fundamental changes to the Horn of Africa conflict system. According to this *pan-Arab* ideology, the Arab world is viewed as one nation and its division into separate states is seen as an aberration resulting from 'foreign designs.'[136] This perceived homogeneity has led to occasional confrontation with non-Arab major powers, in line with the *Huntingtonian*

---

[135] See J. M. Ghalib, *The Cost of Dictatorship: The Somali Experience*, op. cit., p.114.
[136] See B. Korany, et al., "The Global System and Arab Foreign Policies: The Primacy of Constraints," in Bahgat Korany et al., *The Foreign Policies of Arab States*, (Boulder and London: West View Press, 1984), pp.19-39:27.

model of the 'Clash of Civilizations,' whereby global Islam and Arabism is viewed as being a cultural threat to the west [and possibly vice versa].[137]

A contemplation of the dynamic changes can be easily grasped by considering the fact that, in the Horn of Africa, Djibouti and Somalia joined the Arab League, profitting immensely from collective political bargaining as well as from other economic and development oriented packages. Although Somalia's membership in the Arab League in 1979 was accepted unanimously by members of the Arab League nations, Ghalib, however, argues that this did not reflect a sense of Arabism on the part of Somalis, and saw the membership as one based on a reflection of a common destiny of two peoples as a result of historical bonds, geographical proximity, trade connections and the bond of Islam.[138] As a direct outcome of that membership, the Somali government received military and financial aid from several Arab countries that enthusiastically adopted and sustained the totalitarian regime. For its part, Somalia gave support to Eritreans in an effort to please its newfound friends, but also to use Eritrea as part of its animosity against rival Ethiopia. Siyad Barre's major concern at the time was security; underlined by his massive build-up of both soft and hard instruments of power. For example, he created one of the most powerful armies in sub-Saharan Africa.[139] This, it appears, was envisaged as a necessary tool to implement Somali foreign policy, hence inviting hostility from Somalia's immediate neighbours.

From another perspective, the foreign policies of countries in the Horn of Africa were also largely influenced, or rather hampered, by their dependence on the developed world in a variety of ways and at multiple levels. The dependence, more often than not, prevented them from acting rationally and choosing the course of action which would maximize their gains and minimize their losses. The intricacies and strings attached to the dependency on the west, in many cases, functioned to the interest of the west and disadvantage of African countries. That is why, according to dependency theorists, having been an appendage of the western economic system – which forms the core – was also the cause of underde-

---

[137] See S. P. Huntington, "The Clash of Civilizations?" *Foreign Affairs*, 1993.
[138] See J. M. Ghalib, *The Cost of Dictatorship: The Somali Experience,* op. cit., p.143.
[139] See M. H. Mukhtar, "Historical Dictionary of Somalia," *African Historical Dictionary Series No. 87,* (Lanham, Maryland and Oxford: Scarecrow Press, 2003), p.159.

velopment in African countries.[140] As they were part of the periphery, and entities that best serve the interests and priorities of the west more than those of their nations, these countries' foreign policy decisions were utterly designed, formulated, and monitored and evaluated in other capital cities like London, Paris, Washington, Rome, and Lisbon, among others.[141]

In the strict case of the Horn of Africa, classical examples of such dependence include Abtidon's heavy reliance on France and Kenya's political and/or ideological proximity to the United Kingdom. Many observers argue that Britain, which had sent a survey commission to the former NFD in 1962, ignored the local people's overwhelming support and ethnic/nationalist sentiments for unification with Somalia. Instead, it granted Kenya independence in line with colonially divided boundaries, leading to the breaking of [Britain's] diplomatic relations with Somalia.[142] The motivation behind this unilateral decision arose from Britain's massive interest in Kenya, especially guided by the protection and safeguarding of the large number of white settlers and businesses vastly established in many parts of the country.[143]

Most states in Africa, during the period under study, were politically and economically weak and their populations had high expectations for their leaders whose support was sometimes based on clan, ethnic or regional fragmentation, resulting in insecurity among leaders.[144] As a problem of major concern, insecurity among the African leadership, where the head of state felt timidly preoccupied with the survival of his regime, complicated the foreign policy decision-making process by disabling the rationale of sifting personal interest from that which was a national interest. This is because some leaders identified the priorities of their personal interests with those of the country they led and, as a result, some of the

---

[140] See for example T. Dos Santos, "The Structure of Dependence," in K. T. Fann and D. C. Hodges, (eds.), *Readings in U.S. Imperialism* (Boston: Porter Sargent, 1971), pp. 225-236:226.

[141] See A. E. Hillal, et al., "A Literature Survey and a Framework for Analysis," in BahgatKorany et al., *The Foreign Policies of Arab States*, (Boulder and London: West View Press, 1984), pp.5-18:15.

[142] See W. I. Zartman, *Ripe for Resolution: Conflict and Intervention in Africa* (Oxford: Oxford University Press, 1989), p.91.

[143] Ibid.

[144] See D. L. Gordon, "African Politics," in A. A. Gordon and D. L. Gordon (eds.) *Understanding Contemporary Africa* 3rd Ed., (London and New York: Lynne Rienner Publishers, 2001), pp.55-99:58.

decisions they made were not based on wide consensus, but rather on personal preference.[145] This can be surmised, for instance, from Siyad Barre's decision to join the Arab League as this issue fractured his government. The same case applies to Haile Selassie's quest to play a dominant role in the OAU. The Horn of Africa's regional foreign policy environment, therefore, lacked the necessary institutional frameworks and it focused more on individual leaders' personal gain at the expense of the institutions they claimed to represent.

The period 1960 to 1990 was one during which significant changes took place both in world politics – in terms of the Cold War rivalry between the former USSR and the US – but also in the Horn of Africa where countries became pawns in the hands of relentless Superpowers driven by greed and policies of exploitation and manipulation of the weaker African countries. The foreign policy implications of this coercive and in many cases manipulative state of affairs were not only countless in recurrence but realities shaped by the existing opportunities and constraints often considered from perspectives of the superpower. In the Horn region, foreign policy was also informed by the significance, and/or lack of, a country's geographical location, arrangement of neighbours, population and social structure, economic and military capability, as well as its political structure and political economy in general.

Furthermore, the foreign policies of the countries in the region, notably Somalia and its immediate neighbours, were interdependent, despite them being so, by way of rivalry. The interrelatedness, in certain aspects, impacted on the available options: for example, whether to be an ally or not; whether to cooperate, adopt containment, become an isolationist, or stay in the middle and as a result become non-aligned or a coalition-builder. Furthermore, this 'systemic interrelationship' influenced the choice of means and methods: for example, the use of military force or diplomacy, for achieving their objectives. It is within the context of such an elusive and, in some circumstance, ambiguous foreign policy environments that the 1963/64 Somali-Ethiopian War, the 1963 Shifta war with Kenya, and the Somali civil war (first in the north-western part of the country) broke out.

---

[145] Ongoing discussions on the redefinition of the term security and the need to expand and include human security aside, there is also a debate on whether national interest is national interest and not regime (or even group) interest. The same applies to the debate over national security vs. regime/group security.

## Foreign Policy and Conflict in Somalia: An Overview

### *Historical legacy*

History has had, and continues to have, an important role to play in the making and conduct of Somali foreign policy. Somalia is historically as ancient as countries such as Egypt, Greece, Persia and China. The Somali nation [in terms of tribal-nation rather a modern state], therefore, existed long before European colonialism;[146] and in this case before the Westphalian system. At that time, the Somalis constituted a unique but largely homogeneous society that occupied the same terrain, spoke the same language, and shared the same Islamic religion and the same culture and traditions.[147] The European scramble for Africa and its aftermath divided the country and its people into five jurisdictions: two under UK, one under Italy, one under France and the other one under Ethiopia. The Northern Frontier District (NFD) and 'Somaliland' were under UK's rule; Southern Somalia, south-central and north-eastern, was under Italy; while coastal Djibouti was under France.

In Somalia, the colonial concept of division was met with resistance by Sayid Mohammed Abdulle Hassan, the *Dervish* or the Mad Mullah, who in 1899 called for an anti-foreigner insurgence. The *Dervish*, a well-educated Islamic scholar who led a religio-militant, proto-nationalist rebel group was the first in Africa to be fought by the British air force through the use of warplanes. His resistance was supposed to be couched predominantly in a religious idiom. This is where he got the popularly known names of the '*Dervish*', given to him by the Somali people, and 'the Mad Mullah' by British colonialists after he organized his followers into a religious nationalistic movement known as the *Dervishes* (or *Daraawiishta* in Somali).

This movement had three major accomplishments: first, it set the stage for Somali consciousness against colonial rule. Secondly, by attracting large followers who supported his religious (Islamic) teaching and

---

[146] See S. M. Mousa, *Recolonization Beyond Somalia* (Mogadishu: Somali Printing Agency, 1998), p.xiii.

[147] A good example is the early formation of states in Somalia such as the pre-colonial Adal State, the Ajuran State and other mini-states. These states encountered the first European intrusion in the Horn of Africa such as the Portuguese attempt to capture Somali territory. They were also connected with the Ottoman Empire considering themselves inseparable from the rest of the Muslim world.

holy wars (Jihad), Sayid Mohammed established what became known as *pan-Somalism*. Finally, the *Dervish* was seen by Somalis as a national figure who appealed to the patriotic sentiments of both Somalis and Muslims, irrespective of their clan or lineage allegiance.[148] After Sayid Mohammed's death in December 1920, his campaign for Somali unification (liberating Somalia from foreign rule) was taken over by various political parties.

After existing under various titles, the Somali National League (SNL) was founded in British Somaliland in 1935. It pledged a number of development agenda in its programmes. Firstly, the movement aimed to work for the unification of all Somali territories. Secondly, it promised to pursue the advancement of the Somali race by abolishing clan fanaticism and encouraging brotherly relations among Somalis. Thirdly, it pledged to spread education, economic and political development throughout the country. Fourth, it promised to cooperate with the British government or any other local body whose aims were the welfare of the inhabitants of the country.[149] Hence, it carried on with the (early national consciousness) *pan-Somalism* policy established by the *Dervish*. Following Italy's declaration of war on the United Kingdom in June 1940, Italian troops overran British Somaliland and drove out the British Garrison in 1941.[150] Subsequently, British forces began operations against the Italian East Africa Empire and quickly brought the greater part of Italian Somaliland under British control, placing the country under British military administration from 1941 to 1950.[151]

## The Impact of the Second World War

In the Horn of Africa, the principal impetus behind the emergence of nationalism as the most important political force was external.[152] For ex-

---

[148] See K. G. Adar, Kenyan *Foreign Policy Behaviour towards Somalia: 1963–1983* (Lanham, New York and London: University Press of America, 1994), p.87.

[149] See I. M. Lewis, "Modern Political Movements in Somaliland: Part 1," *Africa London*, 28(3), July 1958, p.255., quoted in K. G. Adar, *Kenyan Foreign Policy Behaviour Towards Somalia: 1963-1983* (Lanham, New York and London: University Press of America, 1994), p.88.

[150] See Somalia: Background Note, US Department of State, Bureau of African Affairs, March 2006.

[151] Ibid.

[152] See S. Touval, *Somali Nationalism: International Politics and the Drive for Unity in the Horn of Africa* (Cambridge, Massachusetts: Harvard University Press, 1963), p.76.

ample, instead of evolving from internal events, Touval argues, Somali nationalism sprang mainly from the global wars and their aftermath and further asserts that participation in World War II, service in the armed forces, war propaganda and the UN's ideals influenced developments in most African territories. The Horn of Africa, however, underwent experiences unequalled elsewhere in Africa south of the Sahara.[153]

The Horn of Africa became a major theatre of foreign operations and portions of it changed hands more than once. Moreover, after World War II, the future disposition of the former Italian colony of Somalia became the subject of political struggle and extensive debate, in the course of which the opinions of the population were sought. This solicitation of the wishes of the inhabitants became an especially powerful stimulus to the formation of a nationalist movement. The four power commission which visited Mogadishu in January 1948, and what they saw, is a good example.

The centrality of the 'Greater Somalia' concept was evident in a memorandum presented to the four powers commission by the Somali Youth League (SYL) spokesman, Abdullahi Isse, which concluded:

> We do not pretend that we can stand on our own feet at the moment, but ask the UN Trusteeship Council to decide questions relating to the formation, boundaries and administration of Somali territory to be known as Somalia, this territory to consist of all areas at present predominantly populated by Somalis.[154]

Furthermore, it stated that the union of Italian Somalia with other Somali territories was their primary objective, for which they were prepared to sacrifice any other demand standing in the way of the achievement of 'Greater Somalia.'[155]

In 1948 and 1954, opposition to territorial changes culminated in the establishment of the Somali National League (SNL) and the National

---

[153] Ibid, p.77.
[154] See J. Drysdale, *Stoics Without Pillows: A way forward for the Somalilands*, op. cit., p.63.
[155] See S. Heally, "The Changing Idiom of Self Determination in the Horn of Africa," in I. M. Lewis, (ed.) *Nationalism and Self Determination in the Horn of Africa*, (London; Ithaca Press,1983) pp.93-109, quoted in K. G. Adar, *Kenya's Foreign Policy Behaviour Towards Somalia: 1963-1983* (Lanham, New York and London: University Press of America, 1994), p.89.

United Front (NUF) in the British-administered areas in the north.[156] In 1948, for example, the UK turned the *Ogaden* and neighbouring Somali territories over to Ethiopia.[157] On the eve of the final transfer of some of the British Somaliland rangelands to Ethiopia, the nationalist movements first sought the reintegration of territories ceded from the British and Italian territories, but later on expanded their demands to independence and unification with the rest of the country.[158]

According to Article 23 of the 1947 Peace Treaty, which was negotiated by the victorious wartime allied powers, Italy had to renounce all rights and titles to Italian Somalia. On September 15, 1948, however, the four powers commission referred the question of disposal of former Italian colonies to the UN General Assembly and, on November 12, 1949, it adopted a resolution recommending that Italian Somaliland be placed under an international trusteeship system for 10 years with Italy as the administering authority. This was to be followed by independence for Italian Somalia. In 1959, at the request of the Somali caretaker government, the UN General Assembly advanced the date of independence from December $2^{nd}$ to July $1^{st}$ 1960. One of the many side-effects of World War II was, therefore, the stimulation of a new conception of Somali nationalism: to foster the nationalist agenda of unifying all Somali territories and, at the same time, provide conditions that backed the achievement of this goal.

## *Independence and its Implications on Somali Foreign Policy*

In the 1950s, the preparations for the independence of British Somaliland and Italian Somalia were put underway. The *'Bevin Plan,'* a British-proposed plan, which aimed at the lumping together of all Somali inhabited territories in the form of a British-administered trusteeship, had earlier been rejected. The rejection, in turn, is what led to the referral of the matter to the UN General Assembly. Progress was somehow made in British Somaliland towards self-governance and, as the clock ticked towards independence, the few political leaders who had emerged were ab-

---

[156] See A. M. Jama, "The Destruction the Somali State: Causes, Costs and Lessons," in H. M. Adam and R. Ford, *Mending Rips in the Sky: Options for Somali Communities in the $21^{st}$ Century* (Asmara: Red Sea Press Inc, 1997), pp.237-254:240.
[157] Ibid.
[158] Ibid.

sorbed by a single issue: the question of unity with their neighbour to the south of the United Nations Trust Territory of Somalia.[159]

The politics of independence led to the mushrooming of political parties in the closing years of the 1950s, particularly in response to the overarching need of that particular moment in Somali history. The former British protectorate became independent on June 26, 1960, and five days later, on July 1st 1960, it joined Italian Somalia to form the unified state of the Somali Republic. Almost a year later, by June 1961, Somalia adopted its first national constitution in a country-wide referendum; this provided for the creation of a democratic state with a parliamentary form of government, making the new Somali Republic 'Africa's first democracy.'[160] At this moment, however, those who advised caution were overwhelmed by the nationalist call for unification in the quest for a *pan-Somali* state: in this case 'Greater Somalia' would include *Somali Cote Francais de Somaliens* (Djibouti), *Ogaden* and NFD.[161]

## Somalia and the Horn of Africa: Foreign Policy vs. Conflict

Since its inception as an autonomous state, the Somali Republic has pursued a foreign policy committed to the idea of 'Greater Somalia' – that is, the liberation and voluntary union of all five 'Somalias' divided into alien administrations during and after the European scramble for Africa. From independence in 1960, this idea was at the core of Somalia's relationships with its neighbours and interactions with other actors in the international system. In addition to indirect military involvement in the struggle against the French over coastal Djibouti, Somali diplomats' call for 'the direct decolonization of the Ethiopian-held but Somali inhabited *Ogaden* territory and the self-determination for the Somali people in the former NFD' was an open secret.

The actions of the Somali leaderships were, however, constrained and sometimes promoted by the environment in which they operated. For example, by playing as a client state in the Cold War, Somalia ac-

---

[159] See War-torn Societies Project International, *Rebuilding Somalia: Issues and Possibilities for Puntland* (London: HAAN Associates, 2001), pp.7-30:9.

[160] More on the concept of Somalia as Africa's first democracy see Samatar, A. I., *AFRICA's First Democrats: Somalia's Aden A. Osman and Abdirazak H. Hussen*, (Bloomington, Indiana: Indiana University Press, 2016).

[161] See War-torn Societies Project International, *Rebuilding Somalia: Issues and Possibilities for Puntland* (London: HAAN Associates, 2001), pp.7-30:9.

quired the means to use force, in spite of the inflexibility of the bipolar system, and engaged in coalition building without creating permanent antipathies, using superpower support to its advantage.

Although Somalia also utilized the loophole in the UN which offered support to self-determination by supporting rebel and guerrilla movements, for example in Kenya and Ethiopia, its activities were constrained by the OAU Charter. Another instance is Article III (3) of the OAU Charter, which calls upon all states to respect the sovereignty and territorial integrity of each state.[162] In addition, the fact that the Ethiopian leadership hosted the headquarters of the OAU, and as a result developed a good relationship with other sub-Saharan countries, allowed it to gain strong support for its resistance to Somalia's policies and aims to reunify all Somali inhabited areas in the Horn of Africa region. The idea of playing down Somalia's claim was seen by many as a relevant mechanism to avoid the opening a *Pandora's Box*; because most African leaders believed that successful ethnic-based movements in one African country could encourage others on the continent and, as a consequence, produce destabilizing effects that jeopardise the achievements made and the aspirations for the future.

In 1986, the creation of the Inter-Governmental Authority on Drought and Desertification (IGADD) in Djibouti brought a new window of opportunity that facilitated negotiations between Somalia and Ethiopia. It was responding to the neutralization of the long-stranding animosity between the two neighbours and stabilising the turbulent atmosphere of hatred that characterised the nature of relationship between the rival neighbours. As expected, it led to a shifting of goals from military takeover of the *Ogaden* to opening of its frontiers to population migration and refugee movements. The catalyst, in this case, was the increasing refugee burden. Weakened by drought and diminishing economic resources beyond bilateral aid and Cold War political economy, the Somali government opted to utilize the army in other priority areas than their deployment at battle fronts along borderlines with its neighbours.

Somali claims, though historically justified, operated in the realm of high politics where security is a major issue based on realist ideals. These impacted on the country's relationship with its neighbours as they had to be prepared for possible attacks and threats to their national security. Balancing of power also constrained Somali foreign policy despite its at-

---

[162] See Article III (3) of the OAU Charter.

traction of huge funding from sympathizing states, mainly from the Arab/Muslim world. Somali foreign policy's disregard for low politics – in other words for economic development and democratization – was a key characteristic of dictatorial leadership. As a result, while there was much focus on the *pan-Somalism* project, domestic politics suffered from neglect. For example, resources intended for development had to be diverted to sustain the 'Greater Somalia' project, leading to poverty and disease; as a result, anarchy erupted throughout the country.

The crucial lesson learned here in terms of the conduct of foreign policy is that, by antagonizing its neighbours, Somalia not only sowed the seeds of suspicion but it also shrunk its avenues for possible leverage and influence along peaceful diplomacy of attracting supporters for its cause. For example, the conclusion of a defence agreement between Kenya and Ethiopia was mainly aimed at countering Somali manoeuvres to agitate people and heighten the risk of military confrontation and devastation. If its policies had succeeded, Somalia would have been playing a dominant role in the Horn of Africa by now; its failure, however, had the opposite effect as it encouraged rebel incursions from Ethiopia into Somalia and from Somalia into Ethiopia, leading to the overthrow of both dictators, Siyad Barre and Mengistu, within a short span of five (5) months.

## Conclusions

There are a number of lessons that one can draw from the foregoing discussion that illustrate how the foreign policy a country pursues has implications on conflict. Firstly, it determines whether a country is aggressive or conciliatory towards its neighbours and the international community as a whole. While Somalia adopted a coercive attitude, Djibouti was not reactionary as opposed to Kenya and Ethiopia. The two countries made foreign policy choices based on who they were dealing with: a friendly country or an enemy. Secondly, foreign policy considerations are important in assessing and determining the type, range and number of weapons acquired by a country and the possible purposes behind the acquisition. Due to its policy that predisposed it to war with its neighbours, Somalia not only bought a massive number of weapons but it also kept huge and well-trained armed forces, a military capability many envied. This, in turn, invited the same reaction from Somalia's neighbours, allowing them to counter Somalia's actions if the need were to arise. Under such conditions, wars can easily break out as each party in a dispute feels it has what it takes militarily to impose its wishes on the other.

Finally, foreign policy plays an important role in conflict escalation or de-escalation. In their desire to achieve their foreign policy objectives, states with a coercive approach will be more likely to escalate a conflict faster than others. This is based on the notion that unilateral decisions can lead to war. Somalia's claim to NFD and the *Ogaden* region and its attempts to reclaim, and at the same time militarily support the NFDLF in Kenya and the WSLF in Ethiopia without due regard to the use of international diplomacy, were crucial to the *Shifta* and the *Ogaden* wars.

# CHAPTER THREE

## Conflict in Somalia: The History

### Background to the Somali Conflict

Somalia's long history of migration, conquest and assimilation, coupled with the colonially imported 'nation-state' system, has had a serious impact on the political and administrative health of the nation; so much so that conflict has become not just a recognized part of daily life,[163] but a dynamic one whose possible occurrence could be anticipated. The 'pastoralist' nature of the majority of Somali people has even further exacerbated the already difficult situation.[164]

A pertinent illustration of this premise lies in the works of two Africanist scholars, Richard Burton and Ioan Lewis, both of whom carried out extensive research on Somalia, particularly in the northwestern region. The conclusions they drew from their studies, though in apparent contradiction, clearly illustrate the contradictory and conflicting nature of the Somali psyche. Richard Burton characterized the Somali people as 'fierce republicans;' Ioan Lewis, meanwhile, dubbed them 'pastoral democrats.' Both of these descriptions are correct.

Somalia may have achieved independence, but the country continued being administered through a combination of colonial ideals and practices and political concepts. It could not adhere appropriately either to familiar Somali traditions of governance or to the modern system of western style bureaucratic practices and procedures. In actuality, the dawn of independence brought little that was new. On the contrary, the country's new leaders merely made slight modifications to the colonial systems already in place, paying no significant attention to the escalating levels of corruption, nepotism and political and administrative inefficiency. The result was that the country became a modern example of the worst state collapse ever experienced in the history of post-colonial Africa. Its repercussions were socially, politically and economically devastating, vertically

---

[163] See online journal Somalia Diaspora, Jaaliyadda.
[164] Ibid.

and horizontally. In addition to the loss of lives and destruction of valuable properties, it caused mass displacement, an influx of large numbers of refugees, regional and international interferences, total disintegration of administrative control and the social fabric of the nation. What ensued was, unfortunately, an inconceivable trend of moral corruption and moral decay as displayed in the level of animosity—unparalleled by any that had been experienced in Somalia.

An arid and semi-arid country with seasonally erratic rainfall, only 13 percent of Somalia's land area is arable. Almost half (45%) is devoted to the rearing of livestock. The vast majority of Somalis depend for their livelihood upon livestock, farming, or a combination of the two. Since the outbreak of war, Somalia's non agro-pastoral productive assets have suffered massive losses due to the population's limited access to the scarce resources of the country. Therefore, the deterioration of these culturally practise production lines, coupled with the ever-widening divisions opening within the Horn of Africa region and, along clan lines, within the country; both of which have fuelled escalating internal conflicts, have shaken down development aspirations of the masses. Today, most of Somalia is structurally food-insecure and internally displaced, and the concept of 'development' remains a closed chapter in any book concerned with development. The country has borne the brunt of what one Somali traditional elder called 'a national curse.'[165]

Somalia has experienced three main types of wars. Traditional wars between clans and sub-clans that were triggered by confrontation over wells, camels and women; national wars which involved external actors, and which were fought during the colonial, post-colonial and independence era in Somalia;[166] and civil war which broke out in the late 1980s and it is yet to be fully resolved.

## Pre-colonial Somalia

In pre-colonial Somalia, clans represented primordial cleavages and cultural fragmentation, making conflicts and violence a common feature of

---

[165] Interview with Malaaq Mukhtaar, Nairobi, September 11, 2003.
[166] See S. Hussein, "Somalia: A Destroyed Country and a Defeated Nation," in H. M. Adam and R. Ford, (eds.) *Mending Rips in the Sky: Options for Somali Communities in the 21ˢᵗ Century* (Asmara: The Red Sea Press, inc, 1997), pp.165-192:170.

life,[167] as the idiom of kin, clanship and segmentation formed the structural basis of competition. The competition for resources implied that, in a zero-sum game of sub-clan power, one group's gain was at the expense of another. In harsh times, the circle of trust contracted, excluding those who were genealogically distant.[168] Sub-clan unity was maintained by respecting equality among members who gained equal access to the means of livelihood by which justice was measured. Somali customary law, or *Xeer*, was very important in managing violence.[169] The *Diya* system or blood compensation was negotiated. Members of the group that committed the crime had to pay what was agreed upon with the other group that represents the plaintiff. In Islamic *Sharia* law, the *diya* is 100 camels for men and 50 for women. This is paid to the aggrieved clan as compensation. Presently, due to the Somali customary law- *Xeer*, on the one hand, clans pay what they agree as a standard compensation, which reciprocally also becomes a binding *Xeer* to them when the same type of crime is committed against any of their members. *Xeer*, on the other hand, is the Somali traditional or customary law, which relates mainly to social conventions and contracts. It serves very important roles in managing not only social life but also Somali politics in this new era of statelessness and anarchy.[170]

Therefore, pre-colonial Somalia was characterised by a culture of violence as violent strategies were part and parcel of the harsh way of nomadic life and competition was necessarily fierce.[171] Moreover, clan distinctions also reflected historical experiences and social differences. The latter can be observed in the traditional society of Somalia, which imposed a ranked dimension to a minority of Somali groups who are considered to exist beyond the clan system. One such group consists of

---

[167] See J. Abbink, "Dervishes, Moryaan and Freedom Fighters: Cycles of Rebellion and The Fragmentation of Somalia Society 1900-2000," in J. Abbink, et al, (eds.) *Rethinking Resistances: Revolt and Violence in African History* (Brill, Leiden and Boston; TutaSudAegide Pallas, 2003), pp.328-365:333.

[168] See C. Geshekter, "The Death of Somalia in Historic Perspective," in Hussein M. Adam and Richard Ford, *Mending Rips in the Sky: Options for Somali Communities in the 21st Century* (Asmara: Red Sea Press Inc, 1997), pp.65-98:69.

[169] See I. M. Lewis, *A Pastoral Democracy*, (London: Oxford University Press, 1961).

[170] Ibid.

[171] See J. Abbink, "Dervishes, Moryaan and Freedom Fighters: Cycles of Rebellion and The Fragmentation of Somalia Society 1900-2000," in J. Abbink, et al, (eds.) *Rethinking Resistances: Revolt and Violence in African History* (Brill, Leiden and Boston: TutaSudAegide Pallas, 2003), pp.328-365:338.

those who have paradoxically managed to master rudimentary rural technologies – domestic tools, weaponry, and household utensil-making, leather craftsmanship and knowledge of herbal medicine. A caste – system of oppression was imposed on them.[172]

Furthermore, there was a distinction between and among the four pastoral clan-families, which tend to view the agro-pastoralists [and other communities] as somewhat 'backward,' who in turn considered the nomads to be 'anarchists.'[173] There was, therefore, substantial diversity in lifestyle and prestige. Whatever the diversity, however, the fact remains that ultimately unsettled disputes were left to be resolved through military means and, hence, wars and feuds occurred constantly.[174] In the precolonial period, therefore, there only existed a decentralized form of communal governance that had a richer reflection of the cultural and religious identity of the Somali people. Consequently, violence, as in so many pre-industrial societies, was part of the accepted relations between groups.

### Colonial Somalia: Conflict as a Way of Life

Somalia has always been considered an exception with regard to the rest of Africa on account of its extraordinary (largely) ethnic, cultural, religious and linguistic homogeneity; it is for this reason that Somalia, prior to its independence, was referred to as the nation without a state.[175] In the light of this reality, questions later arose as to how a people seemingly much more coherent and cohesive than others could descend into such chaos and forms of behaviour that are to outsiders inexplicable. While some of the causes are historical, others are more recent and have to do with the country's external relations and conflicts with its neighbours.

---

[172] See H. M. Adam, "Clan Conflicts and Democratization in Somalia," in O. Nnoli, *Government and Politics in Africa: A Reader*, (Harare: AAPS, 2000), p.853. See also Kusow, A. M. (ed,). *Putting the Cart before the Horse: Contested Nationalism and the Crisis of the Nation-State in Somalia*. (Lawrwnceville, NJ: The Res Sea Press, 2004) and Eno, M.A. *The Bantu-Jareer Somalis: Unearthing Apartheid in the Horn of Africa*. (London: Adonis & Abbey, 2008).

[173] Ibid.

[174] See I. M. Lewis, *A Pastoral Democracy* (London: Oxford University Press, 1961), p.27.

[175] See A. A. Botan, "Somalia: Regional State or Cantonization of Clans," in H. M. Adam and R. Ford, *Mending Rips in the sky: Options for Somali Communities in the 21st Century*, (Asmara: The Red Sea Press, 2000), pp.255-270:255.

The modern history of the internal Somali conflict and that between Somalia and its neighbours began in the late 19th century when various European powers began to trade and establish themselves in the area. Gordon, for example, discussing the effects of the 1884-1885 Berlin Conference, which initiated the European Scramble for Africa, notes that in that relatively short period, massive changes took place in the continent that not only established the immediate context for African politics but also continue to constrain and shape its future.[176] The political map inherited by the new African states was based largely on the expedient economic and political strategies of imperial Europe. These not only led to highly divergent and artificial geographical forms but also distorted traditional social and economic patterns.[177]

In Somalia, the British East India Company's desire for unrestricted harbour facilities led to the conclusion of treaties with the Sultan of Tajurs as early as 1840. It was not until 1886, however, that the British gained control over northern Somalia through treaties with various Somali chiefs who were guaranteed British protection. British objectives centred on the safeguarding of trade links to the east and securing local sources of food [mainly meat] and provisions for its station in Aden.[178]

In 1897, the three rival powers in the Red Sea and the Gulf of Aden, namely France, Britain, and Italy sent their representatives to Addis Ababa, within a few days of each other, in order to squeeze concessions out of Ethiopia's Menelik II who had become a formidable figure. It had become apparent to them that they should at least obtain Menelik's formal recognition of their neighbouring acquisition and of their mysterious frontiers with Ethiopia.[179] This second scramble was to be the forerunner of endless strife on the Somali plateau. Furthermore, observes Drysdale, the present frontier between the Somali Republic and Kenya was a historical accident dating from Britain's treaty with Italy in 1895, which par-

---

[176] See D. L. Gordon, "African Politics," in A. A. Gordon and D. L. Gordon, (eds.), *Understanding Contemporary Africa* 3rd Ed., (Boulder: Lynne Rienner Publishers, 2001), pp.55-99:58.
[177] Ibid.
[178] See "Somalia: Background Note," US Department of State, Bureau of African Affairs, March 2006, p.3.
[179] See J. Drysdale, *The Somalia Dispute* (London and Dunmow: Pallmall Press, 1994), p.3.

titioned the Sudan and East Africa respectively to become zones of British and Italian influences.[180]

These historical occurrences have many serious implications for the Somali conflict;[181] including the fact that they created tensions between an ancient pastoral culture and the demands of modern statehood. Somalis were lovers of animals in pre-colonial times and were, according to Mazrui, usually members of stateless societies. They had ordered anarchy and ruled through consensus rather than coercion as opposed to lovers of land who had experienced statehood since pre-colonial times and, therefore, experienced elaborate political and social hierarchal structures even before the impact of the modern state. The European colonization, and with it the idea of state, which includes concepts such as territorial sovereignty and consciousness of frontiers and borders, was often a severe constraint for the nomadic section of the Somali people. The Somali people as a whole found themselves split in five different areas by the Scramble for Africa. In addition to fragmenting the Somali people, colonialism led them to become more conscious of themselves as one Somali family, instead of, as individual clans.

In the colonial period, this brought about resistance and the revolt known as the 1900-1920 *Dervish* rebellion led by Sayyid Mohammed Abdulle Hassan. After the British Consul-General for the coast received a letter from Mohammed Abdulle Hassan accusing the British of oppressing Islam and denouncing those who obeyed or co-operated with the administration as liars and slanders, the British administrator declared the Somali leaders as a rebel and urged his government in London to prepare an expedition against the *Dervishes*.[182] Although Sayyid Mohammed was defeated by the British, using rival Somali elements, he was lauded as a popular hero and still stands as a major figure of national identity to many Somalis.[183] To his credit, the Somali historian Aw Jama Isse argued that, the *Dervish* movement was the first in the history of colonial Africa, which the British used its air force to attack and defeat.[184]

---

[180] Ibid.
[181] See A. Mazrui, "Crisis in Somalia: From Tyranny to Anarchy," in H. M. Adam and R. Ford, *Mending Rips in the Sky: Options for Somali Communities in the 21ˢᵗ Century*, (Asmara: The Red Sea Press, 2000), pp.5-11:8.
[182] See I. M. Lewis, *A Modern History of the Somalia: Nation and State in the Horn of Africa* 4ᵗʰ Ed (Hargeisa: Btec Books, 2002), p.70.
[183] Interview with Abdulkadir Yahya, Co-Director- CRD, Nairobi, June 26, 2005.
[184] Interview with Aw Jama Omar Isse, Somali Historian, Eldoret, December 12, 2002.

## Independent Somalia: Wars with Neighbours, Causes and Issues

After independence in 1960, Somalia has engaged in border hostilities with Kenya and Ethiopia in the mid-1960s and again with Ethiopia in 1977-78 during the *Ogaden* War. Various reasons underlie these wars. Among them, and the most important, is the issue of Somali nationalism. According to Lewis, the first stirrings of nationalism occurred in the 1930s and 1940s in urban centres, especially in Mogadishu.[185] In this rapidly growing urban centre, the impact of Western influence was experienced most keenly and the collective indemnification of wrongs was now less necessary than in the nomadic world of the interior. Amongst merchants and traders, especially, there arose a new feeling of dissatisfaction with the particularism of the past. This, together with the experience of Italian patriotic fervour presented in a new light and the long suppressed reaction to alien rule, provided conditions favourable to the emergence of new aspirations. Thus, in the last few years of the short-lived Italian East African Empire, the first definite steps towards the creation of a modern nationalist movement began in Somalia.

Following the Italian defeat, the whole of the Somali Peninsula (with the exception of French Somaliland) came under British military administration and continued for almost a decade.[186] The most notable development under British military rule was the growth of a new and fervent sense of national awareness. A number of factors helped foster this new attitude. The memory of the *Dervish* nationalist resistance, the unification of the country and the spectre of another dismemberment, the public humiliation of colonial masters (first by the British then by the Italians) hitherto presumed invincible, the progression in education and in economic complexity, the growth of an articulate elite, and the lifting of the ban on open political debate by the new administration were some of the forces that served to give rise to the new nationalist climate.[187] The other reasons were the proposal for eventual independence – since the country was placed under UN trusteeship – and Britain's project for a 'Greater

---

[185] See I. M. Lewis, *A Modern History of the Somalia: Nation and State in the Horn of Africa*, op. cit., p.113.
[186] See D. D. Laitin, and S. S. Samatar, *Somalia: Nation in Search of a State* (Colorado: Westview Press, 1987), p.763.
[187] Ibid.

Somalia' and its encouragement of political parties and, eventually, the country's repartition.[188]

The Somali Youth League (SYL) promoted the idea of Somali unity with neighbouring Somali territories, namely: French Somaliland, the *Ogaden* under Ethiopian rule, the NFD in Kenya and British Somaliland. SYL activists carried flags and banners depicting a white five-pointed star on a blue sky.[189] This idea of 'Greater Somalia' was at the core of Somali foreign policy, fomenting wars with Ethiopia and Kenya. As the people in the disputed areas shared the same culture, language and religion, Somali leaders believed that by merging them into one country under a strong central government, Somalis would achieve a lot.

Attempts to unify all the Somali people in the 1960s did not succeed as the French, Ethiopian and Kenyan British segments could not join with the two larger groupings – Italian in the south and British in the north – to form a new state. Despite independence of the Somali Republic in 1960, the Somali nationalist dream still remained unfulfilled.[190] Because of this *pan-Somali* nationalism, Somalia's relations with its neighbours became sticky and even belligerent. The country supported a proxy-type guerrilla war, by a unionist movement in northern Kenya (usually referred to as the *Shifta*) between 1963 and 1967. It also engaged into a conflict with Ethiopia both in 1964, and later on in 1977-78 by militarily supporting the Western Somali Liberation Front (WSLF) movement in Ethiopia.

A critical observer of the foreign relations and foreign policy systems of the Horn of Africa would not hold Somalia alone responsible for the impasse in the region. For, apart from Somalia, neighbours Kenya and Ethiopia also precipitated the wars and, in certain cases, could be blamed as culprits who 'welcomed' the colonialists' agenda of sowing seeds of hatred by accepting the misappropriation of portions of their neighbour's territory. On Ethiopia's eastern flank, its 19th century acquisition of territory brought it into conflict with Somalia's claims.[191] As an independent

---

[188] See R. Adloff, and V. Thompson, *Djibouti and the Horn of Africa* (California: Stanford University press, 1968), p.119.

[189] See J. Drysdale, *Stoics Without Pillows: A way forward for the Somalilands* (London: HAAN Associates Publishing, 2000), p.71.

[190] See H. M. Adam, et al, *Removing Barricades in Somalia: Options for Peace and Rehabilitation* (Washington United State Institute for Peace, 1998), p.2.

[191] See P. Woodward, *The Horn of Africa: Politics and International Relations* (London and New York: Tauris Academic Publishers, 1996), p.125.

state at the time the Somali-Ethiopian border had been established, Ethiopia was a participant in the negotiations that annexed Somali territory to its land. In other words, the country had not been a helpless victim of the dealings of European colonial powers, but rather a party to the conquest of the Horn of Africa. Most of the *Ogaden* was annexed to Ethiopia only in the 1890s and the contested borders were simply variants of those established in treaties between Ethiopia and Britain in 1897 and between Ethiopia and Italy in 1908. This was followed by the annexing of *Reserve Area* and *Hawd* in 1954 with British consent. The problem was further complicated by the fact that Somalia demanded its land back; about one third of present Ethiopian territory, including the major towns of Harar and Dire Dawa.[192]

The evident greed of Ethiopia, its lust to rub shoulders with European colonialists (for prestige and foolish pride), and its long established religious connection as a Christian nation, interplayed with each other in its favour in the plot against Somalia. But, by crafting this scheme, all three Christian nations—Ethiopia, Britain and Italy—endorsed a catastrophic idea that would significantly hamper the stability and good neighbourliness required to flourish mutual co-existence between the two Horn of Africa countries upon the 'physical' departure of colonialism.

To date, there is not an internationally recognized border, but only a provisional administrative line,[193] which depicts the inadequacy of the OAU's resolution regarding acceptance of border lines as designed by colonialists. Many view such a division as being typically colonial, in the sense that it is a line arbitrarily drawn on the map without regard for ethnic, cultural, or economic realities of the inhabitants; a situation which currently remains a problem and with a potential to flare up into yet another deadly confrontation. As a result of that tripartite decision of annexation, the two neighbouring states engaged in hostilities that cost lives and resources crucially needed for national and human development in both countries. The motivation to go to war, each country claims, was to protect its national interests since losing to the other side meant losing status and prestige; with territory being a major variable of power in in-

---

[192] See E. J. Keller, *Revolutionary Ethiopia: From Empire to Peoples Republic* (Bloomington and Indianapolis: Indiana University Press, 1988), p.162.

[193] See M. H. Mukhtar, "Historical Dictionary of Somalia," *African Historical Dictionary Series* No. 87 (Maryland and Oxford: Scarecrow Press, 2003), p.176.

ternational politics.[194] As mentioned above, Ethiopia also had the curse and concern of being land-locked.

The prestige factor had wide-reaching effects in the person of the Ethiopian emperor, another contributing factor to the conflagration in the region. Due to his imperial inclinations, the Emperor was not satisfied with the 1950 UN resolution to federate Eritrea into Ethiopia, granting it greater freedom and self-governance.[195] This again meant that Ethiopia would be reduced to a land-locked state with endless dependence on other countries for its maritime commerce with the rest of the world. Therefore, it abrogated the federation in 1962, annexed Eritrea and fought rebel forces such as the Eritrean Liberation Front (ELF), causing another massive devastation of human lives and multiple economic resources that would benefit both countries had they adopted mutually negotiated peaceful approaches and diplomatic resolution to their dispute.

This had several implications for the conflict with Somalia: it deepened the suspicions between the two states over their respective intentions; it prompted clientelism and therefore a desire to acquire weapons; and it brought about proxy wars in each other's country. As part of its *pan-Arab* nationalism sympathy, Somalia indeed supported Eritrean liberation movements. Ethiopia, on the other hand, supported Somali rebel groups to counter Somalia's harbouring of what the latter recognized as 'legitimate' freedom fighters. Somalia's concerns lied both in the quest to open different fronts of war to wear out the Ethiopian army while Ethiopia was concerned with the Eritrean port which was an important eco-

---

[194] Moreover, the vision of the two countries was completely different. Ethiopia, for example, considers itself a multi-ethnic country and looks Somali territory as part of the expanded 19th Century Ethiopian empire while Somalia sees itself as a mono-ethnic country that should include all Somalis and considers Ethiopia as part of the colonial powers who took over Somali territories. From this, therefore, Ethiopia is seen as a black colonial power and the liberation movement in the Somali territory as legitimate freedom fighters where self-determination adopted by the UN is applicable to the Somalis in Ethiopia. See for example Abdurahman Abdullahi (Baadiyow), *Making Sense of Somali History Vol. I*, Adonis & Abbey Publishers Ltd (May 12, 2017).

[195] See for example, M. Ottaway, *Soviet and American Influence in the Horn of Africa* (New York: Oxford University Press, 1989).

nomic asset and a strategic point for the supply of weapons,[196] as well as a for the conduct of a vast array of international trade.

As far as Kenya is concerned, Somali nationalism constituted a challenge to its territorial integrity. From the onset of the separation or annexation, Somali nationalists demanded that the eastern portion of northern Kenya be detached from Kenya and re-attached to Somalia, which has now become the Somali Republic. However, the Kenyan leaders of the time were not willing to accommodate the Somali request, a matter which displeased the Somali leaders as nothing but arrogance.[197] For Kenya, it was easy to let go of the huge area in question which covers some 45,000 square miles and comprises about one fifth of the total territory of Kenya.[198] The rejection by both Kenya and Ethiopia to return the annexed territories back to Somalia, according to a section of analysts, gave them a depiction of colonialists, ideologically, not any different from the white invaders.

During independence, the United Kingdom had a certain level of sympathy towards Somalia's dilemma. However, British diplomats were guilty of double-dealing in the 19th Century, which marks the time when the damage had been done. Having signed treaties of protection with Somali leaders, then signing another treaty with Menelik, Somalis feel Britain's contravention of the trust of 'protection' and protectorate. In this view, as Somalis claim, the British put their 'protected' peoples under jeopardy of the jurisdiction of the Ethiopian emperor. To compensate this 'British sin,' Lord Bevin attempted to fashion a united Somali colony in the wake of World War II at a time when the British military administration had control of virtually all Somali lands with the exception of the French colony (today's Djibouti). This proposal, however, failed amid considerable opposition in the UN, especially by the Soviets who saw in the plan another British attempt to expand its empire.

Pretending to be sympathetic to the Somali people, and as a measure not to repeat its early mistake, the British promised the Somalis that the popular will in Kenya's NFD would determine whether it became part of Kenya or Somalia. When a British team travelled to the NFD, it reported

---

[196] See M. Wubneh and Y. Abate, *Ethiopia: Transition and Development in the Horn of Africa* (Colorado: Westview Press, 1988), p.164.
[197] Shafat, A. "The Challenges the Youth of Northeastern Kenya Face: A Historical Analysis," *Journal of Somali Studies*, Vol. 1, No. 1, (2014), pp. 63-90.
[198] See S. Touval, *Somalia Nationalism: International Policy and the Drive for Unity in the Horn of Africa* (Cambridge and Massachusetts: Harvard University Press, 1963), p.147.

an overwhelming desire of the people to join with the Somali Republic.[199] The Somalis of Kenya have sympathized with the Somali nationalist movement since its inception. However, Somali nationalists were increasingly concerned that Kenya's constitutional progress might frustrate their hopes for ultimate unification with the Somali Republic and were reluctant to become subject to Kenya when the country attained independence.[200] For their part, the Kenya nationalists were determined to safeguard the country's territorial integrity and oppose the secession of that territory to the Somali Republic. At this time, British double-dealings resurfaced. In order to make peace with the Kenyan nationalists, seen as essential to an orderly transition of agricultural ownership of British settlers in the white highlands, the British agreed to keep the NFD as a part of Kenya, thus compromising again the desire of Kenyan-Somalis.

This biased intervention and betrayal prompted secessionist feelings among some Somalis in the Northern Frontier District (NFD).[201] In reaction to Kenyan nationalists' refusal to entertain any territorial adjustments in their final negotiations with the British before independence, the Somali government invited Jomo Kenyatta and Ronald Ngala to Mogadishu and showered them with Somali hospitality in order to support the NFD people's right to self-determination. In March 1963, when the British announced on Kenyan radio that the NFD would become an integral part of Kenya, it provoked riots in Somalia and in the NFD. As a result, Kenyan authorities dubbed the Somali nationalists *Shiftas*, (bandits), while their kin in the Somali Republic characterized them as freedom fighters. The agitation by the NFD Somalis was translated by Kenyan leaders as a symptom of disloyalty, thus, prompting Kenya to oppress and kill wantonly its own citizens in the short *Shifta* war.[202] Scholars like Shafat and Aukot put it more explicitly as they suggest that the people of the north [in Kenya] discern no difference between colonial and postcolonial Kenya."[203] As the Kenyan army was well trained in insur-

---

[199] See D. D. Laitin and S. S. Samatar, *Somalia: Nation in Search of a State*, (Boulder, Colorado: Westview Press, 1987), p.133.

[200] See S. Touval, *Somalia Nationalism: International Policy and the Drive for Unity in the Horn of Africa*, (Cambridge and Massachusetts: Harvard University Press, 1963), p.150.

[201] Interview with Ambassador Hussein Ali Dualeh, former Somali ambassador to Kenya and to Uganda, Nairobi, September 11, 2001.

[202] Shafat, A. "The Challenges the Youth of Northeastern Kenya Face: A Historical Analysis," *Journal of Somali Studies*, Vol. 1, No. 1, (2014), pp. 63-90.

[203] Ibid, p.70.

gency warfare during the Mau Mau insurgency, it put down the rebellion quickly; as "Kenyatta's government ironically borrowed heavily from the tactics that the British had been using against the Mau Mau uprising [as] Kenyatta declared a state of emergency [barely] two weeks after independence."[204]

Understandably, Somalia's denouncement of colonially designed borders and annexation fostered the relationship between Ethiopia and Kenya. From that perspective, one can perceptually view that, because a key element in the relationship between Kenya and Ethiopia was Somalia's territorial claims in both Kenya and Ethiopia, which made them targets of Somali guerrilla insurrection, they had to be conscious of the potential threat posed by Somali to the security of their respective countries. In their measure to counter this threat, the two countries signed an agreement of cooperation and mutual defence assistance in 1964 in order to contain the *pan-Somali* claims. The agreement resulted in the Ethiopian-Kenyan border administration commission, which met annually to assess the situation and streamline their operation along their borders with Somalia, which amounted to harsh treatment of Somalis crossing the borders of the two countries. In its January 1983 meeting, the commission condemned Somalia's expansionist ambitions and urged all countries to refrain from arming the Somali regime.

Aside from their joint pact, several events point to the strong ties between Ethiopia and Kenya. During the 1977-78 drought in Ethiopia, Kenya provided food grains to its ally. When Sudan and Somalia supported the Eritrean and Somali guerrillas that attacked and disrupted Ethiopia's access to the Red Sea ports, Kenya came to Ethiopia's help and offered its embattled neighbour the use of the Kenyan port of Mombasa. This offer also facilitated the completion of the Addis Ababa-Nairobi highway, a reality made possible by the cooperation between Somalia's rival neighbours.[205]

In addition, during the *Ogaden* war, where Somalia got the upper hand, Kenya detained aircrafts carrying arms from Egypt to Somalia to the detriment of its relations with Egypt. Kenya was also partly instrumental in preventing Somalia from enlisting US and Western military aid, after its losses in the 1977-78 *Ogaden war*. Kenya, which was also a close

---

[204] Ibid, p.71.
[205] See M. Wubneh and Y. Abate, *Ethiopia: Transition and Development in the Horn of Africa*, op. cit., p.165.

ally of the US at the time, was indeed opposed to any US military assistance to Somalia as it was concerned that such arms might be used to invade and retake NFD. As a result, in 1978, Kenya warned that its Indian Ocean ports may be closed to US warships if Washington sent arms to Somalia.[206]

## Cold War Somalia

Historically, Copson observes that international factors played a role in each of Africa's wars.[207] These factors operated on one or more of three levels: with neighbouring states; with African regional actors; and with powers from outside Africa. Foltz, on the other hand, argues that Africa has a way of periodically phasing in and out of Western consciousness, each time to reappear in a different guise, stimulating a different concern and intrigue or agitating a different set of Western interests and a different set of Westerners.[208] This is derived from the enduring structures governing Africa's interactions with the rest of the world, notably Africa's geographical position and the military and economic weakness of its people in comparison with distinct nations able to reach Africa's shores. Copson further argues that Africa has historically been allotted five roles in great power strategic calculations, namely, the physical obstacle or resting point on the way to some place of importance; the defensive bastion to protect sea lanes heading elsewhere; the launching pad of attack against other territories; the source of military supplies; and finally, the surrogate terrain where great powers could compete symbolically without bearing the full costs of destruction.

The emergence, after World War II, of a global international system, dominated by two Superpowers increasingly affected even such poor and peripheral states as those in the Horn of Africa. Unfortunately, the processes of superpower investments were both uneven and sporadic, being driven sometimes by changing perceptions and priorities in Washington and Moscow, including concerns for the other's actions, and at other

---

[206] Ibid.
[207] See R. C. Copson, *African Wars and Prospects for Peace* (New York and London: M. E. Sharpe Inc., 1994), p.103.
[208] See W. J. Foltz, "Africa in Great Power Strategy," in W. J. Foltz and H. H. Biennen (eds.) *Arms and Africa* (New haven and London: Yale University Press, 1985), p.1.

times by developments within the Horn of Africa itself.[209] The initial rivalry between the US and the Soviet Union in the 1940s and early 1950s centred primarily on Europe, at least until the iron curtain had been effectively lowered across the continent. At that time, Africa was still, overwhelmingly, the preserve of the colonial powers and, in the Middle East, the US was more concerned with Britain's deteriorating position, then with the potential of the Soviet Union. The Suez crisis of 1956 was to jolt that perception severely, because of both the Soviet's approval of Czech arms sale to Egypt and the fact that the concluding events of the crisis demonstrated the shift of the balance of power in the region away from Britain.[210]

Lederach asserts that, during much of the Cold War, the superpowers were never directly engaged in armed conflict in their own territories.[211] Instead, most wars (well over a hundred in the last fifteen years of the Cold War), were fought through, in or over client states. One of the effects of this bipolar context, Lederach posits, was an increase in the volatility, and an exacerbation of conflicts in the developing world, as was the case in the Horn of Africa and Central America.[212] In this case, it created a dominant frame of reference in which the primary explanation for armed conflicts was an ideological struggle between East and West. Lederach further highlights that geographically, the vast majority of wars fought during the Cold War were fought in territories of the periphery; what is variously termed the 'South,' the developing world and the third world: Africa, South Asia, the Middle East, and Latin America.[213]

Having gained independence during the peak of the Cold War, Somalia, together with Ethiopia, was a perfect ground for the period's rivalries. As the Superpowers competed with each other, they fuelled interstate conflict between the two client states. Prior to the shift of alliance in 1977, the Soviet Union used Somalia to fight Ethiopia while the US used the latter to fight the former; after the shift of alliances it was the other way around. Copson concurs that the two powers' foreign policy ambitions and designs could be pursued more easily in Africa [and more so in

---

[209] See P. Woodward, *The Horn of Africa: Politics and International Relations*, (London and New York: Tauris Academic Studies, 1996), p.133.
[210] Ibid.
[211] See J. P. Lederach, *Building Peace: Sustainable Reconciliation in Divided Societies* (Washington D.C.: USIP, 1997), p.5.
[212] Ibid.
[213] Ibid.

the Horn of Africa] than in many other parts of the world.²¹⁴ Here, the risk of dangerous reactions was small and affordable commitments of power could have a great impact. The USSR's Cold War involvement in Africa, for its part, was probably due to the fact that it valued the continent more for its symbolic usefulness in world politics than for its intrinsic value. On the Somalia front, the US military assistance programme was motivated by the Cold War and US strategic interests in the Indian Ocean, the Persian Gulf and the approaches to the Suez Canal.²¹⁵

In addition to fuelling other tensions, the Cold War also triggered the 1977-78 *Ogaden* war. Among other things, the two superpowers poured armaments into both states. Lederach further posits that the reality of the Cold War meant that weapons and the loans needed to finance their purchase as well as ideologies came from the north, while the south contributed its environment: mainly people and national economies.²¹⁶ During this period, more than 95 percent of arms exports came from five countries, all located in the global north, and were destined to countries located in territories housing the most fragile populations.

Cold War Somalia initiated the *Ogaden* War on July 13, 1977 with a strong WSLF drive towards Godey in the southern part of Ethiopia. The Somali decision to invade *Ogaden* may in part be explained by the Somali government's miscalculation. The Somali leadership believed that the Soviets were treaty-bound to Somalia and that they would not provide aid to its adversaries, notably Ethiopia, once Soviet-trained army men with Soviet military equipment engaged in a battlefield with another national army trained and equipped by its superpower rival, the USA. In addition, they could not see why the Soviets would risk what was at the time a secure position in Somalia to support the unstable Ethiopian regime.²¹⁷

---

²¹⁴ See R. C. Copson, *African Wars and Prospects for Peace*, (New York and London: ME Sharpe, Inc., 1994), p.112.

²¹⁵ Ibid.

²¹⁶ See J. P. Lederach, *Building Peace: Sustainable Reconciliation in Divided Societies*, (Washington D.C.: USIP, 1997), p.7.

²¹⁷ The role of Egypt, Saudi Arabia and Iran in pushing Somalia to war with Ethiopia is equally interesting. The trio saw Soviet presence of Somalia as a main security threat and, therefore, used the United States to encourage Somalia to go to war. The aim was to expel the Soviets from Somalia, destroy the Soviet-trained Somali military, and push for regime change in Somalia. However, although the April 1978 coup attempt failed, they succeeded to achieve the two other objectives.

It also appeared that Somalis had tacit encouragement and support from the Carter administration for their planned invasion of *Ogaden*.[218] Barre took advantage of the internal squabbles brewing in Ethiopia and economic difficulties the Mengistu Haile Mariam regime was experiencing, especially the change of guard coupled with the turmoil arising from the nationalist movements in Eritrea who had launched an attack in the provincial capital of Asmara in January 1975. By 1974 -75, massive drought had also weakened Ethiopia and pushed Emperor Haile Selassie's government to a state of collapse. Therefore, Somalia launched an offensive to liberate the Somali people in Ethiopia on the basis that war with weak Ethiopia was winnable.[219]

However, as Somalia was on the verge of victory, Cuba and the Soviet Union came to the rescue of Ethiopia. With the help of thousands of Cuban troops operating sophisticated Soviet Union weapons, the Soviet Union, nursing an opportunistic Cold War strategy, ruptured its long-term relations with Somalia to give full political, diplomatic and military backing to its new Ethiopian ally. Hence, the Ethiopians were able to eject the Somali army from the disputed territories,[220] the Somali foces had captured in the offensive against Ethiopian troops. It is estimated that the offensive destroyed over 75 percent of the Somali tanks and about 50 percent of its combat air force capability while about 800 of its best troops were also killed.[221]

## The Aftermath of the *Ogaden* War

Immediately, in the aftermath of the Ogaden war, Siyad Barre's problems of civil war started, motivated by some senior army officers' dissatisfaction with his decision to relinquish the large territories captured from Ethiopia. However, the situation can be studied mainly from the four principal sets of underlying factors driving civil wars: political factors;

---

[218] See M. Wubneh and Y. Abate, *Ethiopia: Transition and Development in the Horn of Africa*, (Colorado: Westview Press, 1988), p.165.

[219] See A. Simons, "Somalia: A Regional Security Dilemma," in E. J. Keller and D. Rothschild, (eds.) *Africa in the New International Order* (Boulder: Lynne Rienner Publishers, 1996), p.76.

[220] See H. M. Adam, et al., *Removing Barricades in Somalia Option for Peace and Rehabilitation*, (Washington, D.C.: USIP, 1998), p.3.

[221] See M. Robbins, "The Soviet-Cuban Relationship," in R. R. Kanet, (ed.) *Soviet Foreign Policy in the 1980s* (New York: Praegar, 1982 ), p.161.

economic and social factors; cultural and perceptional factors; and structural factors.[222] Some of the causes of internal conflicts include the nature of political power in many African states.[223] Together with the real and perceived consequences of capturing and maintaining power, this is a key source of conflict across the continent. It is indeed frequently the case that political victory assumes 'a winner-takes-it- all' form with respect to wealth and resources. The African situation aside, Somalia had a number of problems: the defeat of the *Ogaden* war led to the disintegrating of the Somali army; there were issues of identity and recognition, participation, marginalisation, and foreign-supported armed opposition. It is against this background that the Somali civil war broke out.[224]

Somalia's descent into chaotic lawlessness did not occur overnight and could have long been predicted.[225] The civilian administration that assumed power after independence became hopelessly corrupt and incompetent and was overthrown by Siyad Barre in a bloodless coup. In an attempt to regain popularity and legitimacy, Barre turned to *pan-Somali* nationalism, leading to the *Ogaden* war, as highlighted above. The defeat of Somali forces in the *Ogaden*, in turn, brought to the surface opposition elements within the Somali armed forces. These elements failed in an attempt to overthrow Barre's military government in April 1978.[226] These were mainly officers from the Majeerteen sub-clan, some of whom consequently escaped and fled abroad, especially to Ethiopia, and played a major role in forming the Somali Salvation Front (SSF), later the Somali Salvation Democratic Front (SSDF) after merger with the Somali Democratic Action (SDA) in October 1981.[227] The SSDF soon began to launch guerrilla raids on Somali army bases and civilian targets across the Ethiopian-Somali border.

---

[222] See M. E. Brown, "The Causes and Regional Dimensions of Internal Conflict," in M. E. Brown, (ed.), *The International Dimensions of Internal Conflicts* (Cambridge and Massachusetts: MIT Press, 1996), pp.1-31; and pp.571-601.

[223] See K. Annan, *"The Causes of Conflict and the Promotion of Durable Peace and Sustainable Development in Africa,"* Secretary General's Report to the UN Security Council, 16 April 1998, p.108.

[224] See M. Robbins, "The Soviet-Cuban Relationship," in R. R. Kanet, (ed.) *Soviet Foreign Policy in the 1980s* (New York: Praegar, 1982), p.161.

[225] See G. B. N. Ayyitey, "The Somalia Crisis: Time for an African Solution," *Policy Analysis* No. 205, March 28, 1994, p.3.

[226] See M. Wubneh and Y. Abate, *Ethiopia: Transition and Development in the Horn of Africa*, op. cit., p.166.

[227] See "Analysis of Somalia," US Department of the Army, December 1993, p.2.

Following the *Ogaden* war, the Somali government violently suppressed opposition movements and clans, particularly the Isaaq sub-clan in the northern region using the military and elite security forces to quash any hint of rebellion.[228] Another consequence of the *Ogaden* debacle was the arrival, from Ethiopia, of more than one million refugees, majority of them settling in the north, which further increased the sense of alienation among the Isaaq.[229] This, compounded with their perception of inadequate representation in the government, led to Isaaq dissidents living in London, forming the second armed Somali rebel group, the Somali National Movement (SNM), with the aim of toppling the government. The SNM armed movement moved its headquarters to Addis Ababa in 1982. The SNM organized and directed its first military operations against the government from Ethiopian bases.

However, it was only in July 1984 that the movement became a serious threat to the Somali government. During this period, the SNM strengthened its relations with other insurgent movements such as the SSDF, since both groups had political and military wings. Proclaiming itself as a nationwide opposition movement, the SNM developed alliances with other sub-clans in the north as well as with non-Isaaq sub-clans in the south.[230]

The Somali government's response to the guerrilla movements included increased nationwide repression of suspected political dissents and brutal collective punishments in the Majeerteen and Isaaq regions. These measures only intensified the opposition to the regime. The government further prevented the opposition from forming a unified front, a situation which had the effect of intensifying both inter- and intra-clan antagonisms. For example, in 1989, the Hawiye clan leaders who had previously cooperated with the SNM decided to form their own clan-based opposition movement, the United Somali Congress (USC), in Rome, Italy. Almost immediately after its formation, the USC split along sub-clan lines within the Hawiye and between Ali Mahdi and the late Gen. Aideed. The latter later received weapons from the SNM with which it became allied. The Siyad Barre government's uneven persecu-

---

[228] See "Somalia: Background Note," US Department of State, Bureau of African Affairs, March 2006, p.5.
[229] See R. Cornwell, "Somalia fourteenth time lucky?" *Occasional paper* 87, Institute for Security Studies, April 2004, p.2.
[230] See for example, M. H. Mukhtar, "Historical Dictionary of Somalia," *African Historical Dictionary*, op cit., p.25.

tions and strategies, therefore, forced the opposition to utilize its own clans [structures] as organized armed forces.[231]

The divisions within the opposition, however, did not work to the government's advantage in the long term as it was gradually alienating an increasing number of the country's clans and sub-clans, including the very lineage of the Dhulbahante and Ogaden sub-clans that had provided the government's most loyal support. In particular, the Ogaden sub-clan living in both Somalia's neighbouring countries Ethiopia and Kenya and which was strongly interested in *pan-Somali* issues tended to blame the Somali government for the country's defeat in the *Ogaden* war. The deteriorating relations between Siyad Barre and former Ogaden supporters climaxed in 1990 with a mass desertion of Ogaden officers from the army leading to the formation of a new opposition movement: the Somali Patriotic Movement (SPM).[232] Finally, in 1990, the Digil-Mirifle, in the Bay and Bakol regions, also formed their own rebel group known as the Somali Democratic Movement (SDM). Motivated by the Isaaq domination of areas captured from government forces, the SDM aimed to essentially protect the unarmed and defenceless Digil-Mirifle peasants in the inter-riverine region from the violence of the warring factions.[233]

## Triggers of the Civil War

The operation of these opposition groups fighting from a rival country forced the Somali government to mount an international effort to cut off foreign aid to the rebels. As a result, the government established diplomatic relations with both Libya (in 1987) and Ethiopia in exchange for the withdrawal of their military support to the opposition groups, especially the SNM, which Ethiopia had allegedly sheltered, armed and trained.[234] In retrospect, the peace accord signed by the Ethiopian and Somali heads of state in April 1988 could be seen as the final precipitant

---

[231] See H. M. Adam, et al., *Removing Barricades in Somalia: Options for Peace and Rehabilitation*, (Washington, D.C.: USIP, 1998), p.4.; See also R. Cornwell, "Somalia fourteenth time lucky?" *Occasional paper* 87, Institute for Security Studies, April 2004, p.2.

[232] Ibid.

[233] See M. H. Mukhtar, "Historical Dictionary of Somalia," *African Historical Dictionary*, op. cit., p.226.

[234] Ibid, p.252; See also R. W. Copson, *African Wars and Prospects for Peace*, (New York and London: ME Sharpe, Inc., 1994), p.141.

of the [Somali civil] war.[235] The accord obliged each party to terminate support for the other's dissidents, to halt subversion, to prevent acts of destabilization and called for troop withdrawal from their common border.

Although one of the intentions of Mengistu was to redeploy troops from the Somali border to the north, it had unintended consequences.[236] Faced with the sudden withdrawal of support by their Ethiopian sponsors in May 1988, the SNM launched an offensive from Ethiopia against the Somali government. Government reprisals had the perverse effect of drawing over larger numbers of Isaaq to the rebellion, including deserters from the army, thus leading to the withdrawal of external support from the donor community.[237] During the final three years of Siyad Barre's rule, there was relatively intense fighting throughout the country as the opposition groups wrested control of extensive areas, with the SNM in the northwest, the SSDF in the northeast, the USC in central Somalia and the SPM in the south.[238] Not only did they establish close relations after a series of informal talks, but the SNM, the USC and the SPM also agreed to pursue a common military strategy against the government and to adopt a united internal and external political front in an agreement signed in September1990.[239]

The inability of the Somali opposition fronts to offer any viable political formula after ousting the central government was rooted in the organisation and strategy that they adopted while fighting the regime. Its underlying weaknesses became dramatically evident with the total collapse of the Somali state and the subsequent disintegration of the various fronts into clan-based armed factions and fiefdoms.[240]

---

[235] I. M. Lewis, *A Modern History of Somalia: Nation and State in the Horn of Africa* 4th ed., (Hargeisa: Btec Books, 2002), p.231.
[236] See R. W. Copson, *African Wars and Prospects for Peace*, (New York and London: ME Sharpe, Inc., 1994), p.130.
[237] See R. Cornwell, "Somalia fourteenth time lucky?" *Occasional paper* 87, Institute for Security Studies, April 2004, p.3.
[238] See "Analysis of Somalia," US Department of the Army, December 1993, p.2.
[239] See M. H. Mukhtar, "Historical Dictionary of Somalia," *African Historical Dictionary*, op. cit., p.233.
[240] See D. Compagnon, "Somalia Armed Movements," in C. Clapham, *African Guerillas* (Kampala: Fountain Publishers, 1998), and p.75.

## Conclusions

Somalia's thirty years of independence were riddled with conflict, first with Kenya and Ethiopia in the early 1960s and later on with Ethiopia in the 1977-78 *Ogaden* war, the latter leading to an internal conflict and a subsequent collapse of the Somali state. Some of the key underlying causes lie in the inter-play of foreign policy and conflict: for example, the rise of Somali nationalism in Somali-populated areas in the Horn of Africa region. The configuration of colonial borders, which divided Somalia into five territories, in turn laid the foundation for Somalia's unification policy leading to its aggressive, conflict-oriented foreign policy and wars and unstable relations with its neighbours.

Along this line, and as will be seen in the following chapters, the foreign policies pursued, not only by Somalia, but also by its neighbours—and other major players in the Horn of Africa politics—played active role as contributory factors to the war in Somalia and in the Horn of Africa region. On the one hand, independent Somalia's foreign policy towards the region, based on the idea of a 'Greater Somalia,' triggered hostile reactions from its neighbours and their backers. This also led to a defence pact between Kenya and Ethiopia in addition to a regionally maintained suspicion over Somalia's future intentions. Although both Somalia and Ethiopia fell into anarchy, Somalia disintegrated and has had no functional central government between 1991 and 2012.

# CHAPTER FOUR

## Somali Foreign Policy, 1960 – 1969

### Domestic Environment

This section analyses Somalia's domestic environment which provides both constraints and opportunities in the pursuit of the country's foreign policy. It is important, however, to recall that since its inception in 1960 the Somali Republic pursued a foreign policy committed to the creation of a 'Greater Somalia.' It is in this context that Somali foreign policy and engagement with other actors in the international system is analyzed.

### Geography

A state's geography obviously has a major impact on its relations with its neighbours and on its actions and influence in the global political arena.[241] This is reflected in the use of the term 'geopolitics' to describe the effect of geographical factors in international affairs. As such, the geographical position of Somalia in the Horn of Africa had important implications for its foreign policy. Somalia lies in the Horn of Africa where the African continent stretches towards the Arab world. Somalia, therefore, has strategic control over access to the Red Sea and is closely linked to the Arabian Peninsula and the Gulf.

The artificial boundaries drawn by colonial powers have caused tense relations between neighbouring states in developing countries as the colonialists failed to take into account geographic, ethnic, and economic considerations. A second issue of great concern is the proliferation of mini-states that lack the right ingredients that would ensure their independent existence. This has resulted in their continued dependence on

---

[241] See S. L. Spiegel, *World Politics in a New Era* (Los Angeles: Harcourt Brace College Publishers, 1994), p.20.

larger countries for economic wellbeing, political support and military assistance.

Somalia has an area of some 640,000 km, which is equivalent to the size of France and Italy combined together. Its 3300 km coastline runs from Bab-Al-Mandab, known as the southern gate of the Red Sea, to Ras Kiamboni at the border with Kenya.[242] Its strategic value was, however, considered to be relatively unimportant over the course of time earlier than the arrival of colonialism—a disadvantage attributed mainly to its lack of physical and economic resources.[243] However, the situation changed later with the opening of the Sues Canal in 1867. At this point, Somalia came in the limelight as a strategically important country, with harbours in Mogadishu, Berbera, and Kismayo that could contribute to superpower leverage during a military engagement within the region or areas of interest in that vicinity.

The influence of geography on Somali foreign policy is necessarily linked to its strategic location and its artificial boundaries. Its location not only attracted the attention of a number of colonial powers, but, in the period under study, attracted the interest of great powers such as Britain, France, and Italy who all sought to provide aid to Somalia and at the same time exploit the advantages it can offer each or any of them against its rivals. Consequently, the importance of Somalia's geography underlined its rapprochement with the West and the Soviet Union, respectively. The division of the Somali people due to the territorial decisions taken by the colonial powers is also significantly related to a geographical issue as Somalia pursued the return of the ceded territories as its principal foreign policy objective, especially in the period immediately after independence.

## Population

Similar to other nations in the world, particularly in the Horn of Africa region, and more specifically in Somalia, the size, composition and geographic distribution of the country's population represent some of the

---

[242] See S. M. Mousa, *Recolonization Beyond Somalia*, (Mogadishu: Horn of Africa Printing Press, 1992), p. xiii.
[243] See C. Legum and B. Lee, *Conflict in the Horn of Africa* (London: Rex Collings, 1977), p.31.

dynamic factors in the calculus of national power.[244] After the union of the two Somali territories, the new Republic had an estimated population of about 2.7 million inhabitants.[245] These inhabitants had one considerable advantage: the homogeneity of the Somali as all the people who lived within the boundaries of Somalia shared a common language, religion, social structure and historical identity. Unlike other African countries in which nationalist elites focused primarily on the problem of cultural unity, Somali leaders faced a different kind of problem.[246] This was based on the fact that, in order to develop a political will to maintain national unity, the Somali nation did not need any kind of "homogenization" of cultures within the borders of the state.[247]

As a result, the appeal of *pan-Somalism* became infectious, making inroads throughout the peninsula. These shared attributes consequently attracted deep popular support for the unity of all other Somali areas in Ethiopia, Kenya, and all of coastal Djibouti (then French Somaliland) under a single Somali flag. Popular support for Somalia's foreign policy at the time towards independence galvanized the Somali people, cementing the formation of three secessionist organizations from ethnic Somalis in neighbouring countries. In Kenya, the Northern Frontier District Liberation Front (NFDLF) was formed while the Western Somalia Liberation Front (WSLF) was incepted in the Ogaden region in Ethiopia as the *Front de Liberation de la Cote des Somalis (FLCS)* emerged in Djibouti.

Apart from the social cohesiveness and national integration that informed Somalia's foreign policy, one other important element is the size of its population. By reclaiming the territories held by their neighbours, Somalia would have been larger and hence would have played a more dominant role in the Horn of Africa. For example, Touval estimated the number of the Somali population in Ethiopia to be between 850,000 and

---

[244] See A. E. H. Dessouki and B. Korany, "A Literature Survey and a Framework for Analysis," in B. Korany and A. E. H. Dessouki, *The Foreign Policies of Arab States*, (Boulder and London: Westview Press, 1984), pp.5-18:14.

[245] See C. Legum and B. Lee, *Conflict in the Horn of Africa*, (London: Rex Collings, 1977), p.31.

[246] See D. D. Laitin and S. S. Samatar, *Somalia: Nation in Search of a State* (Colorado: Westview Press, 1987), p.129.

[247] See L. Laakso and A. O. Olukoshi, "The Crisis of The Post Colonial Nation State in Africa," in A. O. Olukoshi and L. Laakso, *Challenges to the Nation State in Africa* (Uppsala: Nordiska Africa Institute, 1996), p.99.

1,000,000, while the 1962 Kenya census in the Northern Frontier District (NFD) estimates the number of Somalis in that region as being just under 400,000. Whether these figures are true or not, "this, in turn, played a crucial role in Somali foreign policy."[248] In addition, Ethiopia and Kenya hosted a large Muslim population which, in Somali foreign policy calculations, would at least sympathize with the Somali cause.

## Economic and Military Capability

Just like population and geography, foreign policy is also determined by a country's economic and military capabilities.[249] Somalia's lack of physical and natural resources, as most of its land is a desert area unsuitable for cultivation and of little exploitable wealth, was a constraint on both its foreign policy objectives and its means of implementing them. This is corroborated by Somalia's ceaseless search for external aid to build its economy and military capability in order to promote the country's national ambition for unification. Exploiting resources gained through external support, Somalia's military, after independence, grew steadily despite the country's status as one of the poorest states in sub-Saharan Africa. Initially, the weaknesses of the Somali army were exposed in the wars of the 1960s with Kenya and Ethiopia before taking drastic measures to revamp its war capability both in the multiplication of army personnel and increase in military equipment. It is noteworthy mentioning here that, during that time in the sixties, western economic aid was sparse; military support was still not forthcoming and political commitments were largely on the side of Somalia's rivals: Ethiopia, Kenya and French-controlled Djibouti.

In fact, western hostility to Somali designs and ambition was demonstrated when Britain supported Kenya against Somali irredentists in the NFD in the early 1960s and when the US strongly supported Ethiopia whose forces, in 1963-1964, came into military conflict with the poorly equipped Somali army, leading to the defeat of Somalia by both countries. This political, economic, and military scenario laid the foundation

---

[248] See S. Touval, *Somali Nationalism: International Politics and The Drive for Unity in the Horn of Africa* (Cambridge and Massachusetts: Harvard University Press, 1963), p.132. See also, *Kenya Population Census*, 1962, Kenya Statistics Division.

[249] See W. I. Zartman and A. G. Kluge, "Heroic Politics: The Foreign Policy of Libya," in B. Korany and A. E. H. Dessouki, *The Foreign Policies of Arab States*, (Boulder and London: Westview Press, 1984), p.175-196:179.

for Somalia's reorientation of its international relations towards the Soviet Union. During this period, the signing of the defence agreement between Kenya and Ethiopia to counter the perceived Somali aggressiveness further undermined Somalia's capability and hence constrained Somalia's ability to achieve its foreign policy objectives.[250]

## Political Structure

Political structures provide opportunities and impose constraints on decision-makers. In line with this, when the two colonial territories were merged into one state, President Aden Abdulle Osman (Adan Adde) became the first civilian president, with Abdirashid Ali Sharma'arke as the Prime Minister; both were from the southern part of the country. In the parliamentary elections of 1964, Aden Abdulle Osman was elected president for a second term. During that time, Aden Adde dropped Sharma'arke as Prime Minister and appointed Abdirizak Haji Hussein as his replacement.[251]

Later, in the 1967 elections, Sharma'arke teamed up with Mohammed Ibrahim Egal, a veteran politician from the north, to defeat the Osman-Abdirizak political partnership. The opposition won the elections with Sharma'arke as President and Egal as Prime Minister. Aden Abdulle Osman handed over power peacefully and Somalia became the first African country to transfer power from the incumbent president to the opposition without political violence.[252] In fact, this election and the subsequent power transfer from one civilian government to the other gave the Somali Republic the name: the *first African democracy*.

In the nine years that followed its independence, Somalia practiced an electoral parliamentary system of government made up of three branches:

---

[250] See for example K. G. Adar, "Kenya-US Relations: A Recapitulation of the Patterns of Paradigmatic Conceptualization, 1960s-1990s," in M. Munene, et al., (eds.), *The United States and Africa: From Independence to the End of the Cold War* (Nairobi: East African Educational Publishers Ltd., 1995), pp.89-104:98.

[251] See for example A. Y. Farah, "Somalia: Modern History and the End of 1990s" in WSP International, *Rebuilding Somalia: Issues and Possibilities for Puntland* (London: HAAN Associates, 2001), pp.6-29:7.

[252] See also W. Katambo, *Coup d'états: Revolutions and Power Struggles in Post Independence Africa* (Nairobi: Afriscript Publishers, 1985), p.261; See also IRIN Reports, *Somalia: A Chronology of Events Leading to the Interim Government* (Nairobi: IRIN).

the legislature, the executive, and an independent judiciary. The vibrant democracy practiced in those formative early years of independence – along with the remarkable cultural and economic cohesion of Somali society – impressed critical observers and raised premature hopes that Somalia would become a model democracy in Africa.[253]

However, optimists and well-wishers of Africa's new and first experiment with western democracy soon dissipated. Firstly, northwest, which had entered the union at a disadvantage, immediately expressed discontent. For example, the SNL boycotted the June 1961 referendum held to approve the new joint constitution. Seen as a vote of confidence to unity with the south, the northwest region gave it a resounding negative verdict. While the vote was nevertheless carried by a southern majority,[254] the referendum's expression of northern discontent was echoed in popular plays and songs critical of unification. Only six months later, a group of Sandhurst-trained military officers staged an unsuccessful *coup d'etat* in Hargeysa.[255] This rebellion, which was poorly organized, was quickly suppressed.

To further aggravate the delicate situation, the civilian government embarked on an unprecedented behaviour of corruption, malfeasance and a recruitment policy whose main criterion was nepotism and favouritism that left state bureaucracy incompetent and dysfunctional.[256] From the perspective of these recurrent malpractices, one can argue that the praises showered on Somalia as a successful democratic experiment in Africa soon faltered, transforming itself into a predatory state controlled by the corrupt elite who abused power for personal gain and political advantage. Similarly, during the parliamentary era, the civilian elites manipulated *clanism*, and not nationalism, to win elections. The greed to participate in and manipulate the system of corruption became a major foregrounding for the chaotic proliferation of largely clan-based political parties that emerged towards the end of the 1960s, thus heralding a nation-

---

[253] See A. Y. Farah, "Somalia: Modern History and the End of 1990s," in WSP International, *Rebuilding Somalia: Issues and Possibilities for Puntland* (London: HAAN Associates, 2001), p.6-29:7.

[254] See WSP International, *Rebuilding Somaliland: Issues and Possibilities* (Asmara: The Red Sea Press, Inc, 2005), p.10.

[255] Ibid.

[256] See H. M. Adam, "Clan Conflicts and Democratization in Somalia," in N. O. Nnoli. (ed.), *Government and Politics in Africa: A Reader,* (Harare: AAPS, 2000), p.860.

wide disintegration of political institutions and government departments.[257]

The political disintegration, rampant corruption, and embezzlement of public funds not only impeded social and economic progress and squandered foreign aid resources, but also caused public disillusionment with the civilian leadership.[258] Although the two civilian governments were riddled with *kleptocracy* and inefficiency and underwent major changes in their administrations, the basic national objective – unity with other Somali territories – never faltered. The only changes that took place in that respect were related to government tactics and alliance formation as each subsequent leader had his own strategy. This problem also affected the decision-making process in the pursuit of foreign policy. Furthermore, this political discontent became a big blow to the popular support the civilian governments enjoyed in the early days of Somali independence while the political factionalisation diminished the cohesiveness of purpose.

**Foreign Policy Orientation**

*Pan-Somalism (Greater Somalia)*

Somalia's foreign policy orientation in the period 1960 to 1969 can be discerned from its historical legacy, but also from the statements and actions of its leaders immediately after independence. In this period, as is seen from the preoccupation of most of the Somali leaders, the main foreign policy orientation was one of 'Greater Somalia.' The creation of the Somali Republic did not include those Somali nationals living in French Somaliland, *Ogaden*, Eastern Ethiopia and the NFD of Kenya. The situation thus confronting the newly-formed Republic in 1960 was described by Prime Minister Abdirashid Ali Sharma'arke as "Our Misfortune."

Prime Minister Sharma'arke wrote:

---

[257] Ibid.
[258] Ibid., See also, G. B. N. Ayyitey, *The Somalia Crisis: Time for An African Solution*, Policy Analysis, No. 205, March 28, 1994, p.3.; See also A. Y. Farah, "Somalia: Modern History and the End of the 1990s," in WSP International, *Rebuilding Somalia: Issues and Possibilities for Puntland*, (London: HAAN Publishers, 2001), p.7-30:8.

> Our neighbouring countries, with whom, like the rest of Africa, we seek to promote constructive and harmonious relations, are not our neighbours. Our neighbours are our Somali kinsmen whose citizenship has been falsified by indiscriminate boundary 'arrangements.' They have to move across artificial frontiers to their pasturelands. They occupy the same terrain and pursue the same pastoral economy as ourselves, we speak the same language, we share the same creed, the same culture and the same traditions. How can we regard our brothers as foreigners? Of course, we all have a very natural desire to be united. The first step was taken in 1960 when the Somaliland protectorate was united with Somalia. This act was not an act of 'colonialism' or 'expansion' or 'annexation', it was a positive contribution to peace and unity in Africa."[259]

The election of the Somali Youth League (SYL), which had long advocated for the union of all Somalis in the Horn of Africa under one government, laid the platform on which the adoption of the new state's emblem was crafted. The emblem, a five-horned white star on a blue background, symbolized, or rather prefigured, the potential unification of the five Somali groupings living under five different administrations. In that respect, Somalia's frontier disputes are not essentially about land but rather about people and more so about nomadic people.[260] It may, therefore, be argued that the Somali policy was basically about nationalism.[261]

Despite their considerable cultural history and sense of national affinity, Somalis had never before been united in a state of their own. Experience under colonial rule, both local and foreign, bred into them a sense of Somali nationalism[262] which became the chief determinant of the goals set by their new republic. Independence was celebrated only a partial victory on the road to full nationhood; a nation whose independence constitution committed the republic to retrieve the three 'lost hands.'

---

[259] See I. M. Lewis, *A Modern History of the Somali; Nation and State in the Horn of Africa* 4th Ed., (Hargeisa: Btec Books, 2002), p.179.
[260] See J. Drysdale, *The Djibouti Dispute* (London and Dunmow: Pallmall Press, 1994), p.7.
[261] The term 'nationalism' emerged from 18th and 19th century political movements in Europe in which groups of people with a common culture, language and historical traditions claimed the right to self-determination. Examples of early nationalistic movements include the French revolution and the conquests of Napoleon Bonaparte.
[262] See C. Legum and B. Lee, *Conflict in the Horn of Africa*, (Londo: Rex Collings, 1977), p.31.

Another factor responsible for the development of nationalism was Islamic religious antagonism to Christian rule.²⁶³ Islam fosters the belief in its superior moral teachings over other religions; superiority not only by spirituality, but also one to be effected in the field of battle. In Islam, there is in fact no separation between religious and secular matters, as is the case in Christianity. It is exceedingly difficult for a Muslim society to accept non-Muslim rule,²⁶⁴ as became evident during the *Dervish* rebellion discussed earlier.

The issue of Greater Somalia seemed clear to all Somalis and many of those who lived in Somalia's neighbouring countries expressed their desire to live under the jurisdiction of the Somali state. Since the boundaries were arbitrarily created by colonial powers, they questioned why there should not be boundary readjustments based on the popular will of the residents. To Somalis, the issue was simply one that depended on the will for self-determination of subject peoples.²⁶⁵ The Somali peoples living in Ethiopia and Kenya, however, were considered by their governments as just one of the many other minority communities living within their borders and they regarded any desire by the Somalis to break away and unite with the Somali republic as seditious.

The struggle to achieve this national goal informed the foreign policy orientation of Somalia from 1960-1969. As overtly seen, the two civilian leaders in this period followed this path, albeit with different strategies. Thus, by the pronouncement of the ideological frame of Greater Somalia, the newly independent Somali Republic assumed the responsibility, as a sovereign state, to pursue the goal of self-determination of all the Somali people missing from the symbolic star at the centre of the national flag.

## Cold War Clientelism

The impact of the cold war cannot in any way be detached from a discussion of the Horn, be it an advantage or a disadvantage or both. For, it

---

[263] See S. Touval, *Somali Nationalism: International Politics and the Drive for Unity in the Horn of Africa*, (Cambridge, Massachusetts: Harvard University Press, 1963), p.62.
[264] Interview with Sheikh Ismail Moallim Hamud, March 21, 2007, Nairobi.
[265] See D. D. Laitin, and S. S. Samatar, *Somalia: Nation in Search of a State*, (Boulder, Colorado: Westview Press, 1987), p.130.

stands as a unique factor among the significant variables that for some time shaped the political, economic, and military clientelism of the Horn of Africa, particularly the foreign policy orientation of Somalia and its archrival Ethiopia. One other important Somali foreign policy orientation is related to Cold War clientelism; this orientation emanates from the first one because support from outside powers was necessary in order to achieve the goal of uniting all the Somali-speaking population in the region. To achieve this goal, Somalia needed a strong army and sophisticated weaponry as well as a reliable supplier and ally. While it had, in the past, attracted international interests due to its strategic location, at independence, the configuration of the international political system had changed significantly. Not only did new world powers emerge, but these also became engaged in a Cold War whose tentacles spread across continents.

Therefore, in order to protect interests and allies, the superpowers fought proxy wars in other states and in turn many of the small and emerging states negotiated alliances with one or the other of the superpowers. Some nations, like Somalia, were in a position to manipulate situations and play a role by capitalizing on a superpower's threat of the other. The opportunity provided Somalia with a means to extract sizeable grants of military, economic and technological assistance to ascertain its place in the global power play.

Initially, after independence, the issue facing the civilian government was how to win African and world opinion on the issue of *pan-Somalism*. To begin with, Somalia followed the general Afro-Asian pattern of non-alignment within the UN and in its dealings with the two world power blocks.[266] This balance was, however, tilted in favour of the west; hence, it was to Italy, Britain and the US that the Somali government first approached for aid.[267] Several occurrences, however, precipitated the country's re-orientation towards the Soviet Union and China. By late 1964, for example, it had become obvious that the initial campaign to unify all Somalia under a 'Greater Somalia" project had, somehow, failed.

During that same period, Ethiopian forces had established superiority over the Somalis in the Ogaden region and, in Kenya, the government

---

[266] See I. M. Lewis, *A Modern History of the Somali: Nation and State in the Horn of Africa* 4th Ed., (Hargeisa: Btec Books, 20020), p.200.

[267] See C. Legum and B. Lee, *Conflict in the Horn of Africa* (London: Rex Collings, 1977), p.31.

relied on assistance from British counter insurgency experts to clamp down on dissidents and control the Somali-Kenyan insurgency in what was then the NFD. As a result, Kenya's President Jomo Kenyatta and Ethiopia's Emperor Haile Selassie signed a mutual defence agreement aimed at containing what they called 'Somali' aggression.[268] What heightens the significance of clientelism in the Horn is the fact that Ethiopia and Kenya's victories -- over Somalia in the Ogaden War and the *Shifta* War respectively -- were achieved due to support from the west, which did not support or encourage the idea of 'Greater Somalia.' One of the explanations for this was because the west did not want to antagonize Christian Ethiopia, which was its long and trusted ally in the Horn of Africa.

Still on the importance of clientelism, one realizes also that the issue of the NFD, on the other hand, was critical to Somalia's foreign policy re-orientation as the country tried to solicit western support for its cause of unification. With the wave of the Horn politics changing its dynamics towards the approach of independence, Britain backtracked on its promises to Somalia, changing its policy with regards to Kenya's independence: from proposing and supporting the idea of 'Greater Somalia' to making a complete turnaround when it granted Kenya's independence which included the NFD as part of Kenya. In Somalia, popular indignation against Britain and her allies in the west found much resonance with the long history of Britain's conduct with regards to the country's affairs.

On the Somali side of the border, the SYL government, accused of not providing sufficiently a strong leadership on the NFD issue and increasingly becoming unpopular for its management of home affairs, endeavoured anxiously for some dramatic action which might restore its popularity and enhance its position in the lead-up to the upcoming elections.[269] These conditions of disrespected promises and a general atmosphere of despair led Somalia to conclude that it could expect little from the west—an embarrassment to Western-inclined leaders. It was at this critical juncture that some Somali leaders faced off proponents of the

---

[268] See for example K. G. Adar, "Kenya-US Relations: A Recapitulation of the Patterns of Paradigmatic Conceptualization, 1960s-1990s," in M. Munene, et al., (eds.), *The United States and Africa: From Independence to the End of the Cold War* (Nairobi: East African Educational Publishers Ltd., 1995), pp.89-104:98.

[269] See I. M. Lewis, *A Modern History of the Somali Nation and State in the Horn of Africa* 4th Ed., (Hargeisa: Btec Books, 2002), p.200.

West, accusing them of their miscalculation of the nature of the West's relationship toward Somalia and the preference to Kenya and Ethiopia. The ugly situation of political miscalculation and embarrassment were taken as serious matters in the Somali political circles as mistrust of the inhabitants of the missing territories started growing and suspicions were filling at every corridor.

Unlike the West, the Soviet Union, for its part, was quite prepared to take advantage of such an opportunity, especially since 1961 when it granted Somalia a credit of US$53 million.[270] However, without ever completely breaking its ties with the West, the SYL government took a strong decision and re-oriented its foreign policy to a new coarse which it deemed suitable for the attainment of its cause. In another dramatic step, an official announcement came in November 1963 that the Somali Republic had refused an offer of Western military assistance in favour of Soviet military aid.[271] Although Somali seemed to have overcome the huge burden of military supply to its obsolete army, its international relations problems were far from over as there was another obstacle to remove. The third element or obstacle of Somalia's foreign policy orientation was the separation of interests between its roles in the *pan-Africanism* movement and that of *pan-Arabism*, both of which it was longing to have stakes in. Very cautious strategy was required here to balance between the two and make effective use of both at every opportunity they could offer to the country.

## Pan-Africanism vs. Pan-Arabism

Initially, Somalia's post-independence foreign policy orientation was towards black Africa.[272] Within the *pan-Africanist* movement, Somalia had generally found itself aligned with that group of African states which included Ethiopia, notwithstanding the serious local difficulties of the two neighbouring states. This is because, although the *pan-Somalia* issue was clearly vital to Somali national sentiments, it could not be allowed to override the Republic's other interests, especially national development and the wider continental ideology of *pan-Africanism*. In the OAU, Somali

---

[270] See C. Legum and B. Lee, *Conflict in the Horn of Africa*, (Rex Collings, 1977), p.32.
[271] See I. M. Lewis, *A Modern History of the Somali Nation and State in the Horn of Africa* 4th Ed., (Hargeisa: Btec Books, 2002), p.201.
[272] See C. Legum and B. Lee, *Conflict in the Horn of Africa*, (London: Rex Collings, 1977), p.31.

leaders formulated their foreign policy in terms of their desire for self-determination. For example, President Osman's statement at the 1963 OAU Summit was a clear indication of his administration's determination to pursue self-determination for all Somalis in the Horn of Africa.[273] The original 1960 Somali constitution proclaimed that the country would promote, by legal and peaceful means, the union of all Somali territories.[274]

The *pan-Somali* based doctrine of foreign policy orientation marooned Somalia from mainstream African politics. The OAU's principle of adopting resolutions on border issues also proved to be one of the greatest setbacks to the Somali cause as the newly independent African states strongly supported the OAU. This position was also reflected in the OAU Charter and its principle on borderlines was considered sacred by most African states. As a result, Somalia's diplomatic efforts aimed at bringing the complexities of their dilemma to the world's attention were drowned by the country's bellicosity. The battles Somalia engaged in the Horn of Africa region to solve its problems seem to have backfired; leading to the country's diplomatic isolation.

The border issue and Somalia's bellicose attitude were all the more apparent within the OAU,[275] since the organisation's position was upheld by countries like Britain. The Somali Republic was, therefore, by the end of 1963, cast as the odd man out in African affairs.[276] These occurrences were compounded by other factors, which also served to reorient Somalia's foreign policy toward the Arab world, considering Somalia has a long history of cultural, religious and trade ties with the Arab world – particularly the Arabian Peninsula – which lies across the Gulf of Aden. Although Somalis are not Arabs by ethnicity, they identify more with the

---

[273] See K. G. Adar, *Kenyan Foreign Policy Behaviour towards Somalia: 1963-1983*, Lanham, New York and London: University Press of America, 1994), p.98.
[274] See C. Geshekter, "The Death of Somalia in Historic Perspective," in H. M. Adam and R. Ford, *Mending Rips in the Sky: Options for Somali Communities in the 21$^{st}$ Century*, (Asmara: The Red Sea Press, Inc., 1997), pp.65-98:74.
[275] See D. D. Laitin and S. S. Samatar, *Somalia: Nation in Search of a State,* (Boulder, Colorado: Westview Press, 1987), p.138.
[276] See I. M. Lewis, *A Modern History of the Somali Nation and State in the Horn of Africa* 4th Ed., (Hargeisa: Btec Books, 2002), p.199.

Arabs than with their fellow Africans.[277] This identity was propelled by the *pan-Arabism* movement championed by Egypt's Nasser, whose dream was to establish an Arab-Islamic empire whose power base would be Egypt.[278] The philosophy, therefore, courted Somalia to be oriented more towards the Muslim/Arab world which was seen to be more accommodative to Africa's OAU.

## Foreign Policy Decision-Making

Among the objectives of developing states, foreign policy is the desire to maintain the existence of the state, which usually entails the maintenance of the primary elite in positions of power.[279] Furthermore, in developing countries, the number and the relative influence of participants in the decision-making process vary according to the type of political regime and issue-area affected by the particular decision concerned. These differences, however, do not affect the general decision-making pattern which is dominated by executive power.[280] Somali foreign policy decision-making processes from 1960 to 1969 were dominated by the ideals of the SYL and its elites. As a result, the national assembly was very influential in decision-making, mainly because it could elect the president and, by using the Assembly's secret voting system, constrain the prime minister's actions.

In order to perpetuate itself in power, the SYL tried to assuage the deep wound to Somalia's pride caused by British actions by exploring alternative avenues of support. As a result, the government sent the prime minister for a visit to India and China, which culminated in the signing of trade and aid agreements with both countries. The search further aligned Somalia towards the Soviet Union. These new developments enabled the ruling party to increase its popularity and win a majority of

---

[277] Interview with Abdulkadir Yahya, Co-Director, Centre for Research & Dialogue (CRD), Nairobi, June 26, 2005. The late Yahya argued that the Somalis are neither Arabs nor Africans but Somalis.

[278] See J. Gabriel, "The Consequences of Nasser's Futile Dream of an Arab-Islamic Empire," *African Foreign Policy Review*, Vol. 1, No. 2., pp.43-52.

[279] See M. R. Singer, "The Foreign Policies of Small Developing States," in J. N. Rosenau, et al (eds.) *World Politics: An Introduction*, (New York: The Free Press, 1972), p.289.

[280] See A. E. Hillal and B. Korany, "A Literature Survey and a Framework for Analysis," in B. Korany and A. E. H Dessouki, *The Foreign Policies of Arab States*, (Boulder and London: Westview Press, 1984), p.5-18:16.

the seats in the National Assembly elections held in March 1964.[281] The executive, on the other hand, played a crucial role in foreign policy decision-making. Prime Minister Mohammed Ibrahim Egal – with his charismatic appeal and savvy diplomatic traits – managed to moderate the deeply hostile anti-Somali sentiments of Ethiopian officials, on the one hand, and those of President Jomo Kenyatta's government, on the other. With his unwavering effort, and with the cooperation of his counterparts in the other two neighbouring countries, Egal engineered *détente* with Somalia's neighbours and with Britain.[282]

Although the patriotic favour affected the formation of the Republic, the most important of all pervasive elements in Somali politics rested on the loyalty of the individual to his kin and clan.[283] The affiliation to the kin and clan is indicated in the fact that by the mid-1960s, politics in the Somali Republic was characterised by the growing fragmentation of clans and clan alliances, which paved the way for a massive proliferation of political parties.[284] During the competition for parliamentary seats in the 1969 elections, for example, the number of parties has dramatically multiplied to more than 60, with 1,002 candidates in the running. [285] However, in spite of the fact that the elites within government had the capacity to make authoritative decisions, the government maintained consistency, especially with regards to the 'Greater Somalia' issue.[286] This emanated from the views of many Somalis and the participation of the masses, including the intellectual elites, students, workers and bureaucrats, in decision-making. The fact that many Somalis were ready to sacrifice other interests for the sake of unification must, therefore, have influenced the

---

[281] See I. M. Lewis, *A Modern History of the Somali Nation and State in the Horn of Africa* 4th Ed., (Hargeisa: Btec Books, 2002), p.201.

[282] See J. Drysdale, *Stoics Without Pillows: A way forward for the Somalilands* (London: HAAN Associates Publishing, 2000), p.81.

[283] See I. M. Lewis, *A Modern History of the Somali Nation and State in the Horn of Africa* 4th Ed., (Hargeisa: Btec Books, 2002), p.166.

[284] R. Cornwell *'Somalia: Fourteenth time lucky?'Institute of Security Studies*. ISS Paper 87 April 2004.

[285] See A. Y. Farah, "Somalia: Modern History and the End of the 1990s," in WSP International, *Rebuilding Somalia: Issues and Possibilities for Puntland*, (London: HAAN Publishers, 2001), pp.7-30:8.

[286] See R. Cornwell, *Somalia fourteenth time lucky?* Occasional paper 87, Institute for Security Studies, April 2004.

Somali government's decision to go to war with its neighbours; directly or indirectly.

## Foreign Policy Behaviour:

### Somalia and the West[287]

*Italy and Somalia*

From the colonial period throughout its decades of independence and sovereignty, Somalia had dealt with several countries and for different purposes and levels of intimacy. Italy happens to be one of the closest western countries which Somalia interacted with as it had occupied southern Somalia as a colonial power until 1941. Although in the 1947 peace treaty Italy formerly renounced "all rights and title to the Italian territorial possessions in Africa,"[288] it nonetheless returned in 1950, this time under a UN mandate to prepare Somalia for independence. After Somalia attained its independence in 1960, Italy retained its interest in the country. In addition to the colonial ties, some of the factors explaining Somali-Italian relations can be traced back to this UN trusteeship relationship. Having prepared the country for independence, Italy considered itself as having a special responsibility for the future of Somalia.[289] The severing of diplomatic relations between Somalia and Britain further opened up the opportunity for Italy to play a dominant role in the political life of its former colony.[290]

Furthermore, Italy still had the prompting to play the role of a great power and probably in different areas and at different levels. Therefore, Italy's relationship may at a glance be viewed as a sentimental attachment

---

[287] In the late nineteenth century, due to its geographically strategic location, Somalia had been a scene of fierce colonial competition. Moreover, the opening of the Suez Canal in 1869 further enhanced the strategic position of the Horn of Africa region. For more, See more in Hoskyns, C. (1969). *Case Studies in African Diplomacy 2: Ethiopia-Somalia-Kenya Dispute 1960-67*. Dar Es Salam: Oxford University Press. p.ix.

[288] See S. Touval, *Somali Nationalism: International Politics and the Drive for Unity in the Horn of Africa*, (Cambridge, Massachusetts: Harvard University Press, 1963), p.171.

[289] Ibid.

[290] See A. Q. Ali, "The Foreign Factor in the Somali Tragedy," in H. M. Adam and R. Ford, *Mending Rips in the Sky; Options for Somali Communities in the 21st Century*, (Asmara: The Red Sea Press, Inc., 1997), pp.534-563:542.

to Somalia and a desire to protect its own economic investments in the country, particularly in the south, where it had settlers working on huge plantations misappropriated from local, Somali farmers on the wake of the colonial occupation. Italy had also offered scholarships to several of the Somali political elites to prepare them for leadership/administrative roles in post independence Somalia as well as scholarships to the children and relatives of some of the leaders in high positions who could, in one way or the other, influence state decisions.[291]

Even throughout the entire period of the Cold War period, Italy was Somalia's closest European ally after the expulsion of the USSR from Somalia leading up to the 1977 Ethiopia-Somalia *Ogaden* war. This relationship was reflected in the provision of financial and technical aid, military training and educational scholarships that produced some of the core Somali professionals that contributed to the development of the country. Most importantly, and in addition to other development programmes, Italy had underwritten the Somali National University (SNU) where it provided a variety of financial assistance couples with specialized training programmes to its faculty recruited to lecture in one of the institution's faculties.[292]

## Somalia and the United Kingdom

As mentioned above, imperial Britain was one of the countries that had contact and treaties with Somalia well before the latter's independence. Due to that long relationship and, later, as a colonial power controlling the country, Britain was one of the countries engaged in defending and expanding their spheres of influences in Somalia. Consequently, after Britain defeated Italy in the Horn of Africa from 1941 to 1950 and retook previously lost colonial territory, all Somali inhabited areas in the Horn of Africa came under the British military administration which at the time was based in Mogadishu. The UN General Assembly adopted Resolution 289 on November 21, 1949, placing the former Italian colony

---

[291] See more in Eno, M. A. *The Bantu-Jareer Somalis: Unearthing Apartheid in the Horn of Africa.* (London: Adonis & Abbey, 2008).

[292] See more in Eno, M. A. et al, "The Revival of Higher Education in Somalia: Prospects and Challenges," *Journal of Somali Studies*, Vol. 2, Nos 1&2 (2015), pp. 9-45.

of Somaliland under the UN Trusteeship Council.[293] Britain, for its part, was left to administer British Somaliland which later merged with the southern part of the country to form a new state: the Somali Republic.

Prior to independence, two occurrences laid the foundation for Somalia's subsequent foreign policy behaviour towards Britain. First, Britain, under the Bevin proposals, had called for the formation of 'Greater Somalia,' hence stoking the initial fire that lit the ideology of *pan-Somalism*. But on the contrary, it was Britain which in turn signed treaties with Ethiopia, surrendering to it the *Ogaden, Haud* and *Reserve Area* in 1948 and 1954–1955, respectively,[294] In order to submerge the same ideology it had initially fuelled its fire. Britain's 'betrayal' and change of behaviour, not only brought about a huge outcry throughout Somalia but, from another perspective, it also strengthened effectively the Somali sense of unity. Despite the disappointing incident of betrayal, British-Somali relations after independence were still, somehow, influenced by Britain's desire to maintain some dominance in the Republic. Afterwards, and for obvious reasons of appeasement and the desire to be not completely absent from the scene, Britain did not only commit itself to provide financial assistance, but it further provided an aid mission to staff for certain civil service posts. Additionally, it offered a military mission that would remain with the Somaliland scouts for a transitional period of six months. Moreover, in order to extend its assistance to Somalia, Britain made cooperation with Italy in which it provided some military assistance to Somalia.[295]

However, and notwithstanding the principles of cooperation and assistance, Somali foreign policy behaviour towards Britain changed significantly, partly because of the NFD problem in Kenya, and especially after 1962. Approximately about a year prior to Kenya's independence, the special British NFD Commission determined that, despite the fact that the majority of Somalis in this region expressed their will to join the Somali Republic, Britain should grant Kenya independence. It also announced that it would be the obligation of an independent Kenya to decide on the brawl over the NFD matter.

In reaction to Britain's unfavourable decision, the Somali National Assembly, in a vote of 74 to 14, approved a motion allowing the Somali

---

[293] See I. M. Lewis, *A Modern History of the Somali Nation and State in the Horn of Africa* 4th Ed., (Hargeisa: Btec Books, 2002), p.37.
[294] Ibid.
[295] See S. Touval, *Somali Nationalism: International Politics and the Drive for Unity in the Horn of Africa*, (Cambridge, Massachusetts: Harvard University Press, 1963), p.162.

government to break diplomatic relations with Britain. The motion stated that "the National Assembly of the Somali Republic, noting with deep regret that the foreign policy conducted by the United Kingdom damages the interests of the Somali nation, supports the decision of the government to break diplomatic relations with the United Kingdom."[296] As a result of this decision, it was estimated that Somalia lost about $3.6 million worth of aid from Britain.[297]

The break in diplomatic relations with Britain was then regarded by the world press quite sensational as a newly-independent African state had had the gall to break relations with a former metropolitan power and a member of the UN Security Council.[298] In effect, however, this decision led to the *Shifta* war between Kenya and Somalia. Britain's role at this time was consequently confined to training and supplying the Kenya army in its confrontation with Somalia until Prime Minister Egal's *détente* and restoration of diplomatic relations with Britain in 1967.

## Somalia and the United States

Since the founding of the country in 1789 to the end of the Cold War, US foreign policy towards Africa was marked by indifference, at worst, and neglect at best;[299] And Somalia was no different. Accordingly, a consistent axiom of US foreign policy has been that the country has had no permanent friends or enemies, but only permanent interests—a line of argument that is supported by the evolution of US policy towards the Horn of Africa. In this case, when the US could benefit geo-strategically by engaging or disengaging with one or another country, it took necessary steps to do so, without much regards for the nature of the past relationship. Moreover, US engagement in the region was dependent largely on its foreign policy needs and interests in countries outside of Africa.

---

[296] See K. G. Adar, *Kenya's Foreign Policy Behaviour towards Somalia: 1963-1983*, (Lanham, New York and London: University Press of America, 1994), p.97.
[297] Ibid.
[298] J. Drysdale, *Stoics Without Pillows: A way forward for the Somalilands* (London: HAAN Associates Publishing, 2000), p.81.
[299] See R. Lyob and E. J. Keller, "US Policy in the Horn," in D. A. Bekoe, (ed.) *Grappling with a Difficult Legacy in East Africa and the Horn: Confronting Challenges to Good Governance* (London: Lynne Rienner Publishers, 2006), pp.101-125:101.

Somali-American relations have their foundations in the fact that the US participated, after World War II, in the deliberations on the future of the former Italian colonies. During this period, the US, in its attitude toward Somali nationalists, was consistently friendly. In the late 1940s, the compassion was clearly reflected in the general tenor of the remarks of the US representatives on the four-power commission conducting the investigation for the former Italian colonies.[300] Subsequently, during the ten-year period when Somalia was under trusteeship, American goodwill showed itself in the provision of various assistance programmes. For example, American aid was increased after the attainment of independence and the creation of the Somali Republic.[301] Furthermore, the Americans briefly attempted from 1960 to 1964, to buttress western presence by helping to train and equip the Somali police force.[302] The US was also the largest source of non-military aid to Somalia.[303]

Although Somalia's relationship of alignment with the west experienced some ups and downs, it however came at odds sometimes, due to several reasons. First, while developing friendly relations with Somalia, the US also maintained close relations with Ethiopia, a country that was the cornerstone of US foreign policy towards the Horn of Africa. Second, although the US and Ethiopia had diplomatic relations since 1903 and, as a result, concluded treaties of arbitration and conciliation as far back as 1929, a close relationship between the two countries did not emerge until after World War II. At that time, the Ethiopian emperor had determined that events like the Italian occupation should not be repeated and did his best to secure the close support of the US government. A rising superpower, the US, since the early 1940s, coveted a base at Asmara in Eritrea, the *Kagnew* Station along the Red Sea, where it could establish a link for a worldwide radio communications network.[304]

---

[300] Ibid.
[301] See S. Touval, *Somali Nationalism: International Politics and the Drive for Unity in the Horn of Africa*, (Cambridge, Massachusetts: Harvard University Press, 1963), p.172.
[302] See C. Legum and B. Lee, *Conflict in the Horn of Africa*,(London: Rex Collings, 1977), p.9.
[303] See M. H. Mukhtar, *Historical Dictionary of Somalia: African Historical Series*, (Maryland Oxford: Scarecrow Press, 2003), p.253.
[304] See R. Lyob and E. J. Keller, "US Policy in the Horn," in D. A. Bekoe, (ed.) *Grappling with a Difficult Legacy in East Africa and the Horn: Confronting Challenges to Good Governance*, (Boulder and London: Lynne Reinner Publishers, 2006), 101-125:102.

The partnership was formalized when the US and Ethiopia signed a treaty of friendship and economic relations in 1951. Two years later, May 1953, the two countries signed two additional agreements: the Mutual Defence Assistance Agreement and the Agreement for the Utilization of Defence Installations within the Empire of Ethiopia. Following these agreements, the US in effect guaranteed Ethiopia's security and assistance in military equipment, training and communication at a facility in Asmara. Ethiopia also benefited from the presence and activity of the US Military Assistance Advisory Group (MAAG) established in 1954 to work with the poorly equipped Ethiopian military, which at the time was down to the battalion level.[305]

The mutual relationship of the two countries was strengthening gradually as the US was considering Ethiopia as a potential ally in a geostrategically important area. Thus, from 1960 to 1964, a series of secret agreements between the two governments resulted in the modernization and dramatic expansion of the Ethiopian military.[306] The US assistance helped Ethiopia advance its military and political influences in the Horn of Africa region. In fact, one of the stated purposes of this assistance was to prepare Ethiopia's defences for the assumed Somali threat, especially since Somalia had raised its irredentist claims.[307]

A third factor that altered Somali-American relations is that, while it was considerably arming Ethiopia, the US was reluctant to do the same for Somalia. While Somalia was concerned about its military weakness relative to its principle adversary, Ethiopia, its appeal for American assistance in establishing and equipping an army did not bear fruits. The reluctance of the Americans was largely due to the adamant objections of Haile Selassie to any such arms deal between Somalia and the US, a reason for Somalia to sharpen its shopping skills for the Somali army. Somalia's disappointment was greatly augmented by the knowledge that Ethiopia had been receiving substantial American military assistance.

The fourth issue precipitating coldness of US-Somali foreign policy relations was that Somalia did not gain western support for its 'Greater Somalia' ideal. These various factors not merely led to anti-American demonstrations in Somalia, but also bred disastrous results when Ethio-

---

[305] Ibid.
[306] Ibid, p.103.
[307] Ibid.

pian forces clashed with Somalia's, leading the latter to turn to the Soviet Union for help. As a result, Somalia lost western military assistance valued at US$6.5 million in favour of Soviet military aid to the tune of US$11 million, as announced by Prime Minister Sharma'arke in November 1963.[308]

## Somalia and the Soviet Union

Before Somalia's independence, the Soviet Union was not among the prominent European power players in the international relations of the country. Neither did it follow keenly the evolution of the internal political atmosphere in Somalia as did by colonial nations until it became a member of the Four Power Commission appointed by the UN to look into an appropriate solution for the pathway to Somalia's independence. Therefore, the Soviet Union's attitude toward Somali nationalism and quest for sovereignty was not initially marked by affability. However, the Soviets had reservations towards the Four Power Commission's report, which criticized the SYL's political programme, especially after the Soviet Union tended to soften its view toward Somalia, without yet giving any indication of special efforts to court Somali nationalists.[309] In fact, close relations with the Soviet Union began after Somalia attained independence. Disappointed with the handling of its territorial claims and the diminished size of its anticipated borders, and constrained by the virtual absence of worthwhile economic resources or even a good port to revamp foreign trade, the Soviet Union's total grant of USD 50 million was the largest per capita credit given to a foreign state.

From that initiative onwards, Soviet interest in Somalia intensified. For example, a Soviet governmental delegation visited Somalia in April 1961 and, in May that same year, Prime Minister Sharma'arke travelled to the Soviet Union, accompanied by several members of the cabinet and senior officials. The visits became a diplomatic platform on which another agreement under which Somalia was to receive loans and other credit facilities amounting to US$50 million was signed—including other

---

[308] See I. M. Lewis, *A Modern History of the Somali: Nation and State in the Horn of Africa* 4th Ed., (Hargeisa: Btect Books, 2002), p.201.

[309] See S. Touval, *Somali Nationalism: International Politics and the Drive for Unity in the Horn of Africa*, (Cambridge, Massachusetts: Harvard University Press, 1963), p.175.

agreements concerning Soviet technical assistance, commercial relations, and cultural cooperation.[310]

Furthermore, Somalia received a drastically needed US$32 million loan, which was later increased to US$55 million, specifically, for the purpose of equipping its army. In 1963, after Somalia approached it for further military aid, the Soviet Union became the country's leading military patron and an ally to rely on; the kind of relationship Somalia was vehemently looking for. During the civilian administrations, the Soviet Union supplied light arms, artillery tanks, armoured personnel carriers, and MIG-15 and MIG-17 fighter jets. In addition, the Soviet Union trained thousands of Somali students in its higher learning institutions, army pilots, military officers and technicians of various professional categories as well as ideological instruction. The Soviets also helped to build factories, such as a meat processing plant and a dairy plant in Mogadishu while a fish tannery was built in Las Qoray, among other vital projects.[311]

A number of factors explain these warm relations and alliance. First, Somalia was faced with a security dilemma because of the balance of power that was tilted in favour of its erstwhile enemy, Ethiopia. Alignment with the Soviet Union was, therefore, seen as necessary to ensure the country's security in one way or the other. Second, the Soviet Union was interested in the strategic location of Somalia in the Horn of Africa – especially Berbera Port – as this would give it the upper hand over its enemy in naval warfare in the region and in other places of interest. Third, the civilian administration was desperate to pacify domestic anti-western sentiments. Fourth, in order to entice Somalia, the Soviet Union outsmarted rival western powers by offering the highest amount of military aid to the country. Finally, Somalia's rapprochement with the Soviet Union was due to its disappointment with the US which refused to supply arms to Somalia while, at the same time, supporting Ethiopia. Consequently, the quick response to Somalia's dilemma was received favourably by the Soviet Union.[312] Prior to the Soviet's clever move of 1962 and

---

[310] See *New York Times*, June 17, 1961 quoted in S. Touval, *Somali Nationalism: International Politics and the Drive for Unity in the Horn of Africa*, (Cambridge, Massachusetts: Harvard University Press, 1963), p.176.

[311] See M. H. Mukhtar, *Historical Dictionary of Somalia: African Historical Series*, (Maryland Oxford: Scarecrow Press, 2003), p.241.

[312] See for example S. Touval, *Somali Nationalism: International Politics and the Drive for Unity in the Horn of Africa*, (Cambridge, Massachusetts: Harvard University Press, 1963).

1963, several US-led Western powers had offered Somalia packages for arms but the Somali leadership declined.

## Somalia and Its Neighbours

As earlier mentioned in some of the above sections, the ideology of a Greater Somalia was so serious that not just a part with that symbolic nomenclature was formed, but indeed it was allocated a valuable space in the Somali constitution. By constitutionalizing the ideology, the message was to the neighbours that Somalia explicitly challenged the existence of its borders with Ethiopia and Kenya, and the whole of coastal Djibouti. The foreign policy behaviour of the Somali governments towards countries in the Horn of Africa is, therefore, analysed within the context of its 'Greater Somalia' policy, a strategy which led to hostile and belligerent relations with its neighbours.

## Somalia and Kenya

Kenya is one of the few nations Somalia shares borders with. Yet, before the arrival of the colonial powers, there have not been remarkable confrontations people were experiencing, because every community had its own territory. Therefore, the different groups of people in a certain location had ways of co-existing and sorting out their differences in periods of strife or communal confrontation. But these were mostly community based rather than large scale encounters such as organized national military level wars. So, although Somalia contended for control of the NFD, an area covering 102,000 square miles, its foreign policy behaviour prior to Kenya's independence was one of negotiation. At that time, Kenya's nationalists were opposed to any adjustment of borders. Somali diplomats,[313] therefore, felt that if they offered Kenya's nationalist leaders reason and hospitality, it would earn the people of the NFD the right to self-determination.[314] Frequent delegations of clan elders visited Mogadishu to seek support before the National Assembly responded to the

---

[313] It is reported that Somalia had a functioning foreign ministry with an effective diplomatic service at its embassies across the globe three years before Kenya became independent. This includes two-way reporting from the Ministry and the embassies; with analysis and predictions. Notes from the field, 13 September 2005.

[314] See D. D. Laitin and S. S. Samatar, *Somalia: Nation in Search of a State*, (Boulder, Colorado: Westview Press, 1987), p.134.

requests for help by passing a motion, in November 1961, welcoming the union of the NFD with the Somali Republic and urging the government to press for the union by all possible means. Subsequently, the government strongly backed the NFD delegation attending the Kenya constitutional conference held at Lancaster House in February 1962.[315]

In the same year of Kenya's independence, further negotiations were arranged by the UK government at a conference held in Rome, on August 25, 1963, between the governments of Britain, Kenya and Somalia, where Somalia proposed that the NFD area be placed under a special administration.[316] The same issue was also discussed at the UN General Assembly where the Somali delegates reaffirmed their government's position on the issue of the NFD. The delegates stated that since it was the United Kingdom that had annexed the NFD to Kenya, there was an inescapable obligation for that government to reverse the unlawful usurpation of territory of the NFD.[317] In July 1962, the Somali government also invited leading members of Kenya's two African nationalist parties, Jomo Kenyatta from KANU and Ronald Ngala from KADU, to Mogadishu for informal talks.

Although this pursuit of peaceful diplomatic engagement with Kenya can be linked to the desire to adhere to the Somali constitution which advocated for the achievement of the unification of the Somali territories by legal and pacific means, the relations between the two countries worsened when Kenya gained independence and the NFD became the country's North Eastern Province (NEP). Immediately after independence, hostilities between the two countries escalated, with Mogadishu indirectly supporting Somali guerrillas that were dubbed *Shiftas,* or bandits, by the Kenyan government. At the same time, Kenya was undertaking strong measures of suppression in containing the uprising with help from the UK.

---

[315] See I. M. Lewis, *A Modern History of the Somali Nation and State in the Horn of Africa* 4th Ed., op. cit., p.180.
[316] See "Final Communiqué of the British Delegation," quoted in K. G. Adar, *Kenya's Foreign Policy Behaviour towards Somalia: 1963-1983*, (Lanham, New York and London: University Press of America, 1994), p.154.
[317] See 1237th Plenary Meeting, Eighteenth Session, General Debates, United Nations General Assembly, UN Doc APV.1237, 1963, p.6.; quoted in K. G. Adar, *Kenyan Foreign Policy Behaviour Towards Somalia: 1963-1983*, (Lanham, New York and London: University Press of America, 1994), p.101.

The Aden Abdulle Osman-Abdirizak Hagi Hussein administration of 1964-1967 continued with the 'Greater Somalia' policy and, as a result, pursued the NFD issue through the platforms provided by the OAU and the non-aligned movement (NAM). The OAU rejected such a policy through a 1964 OAU Resolution, adopted in Cairo, which explicitly reaffirmed the maintenance of borders as acquired at independence and as determined and demarcated by the colonial powers. Similarly, the NAM Conference held in Cairo in October 1964 reinforced the OAU's decision – a move that was strongly opposed by Somalis, since it jeopardized Somalia's legitimate right to seek self-determination for, and unification of, all Somalis.[318]

However, when Mohammed Haji Ibrahim Egal became Prime Minister, a change of policy occurred in which he pursued *détente* with Somalia's neighbours.[319] At an OAU Summit in Kinshasa, from 11 to 14 September 1967, Kenya and Somalia signed an agreement to honour the OAU ideals and respect each other's sovereignty and territorial integrity.[320] This was followed by the October 28, 1967 Arusha Agreement signed by the two countries; leading to the normalization of relations between Kenya and Somalia after the latter renounced its claims over the NFD.[321]

## Somalia and Ethiopia

In spite of the similarities between the *Ogaden* region and the NFD, several reasons explain the exertion of extraordinary energy, greater effort and broader level of interest by successive governments of the Somali Republic to help liberate the *Ogaden*.[322] First, among the major incentives include the fact that the border between Ethiopia and Somalia was not delineated clearly. Second, had there been any delineation of the border between the two countries, it could change the clan configuration of domestic power. Finally, the Somalis in the *Ogaden* region had constantly

---

[318] See K. G. Adar, *Kenyan Foreign Policy Behaviour towards Somalia: 1963-1983*, (Lanham, New York and London: University Press of America, 1994), p.106.
[319] See also "Somalia: Background Note," US Department of State, Bureau of African Affairs, March 2006, p.4.
[320] Ibid.
[321] Ibid.
[322] See D. D. Laitin and S. S. Samatar, *Somalia: Nation in Search of a State*, (Boulder, Colorado: Westview Press, 1987), p.136.

been humiliated, mistreated, degraded, and oppressed by successive Ethiopian governments. Hostilities, therefore, occurred between Ethiopia and Somalia at an early stage and led to the formation of the Western Somalia Liberation Group (WSLG) in the *Ogaden* in 1961.

The Somalia-backed WSLG aimed at seizing *Ogaden* from Ethiopia by military means, arming militia of the group. Somalia's support of the movement created open hostilities with Ethiopia as the latter was conscious of the former's involvement and backing of the insurgents. As a consequence, and with the absence of peaceful diplomatic approach, the hostilities escalated into an all-out war in the *Ogaden* in 1964. At the same time, leaders of other rebel groups against Ethiopia lived in Mogadishu while Somalis did nothing to root them out.[323] About a year earlier, serious diplomatic clashes occurred between Ethiopia's Haile Selassie and Aden Abdulle Osman of Somalia when the OAU was formed and its Charter signed in Addis Ababa on May 25, 1963.[324] However, when the war broke out, the OAU intervened, trying to create a climate conducive for peaceful negotiation, although its endeavour became a failed effort.

In its last year, however, and with so little to show from the bold pursuit of the Somali cause by his predecessors, the Somali civilian government, under Prime Minister Egal, decided to see what could be achieved through the use of more conciliatory diplomacy, which included halting support for guerrillas and ceasing their encouragement through radio propaganda.[325]

## Consequences of Détente

While not completely abandoning the cause of self-determination for Somalis, the government of Prime Minister Egal's policy of *détente* with Kenya and Ethiopia was a positive step towards peaceful resolution of conflicts, which all the three neighbouring countries needed. The other positive result, emerging from the Kenyan and Ethiopian side, was that the two countries explicitly recognized the existence of a territorial dis-

---

[323] See J. M. Ghalib, *The Cost of Dictatorship; The Somali Experience*, op. cit., p.109.; See also D. Ottaway and M. Ottaway, *Ethiopia: Empire in Revolution* (New York and London: African Publishing Company, 1978), p.163.
[324] See J. M. Ghalib, J. M., The *Cost of Dictatorship: The Somali Experience*, op. cit., p.106.
[325] See "Somalia: Background Note," US Department of State, Bureau of African Affairs, March 2006, p.4.

pute with Somalia and, as a result, expressed their willingness to try to find ways of solving it.[326] It also gave Somalis hope for a better deal in an expanded East African Community (EAC).[327] These developments encouraged the resumption of diplomatic relations with Kenya and with Britain, redrawing another chapter of diplomatic understanding. Finally, the three countries' diplomatic visits began in order to consolidate the peaceful environment created by Somalia's new policy.

While to a great extent the *détente* policy attempted to de-escalate tension in the region, it however had its negative consequences. For example, although Prime Minister Egal claimed that his government's new diplomacy did not make any concessions to Ethiopia or Kenya, it indeed represented a new understanding of the Somali point of view, particularly in Addis Ababa and in Nairobi, where it was tempting to interpret the new Somali policy as one of capitulation. This view was also adopted by the Somali premier's political opponents in Mogadishu, where demonstrators accused him of being a sell-out.[328] Similarly, the move towards reconciliation with Ethiopia made many Somalis – including the army – furious. In Somali circles, Prime Minister Egal's reconciliation efforts toward the region, particularly Ethiopia, were widely seen as part and parcel of the principal factors that provoked the October 21$^{st}$ 1969 bloodless *coup d'état*,[329] diligently executed by the Somali Armed Forces under the leadership of Mohamed Siyad Barre.

## Somalia and Djibouti

While Somalia was engaged in diplomatic negotiations and military confrontations with Ethiopia and Kenya, Djibouti remained under French colonial administration, but not really off the Somali unification lens. However, prior to its independence, two referendums, one in 1958 and the other in 1967, were organised by the French to determine the future of the colony. In the hope of incorporating this territory into a 'Greater

---

[326] See K. G. Adar, *Kenya's Foreign Policy Behaviour towards Somalia: 1963-1983*, (Lanham, New York and London: University of America, 1994), p.122.
[327] See P. Woodward, *The Horn of Africa: Politics and International Relations*, (London and New York: Tauris Academic Studies, 1996), p.126.
[328] See I. M. Lewis, *A Modern History of the Somali Nation and State in the Horn of Africa* 4$^{th}$ Ed., (Hargeisa: Btec Books, 2002), p.203.
[329] Interview with Ambassador Hussein Ali Dualeh, former Somali ambassador to Kenya and to Uganda, Nairobi, September 11, 2001.

Somalia,' Somali foreign policy behaviour towards the colony was one of involvement in and support for its struggle for independence.[330] In the May 1967 referendum, for example, suspicious of French interference, the Somali Republic called upon the UN to provide observers for the referendum.[331] The Somali government also used its media outlets, both print and electronic, mainly the radio, to point out French atrocities and irregularities, while aiming to influence the residents of the French colony to vote for independence.[332] The French conducted an unsupervised election and used the tactics of divide and rule to orchestrate an endorsement of French continuance of control and rejection of outright independence before 1977.

## Somalia in the OAU and the Arab World

In June 1961, Prime Minister Sharma'arke told parliament that:

> While acknowledging its traditional friendly ties, the Somali Republic wished to establish relations with the largest possible number of independent countries and to remain outside any bloc or political coalition, thus confirming as the goals of its international activity the maintenance of peace and respect for the neutrality principle, co-operation and solidarity among countries, and in particular among the African and Muslim nations.[333]

He further said that the new government placed above anything else, not only in thought but also in action, the intention of achieving the unification of the Somali territories by legal and peaceful means.[334] The idea was meant to set the pace for Somalia's *pan-African* endeavours and as a result, it was presented at the signing of the OAU Charter in Addis Ababa on May 25, 1963.

---

[330] See J. M. Ghalib, *The Cost of Dictatorship: The Somali Experience*, (New York: Lilian Barber Press Inc., 1995), p.114.
[331] See M. H. Mukhtar, *Historical Dictionary of Somalia: African Historical Series*, (Maryland Oxford: Scarecrow Press, 2003), p.76.
[332] See S. Touval, *Somali Nationalism: International Politics and the Drive for Unity in the Horn of Africa*, (Cambridge, Massachusetts: Harvard University Press, 1963), p.138.
[333] See *The Somali* News, 25 August 1961.
[334] Ibid.

In the period 1960 -1967, Somalia used the OAU as an arena for the pursuit of its 'Greater Somalia' policy, as was evident from statements by President Osman and the Somali Minister for Foreign Affairs. The OAU, however, firmly held the principle of respect for the sovereignty and territorial integrity of each state, denying, for example, Somalia's claims for control of the NFD.

Following the *Shifta* war of 1963, a cease-fire agreement between Somalia and Kenya was finally reached in Khartoum, Sudan, on March 30, 1964. Again, when border disputes flared up between Somalia and Ethiopia in 1968, Somalia appealed to the OAU to send a fact-finding mission, but Ethiopia denied the Somali claims. Similarly, the OAU Council of Ministers meeting in Lagos, Nigeria, adopted a resolution which called for negotiations between Kenya and Somali due to the *Shifta* activities.[335] At the July 1964 OAU conference in Cairo, the OAU reaffirmed the strict respect by all members of the organisation to the principles laid down in paragraph 3 of the OAU Charter. In practice, the OAU therefore continued to be an impediment to Somalia's ambitions.

Indeed, the Somali national assembly subsequently passed a motion rejecting the 1964 OAU decision. The motion stated that the OAU resolution regarding the borders was in no way binding on the Somali Republic or applicable to the disputes the Somali Republic had with Kenya and Ethiopia. Somalia indeed claimed that such disputes could only be satisfactorily settled by recognition of the right to self-determination of the Somali people and the denunciation of all forms of colonialism.[336]

The result of the Somali claims vis-à-vis the OAU's position led to Somalia's diplomatic isolation.[337] The OAU mechanism was, however, crucial during the Egal era of *détente*, since it was under its ambit that the Arusha Declaration was negotiated and signed.

---

[335] See Resolutions and Recommendations of the Second Extra Ordinary Session of the Council of Ministers, Organization of African Unity, Dar e Salaam, 12-15 February 1964, OAU Mimeographed Texts, February 1964, OAU Doc Ecm/Res3(11) quoted in K. G. Adar, *Kenya's Foreign Policy Behaviour Towards Somalia: 1963-1983*,(Lanham, New York and London: University of America, 1994), p.101.

[336] See "Somalia to Ignore OAU Frontiers" *East African Standard*, Nairobi, October 1964, quoted in K. G. Adar, *Kenyan Foreign Policy Behaviour Towards Somalia: 1963-1983*, (Lanham, New York and London: University of America, 1994), p.106.

[337] See D. D. Laitin and S. S. Samatar, *Somalia: Nation in Search of a State*, (Boulder, Colorado: Westview Press, 1987), p.199.

On the Arab front, Somalia, which was firmly part of Nasser's agenda of expansionism, received considerable aid from Egypt, which viewed it as an Islamic ally. Along with Egypt, other Arab and Muslim countries like Syria and Iraq also provided scholarships to pre- and post-independence Somalia. Egypt also established schools in Somalia from primary to secondary levels during the Italian-administered UN trusteeship period. After independence, however, Somalia looked to the Arab world for diplomatic and economic support.[338] In fact, *pan-Somalism* tended to undermine support for *pan-Arabism*, often rendering Somalia moderate in its stand on Arab nationalism. Egypt was also placed in a difficult position by *pan-Somalism*, as it was forced, for instance at OAU conferences, to adopt a position of uneasy neutrality as it did not want to commit itself to the Somali side [nor turn against].[339]

## Conclusions

It is evident that Somalia was active in the foreign policy arena during the civilian governments by pursuing a foreign policy of 'Greater Somalia,' which consequently led to hostilities between the country and its neighbours: mainly Kenya and Ethiopia. This policy was also pursued up to the OAU, leading to Somalia's diplomatic isolation. Somali foreign policy was also externally-oriented in order to attract military and economic aid from the west, the Soviet Union and from the Arab/Muslim world. These external actors also had various motives and intentions in their interaction with Somalia and hence contributed – in one way or the other – to the escalation and de-escalation of the conflicts in the Horn of Africa region.

---

[338] See M. H. Mukhtar, *Historical Dictionary of Somalia: African Historical Series*, (Maryland Oxford: Scarecrow Press, 2003), p.40.
[339] See I. M. Lewis, *A Modern History of the Somali Nation and State in the Horn of Africa* 4th Ed., (Hargeisa: Btec Books, 2002), p.199.

# CHAPTER FIVE

## Somali Foreign Policy, 1969 – 1990

### Background

In the 1968 National Assembly elections, Abdirashid Ali Sharma'arke's party, the SYL, won an overwhelming majority of parliamentary seats. There were allegations, however, that the elections were widely rigged. Several parties in various constituencies appealed to court against the outcome. As a result, Sharma'arke and his regime became very unpopular. President Sharma'arke appointed Mohammed Ibrahim Egal as the Prime Minister whose government took a peaceful approach to solving crises with its neighbours. Based on the reality on the ground at the time, particularly the superior military power of Somalia's adversaries – notably Kenya and Ethiopia, who had recently signed a defence pact – and the country's isolation from most African countries, the Somali government had to seek a policy of *détente* with Ethiopia and Kenya. This approach was, however, not well received at home. If anything, it was interpreted by rival opposition figures as an astounding compromise of the sacred ideology of Greater Somalia. On 15 October, 1969, on grounds of what was believed to be vengeance for the rigged elections, President Sharma'arke was assassinated while visiting his hometown in North-eastern Somalia. On October 21, 1969, a bloodless *coup d'état* transformed the entire country's socio-political landscape. After the successful removal of the leaders of the civilian government and subsequently putting them in custody, the architects of the coup swiftly moved to the formation of a military government under a Supreme Revolutionary Council (SRC) chaired by Siyad Barre. Although few Somalis relished the prospect of military rule, this development was received as a welcome alternative to the Somali society's disappointments with the civilian rule, particularly their pacifist foreign policy which many Somalis interpreted as unpatriotic.

The first phase of Gen. Barre's military rule, roughly up to 1974, was characterized as a period of concentration on dealing with internal problems, namely: the focus on local development and the consolidation of the government's authority.[340] During that period, Barre's authoritarian regime enjoyed an unparalleled degree of popular support largely because it performed to the satisfaction of the masses, acted with a high degree of decisiveness not displayed by the civilian governments of the 1960s, and, as a result, attracted a massive amount of praise and unreserved extent of loyalty from the citizens. Even the 1970 *coup* attempt failed to affect the stability of the government.[341]

The fact that Barre's military coup was bloodless demonstrated the lack of support for the previous governments. There was no shortage of areas to be capitalized on as far as the misdeeds of those governments were concerned. Unlike the previous civilian regime, Barre's first government consisted of experienced men of integrity and intellectuals, whose careful appointment immediately paved the way for the restoration of public confidence in the day to day handling of national as well as international issues. Barre vowed to eliminate rampant corruption, restore security and stability and, on this basis, called for public support for a wide range of programmes of reconstruction based on self-help (*Iskaa wax u qabso* in Somali) in order to solve the country's socio-economic ills. There was a genuine and spontaneously positive response across the country, which consolidated his power base for the increasingly totalitarian rule.[342] This background laid the foundation for Barre's foreign policy orientation and decision-making process – which included making Somalia a socialist country with personalized, dictatorial decision-making processes.

---

[340] See M. H. Mukhtar, *Historical Dictionary of Somalia: African Historical Dictionary Series*, No. 87 (Maryland Oxford: Scarecrow Press, 2003), p.226.

[341] Interview with Ambassador Hussein Ali Dualeh, former Somali ambassador to Kenya and Uganda, Hargeisa, 'Somaliland,' March 7, 2004.

[342] See J. M. Ghalib, *The Cost of Dictatorship: The Somali Experience* (New York: Lillian Barber Press Inc, 1995), p.120.

## Domestic Environment

### *Geography and Population*

Notwithstanding the rule of the military government, the superpowers continued to show interest in the country as they considered it to be of great strategic value. Similarly, as Somalia still had few natural resources to use for its socio-economic growth and development of military capability, its foreign policy was in many cases tailored to attract foreign aid. Its location also affected its relations with neighbouring countries. For example, Ethiopia and Somalia's respective interests in colonial Djibouti had an impact on that country, Somalia and the Horn of Africa as a whole. As a result, the two countries had a difficult relationship which led to an arms race, prompting dependence on external actors for armaments and military training.

Somalia had an estimated population of about eight to ten million people before the civil war. Since the population was considerably small; the country could not produce enough wealth to generate power capabilities, which reinforced its external orientation and quest for external support. In turn, the size of the Somali population and its effect on its foreign policy also had an impact in terms of public opinion: for example, there was a long suppressed public antagonism and resentment felt towards Somalia's official friends. This brought about an anticipated breach with the Soviet Union and her satellites, especially Cuba, riding on a wave of popularity for the Mogadishu government.[343]

On the other hand, the Somali public still had a desire to be united with their brothers in the *Ogaden* and NFD regions, as was stimulated to a large extent by Somali literacy. This led to Gen. Barre's decision to invade *Ogaden* in order to gain a patriotic status and increase his popularity and legitimacy.[344] The anticipated support that such a course of action would gather was a factor in Barre's decision to employ all available capabilities in order to gain credibility.

---

[343] See I. M. Lewis, *Modern History of the Somali: Nation and State in the Horn of Africa* 4th Ed., (Hargeisa: Btec Books, 2002), p.235.
[344] See H. M. Adam, et al, *Removing Barricades in Somalia: Option for Peace and Rehabilitation* (Washington, DC.: USIP, 1998), p.3.

## Economic and Military Capabilities

Although the riverine areas of Somalia's Jubba and Shabelle rivers enjoyed considerable rates of production in pre-colonial days,[345] colonial and post-colonial Somalia has not experienced development of available opportunities to enhance the overall agricultural economy of any other sector that could have had economic resource. The oversights of vital economic resources are compounded by the fact that Somalia is a land of sparse rainfall where more than half of the population consists of pastoralists and agro-pastoralists who raise camels, cattle, sheep and goats or practise farming, mainly for subsistence. A small number relies on fishing, while the rest are urban dwellers. As such, livestock exports to neighbouring Arab countries and to Italy have provided the mainstay of the modern Somali economy. Banana plantations established around the two main southern rivers, the Shabelle and the Jubba, have provided the second important export to those same states. In 1990, agriculture contributed about 65 per cent of the country's GDP, of which livestock was responsible for just over 50 per cent, crops for 38 percent and forestry and fisheries for about 1 per cent.[346] The country's poor economic performance is attributable to the nationalization of the commercial sector and military-led authoritarianism in a 'Somali' socialist fashion.

The implications of this weak economy were numerous. First, the economic infrastructure was incapable of satisfying the economic needs of the population, thus increasing the need for foreign aid.[347] The desire to satisfy individual and group needs indeed generated pressures on political leaders to look outside their borders to obtain the means for sustenance. Consequently, the country's foreign policy was tailored to achieve this, mainly through reliance on the Soviet Union, Italy and various Arab/Muslim states, among others. Secondly, as the economy of a state is

---

[345] K. Menkhaus, (1989). Rural Transformation and the Roots of Underdevelopment in Somalia's lower Jubba Valley. PhD Dissertation, University of South Carolina, Columbia.

[346] See H. M. Adam, "Somalia: Personal Rule, Military Rule and Militarism," in E. Hutchful and A. Bathily, *Military and Militarism in Africa*, (Dakar: CODESERIA, 1998), p.359.

[347] See A. E. H. Dessouki and B. Korany, "A Literature Survey and a Framework for Analysis," in B. Korany and A. E. H. Dessouki, *The Foreign Policies of Arab States* (Boulder and London: Westview Press, 1984), pp.5-18:14.

fundamental to its capability,[348] that of the Somali state was limited—in natural resources as well as in physical resources.

After Somalia gained independence in 1960, its military personnel consisted of about 5,000 troops strong, largely under Soviet patronage, later expanding to around 23,000, and then to 37,000 on the eve of the *Ogaden* war. Similarly, the country's army swelled from about 32,000 in 1977 to 65,000 in 1987.[349] Siyad Barre continued to increase the strength of the army with observers arguing that it had increased to 120,000 in 1982; much larger than the Nigerian army, a country of over 100 million people.[350] Barre, therefore, built an army, which his neighbours had to reckon with. As a result, it was no longer possible for the Ethiopians to boast, as the late Gen. Aman Andom once did, that they could march to Mogadishu in a day.[351] In fact, it was the opposite in the 1977-1978 Somaila-Ethiopia war when the Somali troops pushed their Ethiopian counterparts deep into their country and almost captured Addis Ababa before Russian and Cuban troops pushed the Somali soldiers back in a retreat.[352]

Policies of arms acquisition have a great influence on foreign policies, often leading to war as militarization can entail an offensive external doctrine.[353] The existence of large armies may entice decision-makers to use the military as a predominant component of their foreign policy.[354] In the case of Somalia, proliferation of war arsenal and preparation of this large army was a potential instrument to achieve the government's objectives; mainly Somali nationalism. It not only led to the increased strength of Somalia relative to the rest of the countries in the Horn of Africa, but it

---

[348] R. Little, and M. Smith, *Perspectives in World Politics* (eds.) 2nd Edition (London and New York: Routledge, 1991), p.62.
[349] See R. Lyob and E. J. Keller, "US Policy in the Horn," in D. A. Bekoe, *Grappling with a Difficult Legacy in East Africa and the Horn: Confronting Challenges to Good Governance* (Boulder and London: Lynne Rienner Publishers, 2006), pp.101-125:101.
[350] Interview with Abdirahman Moallim Abdullahi, former colonel in the Somali National Army, Nairobi, April 22, 2005.
[351] See C. Legum and B. Lee, *Conflict in the Horn of Africa* (London: Rex Collings, 1977), p.32.
[352] Dualeh, H. A., *Search for a New Somali Identity* (Nairobi, 2002).
[353] See J. D. Fearon, "Domestic Policies, Foreign Policy, and The Theories of International Relations," *Annual Review of Political Science*, 1998, pp.289-313:302.
[354] See A. E. H. Dessouki and B. Korany, "A Literature Survey and a Framework for Analysis," in B. Korany and A. E. H. Dessouki, *The Foreign Policies of Arab State*, (Boulder and London: Westview Press, 1984), pp. 5-18:14.

also set the stage for an increased arms race with its main adversary, Ethiopia, seeking a balance of power in its favour. Somali analysts argue that the perception of having a more superior military capability, in addition to other remote and immediate causes, must have influenced the Somali government's decision to attack Ethiopia in 1977.[355]

However, the Somali army was not only intended to shield the country against external threats and to protect its territorial integrity; it was also a symbol of national independence – as is the case of many developing countries[356] – and an embodiment of the nation's identity and dignity. Although the Somali government failed in its attempts to win the *Ogaden* war with Ethiopia, there was a feeling that the country could still field one of the best armies in Africa.[357] Furthermore, the army was also used to maintain the country's internal security, by waging war against armed rebel groups challenging the military government.

## Political Structure

The first few years of military rule in Somalia were as charged as the period before and immediately after independence. General Barre and the Supreme Revolutionary Council (SRC) – which originally consisted of 25 members – received a tumultuous welcome. The Council members, and the entire army, were seen as heroic patriots who had left the barracks to save the nation. This feeling was reinforced by the trials of civilian politicians, the new and inflated rhetoric of nationalistic statism, the selection of an official orthography for the Somali language, and the subsequently massive campaign of adult literacy.[358]

The SRC banned political parties, abolished parliament and suspended the constitution in the name of radical change, according to Marxist

---

[355] Interview with Ambassador Hussein Ali Duale, former Somali Ambassador to Kenya and Uganda, Nairobi, September 11, 2001. Amb. Duale argues that he wrote a confidential policy cable back to Mogadishu advising the government against the *Ogaden* war and that he was recalled back to Mogadishu, the capital where he was redeployed to the battlefront in the *Ogaden* region.
[356] Ibid.
[357] See for example, H. M. Adam, et al, *Removing Barricades in Somalia: Options for Peace and Rehabilitation*, (Washington, D.C.: USIP, 1998), p.4.
[358] See A. I. Samatar, "Under Siege: Blood, Power and the Somali State," in P. Anyang Nyong'o, *Arms and Daggers in the Heart of Africa: Studies on Internal Conflicts* (Nairobi: African Academy of Sciences, 1993), pp.67-100: 85.

precepts. As such, in October 1970, the SRC adopted what it referred to as *'Scientific Socialism'* and declared Somalia a socialist country. The First Charter of the Revolution vested the SRC with all the functions previously performed by the President of the Republic, the Parliament, the Council of Ministers and the Supreme Court combined. Though several key ministries were held by military officers who were members of the SRC, there were also 'civilian secretaries of state' who formed a cabinet of ministers called the Council of the Secretaries of State (CSS), which also reported to the SRC.[359] The SRC-led government promised to end corruption, eliminate clannism, eradicate hunger and provide an efficient government, although the euphoria of the military coup began to wane in the mid-1970s. By then, it had become obvious that the SRC was not intent on restoring democracy as they had promised when they resumed power, but would instead give themselves more concrete powers and privileges.

In 1976, Gen. Barre formed a Soviet-style single party, the Somali Revolutionary Socialist Party (SRSP), and assumed the title of Secretary-General of the party and Chairman of the *Politburo* of the party composed of five members. As a result, the SRC dissolved itself and handed its powers back to themselves under a new institutional name now called the SRSP. In 1979, the Somali government introduced a draft constitution, which institutionalized both the military junta's apparatus and practices and the SRSP as the only legitimate party in the country. The draft constitution was approved in a referendum in which the government claimed to have received more than 99 per cent approval rate from the electorate, although the ballot paper had only one party. This was followed by parliamentary elections, where members were nominated by the *Politburo*, approved by the SRSP's Central Committee and elected as a single list of uncontested candidates. The National Assembly, in turn, elected Gen. Barre as President in a process that was routinely repeated every four years.[360]

The government structure in Somalia implied a number of foreign policy constraints and opportunities. Personalized rule was crucial in decisions such as going to war with Ethiopia in 1977, joining the Arab

---

[359] See M. H. Mukhtar, *Historical Dictionary of Somalia: African Historical Dictionary*, (Maryland Oxford: Scarecrow Press, 2003), p.243.

[360] Ibid, p.237, See also M. A. Jama, "The Destruction of the Somali State: Causes, Costs and Lessons," in H. M. Adam and R. Ford, *Mending Rips in the Sky: Options for Somalia Communities in the 21$^{st}$ Century* (Asmara: Red Sea Press Inc, 1997), pp.237-254:240.

League and engaging in a policy of *détente* with neighbours. The military government was also grappling with the issue of legitimacy and lack of public support. The link between foreign policy and domestic policy was, therefore, glaring as the government conducted its foreign policy for the achievement of its domestic objectives. It indeed invaded *Ogaden* in an attempt to mobilize popular support through manipulating the surviving elements of the military government's version of *pan-Somali* nationalism.[361]

## Foreign Policy Orientation

It is a known fact that foreign policy decisions do not seem to change much when the national leadership shifts to the hands of the military,[362] because the military officers appear to have set their nation's international course according to much the same criteria of national interest as the civilian governments did. The SRC pledged to maintain pan-Somalism and to follow a non-aligned foreign policy.[363] Non-alignment, as a concept, was originally adopted by countries whose governments did not feel that the conflict between the Soviet Union and the west concerned them and as a result refused to take sides. In that sense, this course of action was merely a slightly different version of classical neutrality.[364] Non-alignment was, however, mere rhetoric in most African countries as, for example, Barre's regime aligned itself first with the Soviet Union and then with the USA. It was able to switch from one to the other rival power as a way of maintaining itself; both in economic terms and in military capability. This mainly arose because, during the Cold War, both the US and the Soviet Union vied for influence and control over the country [and] in the light of its strategic location along oil routes from the Persian Gulf.[365]

---

[361] See for example, WSP International, *Rebuilding Somaliland: Issues and Possibilities* (Asmara: The Red Sea Press, Inc., 2005), p.11.
[362] See H. S. Biennen, "The Role of The Military in Foreign Policy," in J. F. William and H. H. Biennen (eds.), *Arms and Africa* (New haven and London: Yale University Press, 1985), p.157.
[363] See M. H. Mukhtar, *Historical Dictionary of Somalia: African Historical Dictionary*, (Maryland Oxford: Scarecrow Press, 2003), p.243.
[364] See T. W. Scott, "The Third World and the Conflict of Ideologies," in T. W. Scott, (ed.) *The Third World Premises of US Policy* (San Francisco: ICS, 1978), p.13.
[365] See for example M. Bezboruah, *US Strategy in the Indian Ocean: The International Response* (New York: Praeger Publishers, 1977).

## Pan-Somalism

When Siyad Barre came to power, he declared that his government would pursue a policy of *détente*. Referring to Somalia's relations with its neighbours, the leader once said in a speech: "we are determined as ever to come together with our friends at the round table to reach solutions honourable and satisfactory for all."[366] Although, in theory, this meant that Somalia was to pursue a policy of *détente* with its neighbours, mainly Kenya and Ethiopia, this was contradicted by two factors. First, the SRC had pledged to maintain *pan-Somalism* as a central ideological tenet in its international relations and diplomacy; and, secondly, Somalia, under Barre, was virtually preparing for war by assembling one of the largest and best equipped armies in Africa.

The inconsistency of Somalia's foreign policy was not only highlighted by the fact that Barre was initially relatively cautious with regard to the country's neighbours, but actually by the government's eventual foreign policy behaviour towards Djibouti, Kenya and Ethiopia. These decisions were not only erratic, but were, according to some analysts suggest, a betrayal of *pan-Somali* objectives. They, however, make part of the several ways of understanding Somalia's foreign policy, both in its general approach to international issues as well as in specific matters related to dealing with certain countries. Accordingly, Somali foreign policy, just like that of many other states, is related to the core objective of state survival. This includes protection of the lives of the citizens, territorial integrity, sovereignty and political independence. Addressing the issue of self-determination for 'lost' territories was 'core' to Somalia's quest to build its military capability in order to have the upper hand in its dealings with neighbouring countries. In principle, Somalia's efforts to identify with the ethnic kin in the Somali Horn of Africa region were a pride and a national duty. It was not, therefore, secret that this pride has greatly influenced Barre's support for the Western Somali Liberation Front (WSLF) incursions in Ethiopia. Since its assumption of power in 1969, the military had frequently acknowledged their abiding commitment to the liberation of those parts of the Somali nation, which still languished under foreign

---

[366] See M. Wubneh and Y. Abate, *Ethiopia: Transition and Development in the Horn of Africa*, (Colorado: Westview Press, 1988), p.166.

rule: the French territory of the Afars and Issas (Djibouti), the *Ogaden* and the NFD.[367]

But Siyad Barre's approach to *pan-Somalism* was smart; sometimes cunning, and other times opportunistic. He, for example, gave up attempting to conquer Djibouti after being assured that the Issa, the Somali ethnic group in the country, would not be discriminated against during the exercise of the referendum. Neither did Barre insist in unification even after Djibouti's declaration of its intention to remain an independent nation. Similarly, he gave up claims to the NFD after President Moi's proactive approach of accommodating Kenyan-Somalis in the socio-political and socio-economic life of mainstream Kenya.[368] It was, therefore, no longer feasible for Somalis in capitalist Kenya to rejoin socialist Somalia which was in many ways staggering—politically, economically or otherwise. However, to Barre, *Ogaden* was the major stake; but he knew that he stood no chance of success without making a significant concession elsewhere.[369] As Somalia was surrounded with enemies, not only in Africa but also across its northern waters with Marxist South Yemen, and others with hidden agendas in the Arabian Peninsula, it conceded to the desires of regional leaders out of fear of further weakening its own position.[370]

When conquest of the *Ogaden* region re-emerged as a feasible option, Barre sought to recapture it out of sheer opportunism. As the flush of enthusiasm for Barre's 'revolution' began to fade in the mid-1970s, he turned to the *pan-Somali* dream to reinvigorate his flagging support base.[371] Somalia's defeat in the *Ogaden* war with Ethiopia, however, decisively buried the dream of a *pan-Somali* state. The death certificate of the ideology was underscored, at least with Kenya, in Somalia's signing, in 1984, of an official agreement with Kenya relinquishing the idea of 'Greater Somalia.'

---

[367] See for example, I. M. Lewis, *A Modern History of the Somali Nation and State in the Horn of Africa* 4th Ed., (Hargeisa: Btec Books, 2002), p.227.

[368] Interview with Ambassador Hussein Ali Dualeh, former Somali ambassador to Kenya and to Uganda, Nairobi, September 11, 2001.

[369] See J. M. Ghalib, *The Cost of Dictatorship: The Somali Experience* (New York: Lilian Barber Press Inc, 1995), p.112.

[370] Notes from the field, September 13, 2005.

[371] See WSP International, *Rebuilding Somaliland: Issues and Possibilities* (Asmara: The Red Sea Press, Inc, 2005), p11.

## Somalia and the Latter Part of the Cold War

As the rivalry between the Superpowers, the USA and the USSR, grew, the duo went far afield across continents, engaging each other in a strategically motivated geopolitical competition. Both Superpowers wanted to expand their influence in strategic locations around the world to the disadvantage of its rival. On the one hand, the Soviet Union and its allies, notably Cuba, persistently attempted to keep both Ethiopia and Somalia within the socialist camp; but not knowing exactly how to achieve it. The new conundrum, though, in its pragmatic reality, meant more than trying to merely dampen Ethiopian-Somali hostilities, in particular the territorial claims of the Somali government. The socialist negotiators encountered a colossal stalemate too burdensome to overcome. For, while the Soviet Union and its supreme loyal ally, Cuba, were negotiating with the Horn of Africa rivals for the sake of upholding the socialist ideology, Somalis viewed the whole scenario, the entire process, as an erroneous exercise— in that: while fundamentally it was (re)vitalizing socialist ideology for the advantage of the Soviet union, it was at the same time jeopardizing inconsiderately the Somalis' sacrosanct ideology of 'Greater Somalia.'[372] So, from the perspective of the Somali leaders, now left in shock and dismay, the two ideologies, the indigenous and the alien, seem to be contrastively incomparable. Feeling insulted, the Somalis interpreted the intervention as nothing less disloyalty, socialist hypocrisy, and betrayal of an old ally. As the situation kept deteriorating with no feasible solution, Somalis had to make a decision, an expeditious decision whose consequences would be far reaching more than anyone could anticipate—politically, socially, economically, and, in geopolitical terms, strategically.[373]

A historical review, prior to the onset of the Cold War, shows that the only significant American presence in the Horn of Africa was found in Ethiopia. At the height of the Cold War, however, and as US interests shifted toward countering the Soviet Union's efforts at securing physical presence in the region, its key allies shifted to the countries surrounding pro-Soviet Ethiopia, such as the Sudan and Somalia.[374] The move can be

---

[372] Notes from the field, September 13, 2005.
[373] Ibid.
[374] See R. Lyob and E. J. Keller, "US Policy in the Horn," in D. A. Bekoe, *Grappling with a Difficult Legacy in East Africa and the Horn: Confronting Challenges to Good Governance* (Boulder and London: Lynne Rienner Publishers, 2006), pp.101-125:101.

explained in the context of what can be termed as the 'policy of encirclement.' The two superpowers, therefore, played off the opposing clients at different times, realigning themselves either as strategic friends or enemies.

The posturing of the superpowers in the Horn of Africa circumstance had a number of effects. First, it sparked an arms race between Ethiopia and Somalia. For example, the size of the Ethiopian army grew from 54,000 in 1977 to more than 300,000 a decade later; while Somalia's army swelled from about 32,000 in 1977 to 65,000 in 1987. Their defence expenditures in the same period (1977-1987), also grew from $103 million to $134 million respectively.[375] This level and pattern of growth in military expenditures could not have taken place had the countries of the Horn of Africa not been able to rely on superpower patrons who provided them with increasing levels of military assistance.

Secondly, the superpowers' actions not only fanned the fire of hostility among the two neighbours, but they played a role in the escalation of the hostility to a full-blown proxy war pitting Somalia against Ethiopia.[376] In addition to fuelling instability in the region due to an ideological struggle for supremacy, it also exacerbated the degree and intensity of the conflict between the two countries and later within each individual country. On the one hand, Barre believed that the Soviets were bound by treaty to Somalia and that they should not provide aid to its adversaries, while on the other hand he evidently believed that Washington had flashed him, at least, a dim green-light, to attack Ethiopia. The percept of the tacit encouragement and support has been denied by US officials as a misperception of their country's position.[377] It can nonetheless be argued that this foreign policy orientation facilitated inter-state war between Somalia and Ethiopia and later, as mentioned earlier, intra-state wars that toppled both regimes at the hands of rebellious armed insurgents ambitious for change.

---

[375] Ibid, p.106.
[376] See J. G. Hershberg, "Anatomy of Third World Crisis: New East Bloc Evidence on the Horn of Africa 1977-1978," *Cold War International History Project*, CWIHP Bulletin 8/9, Winter 1996, p.1.
[377] Ibid; See also M. Wubneh and Y. Abate, *Ethiopia: Transition and Development in the Horn of Africa*, (Colorado: Westview Press, 1998), p.166.

## Foreign Policy Decision-Making

State policy, be it internal or external, entails considerations and a long process of studies of options and analyses of the available choices and the judgements that follow in reaching the final decision. The foreign policy decision-making process under Barre's rule was one that placed primacy on the executive. Decisions were, therefore, dominated by the president himself, although top members of the politburo, as handymen, would be consulted and/or discussed with on certain issues. But the single-handedness for the decision-making authority could be attributed to several factors, the first being the country's low level of political institutionalization. For example, following his election by members of the 'people's parliament' where all members belonged to one party, the SRSP, Barre could, and more often than not did, reshuffle the cabinet at his prerogative will, if not by constitutional right, thereby abolishing the positions of the three vice presidents. He reshuffled the cabinet for about three times between November 1969 and June 1972. This was followed by another reshuffle in October 1980 in which the old SRC was revived. This particular move resulted in three parallel and overlapping bureaucratic structures within one administration: the party's *politburo*, which exercised executive powers through its central committee; the Council of Ministers; and the SRC. The resulting confusion of functions within the administration left decision-making solely in the president's hand.[378] However, whether this was intentional or not is another debate beyond the scope of this study.

The confusion prevailing in this situation was further entrenched by state censorship of the press and the lack of organized opposition movements or parties to confront the ruling military government. Using dictatorial methods based on personal rule, the government made it a capital offence for anybody to become a member of an opposition political organization. It also ruled, without any serious attempt, to encourage the opposition either to talk to the government or to join them rather than go public and therefore suffer dire consequences. Power was restrictedly centralized and Mogadishu became the nerve centre of the

---

[378] Interview with Ambassador Hussein Ali Duale, former Somali ambassador to Kenya and Uganda, Nairobi, September 11, 2001.

whole country,[379] as development projects were not going beyond the capital and other specific areas where individual officials' interests or state stakes were the priority for consideration. Within the capital itself, power and authority were centralized in the president's political office and extended down to the regional and district levels with a formidable array of subordinate organisations, each with its own power base which ultimately connected to the president either directly or via members of the SRC.[380] Barre effectively shifted the responsibility of the state organs and national institutions in favour of his office, affecting, as a result, the foreign policy decision-making process.

Another main factor is that, as the chief of state, a leader embodies the national interest more than anyone else. He is at the top of the political pyramid and somehow responsible for bringing together all the separate individual and group interests.[381] This is highlighted by the fact that a leader may take a hawkish or poor decision and initiative and, with the authority and respect he/she commands, still be backed by a substantial portion of the population. In this regard, Barre was supported by his clan, and by his cronies, from friendly clans, and those whose interests were served in the *politburo*. At the same time, however, and with regard to membership of the Arab League, another of Siyad's innovations, many Somalis questioned whether it was at all necessary to join. Ghalib, for example, poses the question whether the Arabs themselves ever accepted the Somalis as genuine Arabs.[382] As of to-date, this is still an ongoing debate.

The military regime's decision-making process, was therefore, not rational; rather, it was informed by Barre's idiosyncrasies, one being his egoist tendencies. This indeed appears to have prompted him to replace Omar Arte, a formidable and influential foreign affairs minister at the time, with his own cousin, Abdulrahman Jama Barre, known for his incompetence, hence leading to the ineffectiveness of the ministry in terms

---

[379] See J. G. N. Yoh, "Peace Processes and Conflict Resolution in the Horn of Africa," *African Security Review*, 12 (3) 2003.
[380] See WSP International, *Rebuilding Somalia Issues and Possibilities for Puntland* (London: HAAN Associates, 2001), p.9.
[381] See B. Russet, and H. Starr, *World Politics: The Menu for Choice*, (New York: W. H. Freeman and Company, 1989), p.241.
[382] See J. M. Ghalib, *The Cost of Dictatorship: The Somali Experience*, (New York: Lilian Barber Press Inc., 1995), p.142.

of foreign policy decision-making.[383] At the same time, the diplomats entrusted with conducting Somalia's foreign relations and representing the state abroad were chosen from government loyalists as well as graduates with history and English language backgrounds regardless of their acquaintance with diplomacy and foreign policy. Like most African leaders at the time, this further entrenched unaccountability to the people, making the president the only one responsible for foreign policy.

Siyad Barre's foreign policy decision-making process did not occur in a vacuum. He used his solid base within the army, together with controlling other state actors and civil society through institutions and organisations such as security, paramilitary, an elitist vanguard party, and so called mass organisations, which as a personal ruler he had the autonomy to operate.[384] The decision-making process behind Somali foreign policy, therefore, relied on Barre's personality and perceptions and the competition between various cronies and groups which had an influence on him and on each other; typical of what has been branded as the psychological model of decision making.[385]

An analysis of the Somali foreign policy decision-making process, under Barre, would be incomplete without highlighting the influence of external actors which penetrated the leader's decision-making process and consequently participated authoritatively in the allocation of resources and the determination of national goals. For example, the US appealed for Somalia's withdrawal from the *Ogaden* in exchange for aid, pressuring him to renounce the 'Greater Somalia' ambitions by withholding the military aid[386] the country needed. The Arab League also had its influence on Barre especially, from the time Somalia joined the League; the same also applies to old European colonialists who ruled Somalia, mainly Italy, which stayed in close touch with Siyad Barre with its support up to the last minute of his government.

---

[383] Ibid, p.110.
[384] See H. M. Adam, "Somalia: A Terrible Beauty being Born," in W. I. Zartman, *Collapsed State: The Disintegration of Legitimate Authority* (Boulder and London: Lynne Rienner Publishers, 1994), pp.69-89:71.
[385] For more on this see, for example, T. L. Brewer, *American Foreign Policy: A Contemporary Introduction* 3rd Ed (New Jersey: Prentice Hall, 1980), p.29.
[386] See for example, D. D. Laitin and S. S. Samatar, *Somalia: Nation in Search of a State* (Colorado: Westview Press, 1987), p.143.

## Foreign Policy Behaviour

### *Somalia and the East (the Soviet Union)*

When, in October 1970, the Somali government declared Somalia to adopt socialism as the political approach for the country, the Soviet Union recognized it as part of the socialist bloc. To the Somali government, the aim of this new political concept of *Hantiwadaagga Cilmiga ku Dhisan 'Scientific Socialism'*, as Barre announced, was to correct the errors of the past corrupt civilian regimes and place the country's fortunes on a firm footing; based on this ideological orientation. Barre's new choice of direction, already foreshadowed in the retrospective transformation of the *coup de'tat* into a revolution, included mass organisation based on togetherness and a national campaign against clannism.[387]

Siyad Barre eloquently preached *'Scientific Socialism'* out of sheer expediency without much knowledge or personal commitment.[388] The adoption was basically due to Somalia's increasing dependence on Soviet aid but not to any ideological conviction.[389] In other words, it reflected the army's growing dependence on Soviet equipment and advisers in contrast to the complementary connection of the police force with America and the west.

One of the reasons for this dependence on the Soviets is that the new Somali leader at the time, a product of the former Italian army himself, a man of old-fashioned virtues and a staunch Muslim, had been 'converted' to Marxism because of his disillusionment with the west, mainly over its 'hostility' to Somalia's aspirations. Siyad Barre, like other Somali leaders, had lost his faith in the earlier policy of trying to befriend the 'hostile alliance' of Ethiopia, Kenya, the US, the UK, France and Israel.[390] In fact, this was highlighted in the early years of Barre's revolution through foreign policy pronouncements that emphasized the evils of US imperialism in Southeast Asia and the Zionist imperialism in the Middle East. It was

---

[387] See I. M. Lewis, *A Modern History of the Somali: Nation and State in the Horn of Africa* 4th Ed., (Hargeisa: Btec Books, 2002), p.209.

[388] See J. M. Ghalib, *The Cost of Dictatorship: The Somali Experience*, (New York: Lilian Barber Press Inc., 1995), p.126.

[389] See R. Cornwell, "*Somalia fourteenth time lucky?*" *Occasional paper* 87, Institute for Security Studies, April 2004, p.2.

[390] See C. Legum and B. Lee, *Conflict in the Horn of Africa*, (London: Red Collings, 1977), p.32.

also natural that the idealistic young intellectuals associated with the new government should look to the Soviet bloc for inspiration, since the previous civilian governments had on the whole been inclined towards the west despite the military aid agreement of 1963 with the Soviet Union.

By all accounts, dependency was key to the relationship between Somalia and the Soviet Union. Somalia, as the periphery state, had a lot to gain from the Soviet Union for arms supply and military and professional training while the Soviet Union, as the core, was interested in expanding and improving its naval capabilities. The interest of both countries was evident in the agreement they made for the construction of the port of Berbera, which became an important Soviet military base to counter US activities at bases in the Indian Ocean and the Red Sea.

In its desire to reduce vulnerabilities and diminish threats, Somalia therefore, entered into an alliance with the Soviet Union. The relationship of the two nations reached a peak with the 1974 Treaty of Friendship and Co-operation Somalia signed with the Soviet Union. Through the treaty, Somalia upgraded its military potential; building up substantially strong and enviable national armed forces.[391] The Somalis benefited from training in the Soviet Union, Eastern Europe and Cuba, as well as acquiring advanced military hardware that included 150 T-35 and 100 T-54 tanks mostly fitted with 105mm guns.[392] The Soviets also supplied the Somali army with more than 300 armed personnel carriers, 200 coastal batteries, 50 MIG fighters and supersonic jet fighters, a squadron of II-28 bombers, a SAM-2 ground-to-air missile complex, an SAM-2 missile defence system for Mogadishu, the capital city, and modern torpedo and other advanced landing crafts for the navy.[393] To match the broadened scale of the project activities and adhere to the commitment to success, the number of Soviet advisers had to be increased.[394] Finally, as the two allies' loyalty and commitment to each other reached new heights, the Soviets agreed to write off Somalia's arms debts and set up the Somali army intelligence apparatus and the National Security Service (NSS).

---

[391] See D. D. Laitin and S. S. Samatar, *Somalia: Nation in Search of a State*, (Boulder, Colorado: Westview Press, 1987), p.139.
[392] Ibid.
[393] Ibid.
[394] Ibid, p.140; See also M. H. Mukhtar, *Historical Dictionary of Somalia: African Historical Dictionary*, (Maryland Oxford: Scarecrow Press, 2003), p.241.

In spite of these developments, which ensured Somalia's preparedness in case of war, a lot of discontent began to emerge among the Somali public. Ali observes "the Soviet Union was not eager to finance development projects unless they fit its plans of exploitation; this culminated in 1974 with the making out of the national territory a large military facility for the superpowers."[395] Furthermore, since major ideologies are themselves a product of the conditions and mental attitudes of the advanced world, Somalia's *'Scientific Socialism'* and its misuse brought about resentment towards the Soviet Union as it was viewed as perpetuating violence and oppression against the Somali people.

## Somalia and the West:

### *The US and the European Union (EU)*

Unlike Somali relations with the Soviet Union, Somali-American relations constantly fluctuated in response to evolving Somali foreign policy and American interests in the volatile Horn of Africa. Indeed, there was lack of a consistent (foreign) policy, or diplomacy, on both sides.[396] For example, the relationship between the US and Somalia deteriorated after the installation of the military government in 1969. For a decade, US-Somali relations were reduced to the formal presence of diplomatic missions in Mogadishu and Washington and, on behalf of the Kremlin, the Somali government participated in the Cold War in full swing.

In the early 1970s, the military government, dizzied by Soviet generosity in arms and military advisors, undertook an anti-American rhetoric which echoed in Somalia and in all forums to which the Somali government had access. Somali citizens were in danger as long as they had any sort of ties, even genuine, with the US. Unless they publicly repudiated their country, US officials and citizens had their freedom of movement in Somalia and contacts with Somali citizens and officials restricted in the

---

[395] See A. Q. Ali, "The Foreign Factor in the Somali Tragedy," in H. M. Adam and R. Ford, *Mending Rips in the Sky: Options for Somali Communities in the 21st Century*, (Asmara: The Red Sea Press, Inc., 1997), pp.534-563:539.

[396] See M. H. Mukhtar, *Historical Dictionary of Somalia: African Historical Dictionary*, (Maryland Oxford: Scarecrow Press, 2003), p.253.

country, as obtaining a Somali visa became arduous for US passport holders.[397]

Siyad Barre's friendship with the US began with the Carter administration when the former was planning to wage war against Ethiopia and the military government approached Washington in the hope of obtaining backing.[398] However, it was not until 1977 that US-Somali rapprochement actually began. One of the events leading to this was the change in US-Ethiopia relations when the Mengistu-led *Derg* movement overthrew Emperor Haile Selassie in a bloody *coup d'etat* on February 3, 1974, leading to Mengistu's accession to power. The first leader from the communist states to meet the new Ethiopian leader was Cuba's Fidel Castro. The *Derg* immediately embraced socialism; leading to US discontent. Gradually, Washington reduced its foreign aid to Ethiopia, beginning on February 25, 1977 when US Secretary of State Cyrus Vance announced that US foreign aid was being reduced in three countries – Ethiopia, Argentina and Uruguay – due to human rights violations.[399]

Although US arms supplies to Ethiopia continued on an irregular basis for the first three years of the *Derg* revolution, they did not match the dramatic increase in Soviet shipments to Somalia which took off after 1974 and reached a peak in 1976 -77 when the danger of American retaliation had virtually disappeared.[400] In spite of this support, the Soviet Union lacked sympathy for Somalia's *Ogaden* aspirations; it not only counselled patience to Barre, it also attempted to fashion a socialist alliance among South Yemen, Ethiopia and Somalia.[401] Barre, however, wanted to take advantage of the temporary balance of power, which favoured his

---

[397] See A. Q. Ali, "The Foreign Factor in the Somali Tragedy," in H. M. Adam and R. Ford, *Mending Rips in the Sky: Options for Somali Communities in the 21st Century*, (Asmara: the Red Sea Press, Inc., 1997), pp. 534-563:544.

[398] Ibid, p.545; See also A. Mazrui, "Crisis in Somalia: From Tyranny to Anarchy," in H. M. Adam and R. Ford (eds.), *Mending Rips in the Sky: Options for Somali Communities in the 21st Century* (Asmara: The Red Sea Press, 1997), pp.5-11:8.

[399] See M. Ottaway, *Soviet and American Influence in the Horn of Africa* (New York: Praeger, 1982), p.142; See also C. Legum and B. Lee, *Conflict in the Horn of Africa*,(London: Rex Collings, 1977), p.69.

[400] See C. Clapham, "The Horn of Africa: A Conflict Zone," in O. Furley, (ed.), *Conflict in Africa* (London and New York: Tauris Academic Publishers, 1995), pp.72-91:78.

[401] See D. D. Laitin and S. S. Samatar, *Somalia: Nation in Search of a State*, (Boulder, Colorado: Westview Press, 1987), p.142.; See also G. B. N. Ayyitey, "The Somalia Crisis: Time for An African Solution," *Policy Analysis*, No. 205, March 28, 1994, p.3.

country at the time, and invaded *Ogaden* against Soviet advice to refrain from waging war. This was the genesis of the rupture of the country's relationship with the Soviet Union.

The diplomatic relationship between the two countries was already rather grim when Barre visited Moscow shortly before the 1977-78 *Ogaden* war. Not only did Brezhnev have little time for Barre during his visit, making it rather fruitless, but encouraged by the increasingly socialist rhetoric and policies of the Ethiopian revolutionaries, the Soviets felt that they had greater affinities with that country.[402] They were consequently true to their word and abandoned Somalia after mediation efforts failed, in August 1977. Subsequently, the Soviet Union suspended arms shipments to Barre's government and accelerated military deliveries to Ethiopia. Three months later, Somalia renounced the treaty of friendship and cooperation, expelled all Soviet advisors and personnel from Somalia and, at the same time, broke diplomatic relations with Cuba.[403]

Therefore, not only did the *Ogaden* war cement Somalia's defection from the Soviet bloc and its defeat, it also elevated the conflict to a superpower-level crisis, as Washington accused Moscow of employing Cuban proxy forces to expand its influence in Africa. Moscow and Havana, for their part, maintained that they had only helped Ethiopia defend itself from a US-backed assault from Somalia, with the additional support of various reactionary Arab countries.[404]

Following the *Ogaden* war, Barre was desperate to find a strong alliance to replace the Soviet Union. His main magic card was the strategic value of the port of Berbera, which was capable of handling large bombers. When the Shah of Iran fell in 1979, the US lost its closest ally in the Gulf, and its strategic planners felt that the country could no longer adequately protect western oil interests. President Carter deemed it unwise to rely on any single country in that region and, therefore, plotted to build up a Rapid Deployment Force (RDF) capable of a quick response to any emergency situation in the Middle East. With the Soviet Union out of

---

[402] See for example, M. Ottaway, *Soviet and American Influence in the Horn of Africa,* (New York: Praeger, 1982).

[403] Interview with Mohammed Haji, former Assistant Minister, Nairobi, April 22, 2005.

[404] See for example, J. G. Hershberg, "Anatomy of Third World Crisis: New East Bloc Evidence on the Horn of Africa 1977-1978," *Cold War International History Project,* CWIHP Bulletin 8/9, Winter 1996.

Somalia, Berbera became a possible facility for the strategic activities of the RDF.[405]

Ronald Reagan came to office and persuaded that his predecessor had failed to stand up for his friends and ensure that the country was respected by its adversaries,[406] accelerated US-Somali *rapprochement*. This culminated in a 1980 agreement allowing the US access to, and use of, ports and airfields in Berbera, Mogadishu and Kismayo for which Somalia received in exchange US$40 million in military aid and US$53 million in economic assistance.[407]

In the summer of 1982, Ethiopian forces invaded Somalia along the central border, mainly Galdogob and Balanballe, and the US provided two emergency airlifts to help Somalia defend its territorial integrity. From 1982 to 1988, the US viewed Somalia as a defence partner in the context of the Cold War and Somali officers of the national armed forces were trained in US military schools, incorporating civilian and military studies.[408] Somalia also received considerable refugee aid, with USAID funding projects in agriculture, livestock, and other development sectors. Military aid totalled more than US$200 million in the 1980s, whereby the US was able to counter the Soviet presence in Ethiopia and, as a result, obtained a strategic foothold at a crossroad with the Middle East.[409]

This *rapprochement* was, however, cautious because Somalia still had ambitions to retake *Ogaden* and could use US arms to achieve that aim, thereby prompting a massive counterattack by Ethiopia. In addition, the relationship was riddled with controversy due to the Somali government's human rights policies. The policy of repression of both individual rights and opposition groups in the north indeed aroused criticism of the

---

[405] See D. D. Laitin and S. S. Samatar, *Somalia; Nation in Search of a State*, (Boulder, Colorado: Westview Press, 1987), p.144.

[406] See A. Q. Ali, "The Foreign Factor in the Somali Tragedy," in H. M. Adam and R. Ford, *Mending Rips in the Sky: Options for Somali Communities in the 21st Century*, (Asmara: The Red Sea Press, Inc., 1997), pp.534-563:545.

[407] Ibid.

[408] See "Somalia: Background Note," US Department of State, Bureau of African Affairs, March 2006.

[409] See for example, A. Q. Ali "The Foreign Factor in the Somali Tragedy," in H. M. Adam and R. Ford, *Mending Rips in the Sky: Options for Somali Communities in the 21st Century*, (Asmara: The Red Sea Press, Inc., 1997), pp. 534-563:546.

government in the US Congress.[410] This strained relations to the extent that, in 1989, under Congressional pressure, the US terminated its military aid to Somalia although it continued to provide economic and food assistance.[411]

In 1990, Washington revealed that Mogadishu had been defaulting on loan repayments for more than a year. This, under the terms of the Brooks Amendment, meant that Somalia was ineligible to receive any further US aid. Relations between the two countries further deteriorated when, during the height of the civil war in Mogadishu in January 1991, the US closed its embassy and evacuated all its personnel from the country.[412]

The Somali government, on the other hand, maintained its relations with the European Commission (EC). The EC was an important ally which never encouraged its member states to suspend their aid to the government, even after it had come to wage an open war against its people and human rights organisations and the European media had denounced its atrocities. Chief among these countries was Italy which spent, between 1980 and 1990, more than US$1 billion to sponsor 114 projects. For example, US$20 million was spent on the Garowe-Bosaso road that stretches 450 kilometres across [the] barren desert.[413]

**Regional Goals**

Barre envisioned Somalia being simultaneously at the centre of African and Arab relations. In the African context, for example, the Somali government successfully played a mediation role in the confrontation between Uganda and Tanzania in 1972. Having joined the Arab League as the only non-Arabic speaking member state, this dual policy assumed

---

[410] See "Somalia: Background Note," US Department of State, Bureau of African Affairs, March 2006.
[411] Ibid.
[412] See M. H. Mukhtar, *Historical Dictionary of Somalia: African Historical Dictionary*, (Maryland Oxford: Scarecrow Press, 2003), p.245.
[413] See A. Q. Ali, "The Foreign Factor in the Somali Tragedy," in Hussein M. Adam and Richard Ford, *Mending Rips in the Sky: Options for Somali Communities in the 21st Century*,(Asmara: the Red Sea Press, Inc., 1997), 534-563:543; G. B. N. Ayyitey, "The Somalia Crisis: Time for an African Solution," *Policy Analysis* No. 205, March 28, 1994, p.4.; A. Wolfgang, "The Italian Connection: How Rome Helped Ruin Somalia," *The Washington Post*, January 24, 1993, p.1.

much greater prominence, at least on the African political scene, when in 1974 Somalia hosted the OAU summit in Mogadishu.

No expense was spared in using this opportunity as a way to promote the image of Somalia -- in the eyes of the African, Arab and international community -- as a proudly independent, progressive, socialist state. In seeking a more prominent and forceful role in African affairs, the government stressed how well-placed Somalia was geographically to act as a natural mediator between the Islamic world and sub-Saharan Africa.[414]

## Somalia and the Arab/Muslim World

Although Siyad Barre's regime was identified with Marxist socialist ideologies, it nevertheless tried to play roles wherever opportunities arose. In one of such instances, Somalia sought membership to become among the counties of the Arab League, for calculated political and economic principles. Several reasons explain why, notwithstanding Somalis' reluctance to be called Arabs, Somalia joined the Arab League. First, the government paid lip service to the Arab and Palestinian cause; to care about Arab problems. Second, these were the years of petro-dollars and the rich Arab Gulf countries had given employment opportunities to Somali workers and economic assistance to the government.[415] Third, most of the young officers who participated in the 1969 military coup were graduates from Egyptian and Iraqi military academies, as were a number of civilians in the military government machine such as Omar Arte Ghalib (who was foreign minister between 1970 and 1975) and were favourable to the Arab League. However, it was Foreign Minister Omar Arte Ghalib who engineered Somalia's entry into the Arab League, following a long-standing invitation, declaring that Somalia was ready to play its role fully in the service of the great Arab cause.[416]

---

[414] See I. M. Lewis, *A Modern History of the Somali Nation and State in the Horn of Africa*, 4th Ed., (Hargeisa: Btec Books, 2002), p.227. Also, note that – dubbed as the MENA region – Africa north of the Sahara or northern Africa is more Arab than African and it is counted as part and parcel of the Middle East regional political context.

[415] See A. Q. Ali, "The Foreign Factor in the Somali Tragedy," in H. M. Adam and R. Ford, *Mending Rips in the Sky: Options for Somali Communities in the 21st Century*, (Asmara: The Red Sea Press, Inc., 1997), 534-563:547.

[416] Ibid, p.546,; See also D. D. Laitin and S. S. Samatar, *Somalia: Nation in Search of a State*, (Boulder, Colorado: Westview Press, 1987), p.145.; H. M. Adam, "Somalia: Personal

Finally, Barre sought to gain geopolitical advantages by strengthening the country's alliance system and tapping into various categories of Arab aid and Arab development funds. Joining the Arab League was intended to diversify Barre's diplomatic and foreign aid options, particularly in light of the shift in global power and resources brought about by the oil shock of 1973.[417]

While Somalia provided the rich Arab countries with a cheap vote in international forums, it was also at times at crossroads with some Arab countries. For example, Somalia broke its diplomatic relations with Libya from 1981 to 1985, accusing the country of having supported Somali dissident groups.[418] Furthermore, there were conflicts with the wealthier and conservative Arab states, especially Saudi Arabia, over the adoption of *Marxism-Leninism* rather than Islam. Arab states also insisted that if Somalia was truly an Arab state, it should have placed less emphasis on the development of the Somali language.

In response to this, the Somali government put more efforts into having many officials in the Ministry of Education re-assigned to enhance the Arabic language curriculum. Finally, Barre shocked the orthodox Arab states by executing ten Imams who preached against his secularism in 1975, over the sensitive subject of gender equality as viewed from an Islamic perspective. [419] The executions targeted Imams who went public inside the mosques and in other gatherings, contradicting the government and preaching about the issue of equality in the family law known as '*Xeerka Qoyska*,' a newly introduced section of the government's penal code which provided for equality between men and women.

Altogether throughout the 1980s, Somalia became increasingly dependent on economic aid from Kuwait, Qatar, Saudi Arabia and the United Arab Emirates (UAE). This dependence was a crucial factor in the government's decision to side with the US-led coalition of Arab

---

Rule, Military Rule and Militarism," in E. Hutchful and A. Bathily, *Military and Militarism in Africa*,(Dakar: CODESERIA, 1998), p.367.

[417] See H. M. Adam, "Somalia: Personal Rule, Military Rule and Militarism," in E. Hutchful and A. Bathily, *Military and Militarism in Africa*,(Dakar: CODESERIA, 1998), p.368; See also C. Legum and B. Lee, *Conflict in the Horn of Africa* (London: Red Collings, 1977), p.32.

[418] Interview with Matt Bryden, ICG regional analyst, Nairobi, April 22, 2005.

[419] See M. H. Mukhtar, *Historical Dictionary of Somalia: African Historical Dictionary*, (Maryland Oxford: Scarecrow Press, 2003), p.40; See also H. M. Adam, "Somalia: Personal Rule, Military Rule and Militarism," in E. Hutchful and A. Bathily, *Military and Militarism in Africa*, (Dakar: CODESERIA, 1998), p.368.

states that opposed Iraq following its invasion of Kuwait in 1990. Although Somalia supported Iraq in the initial stages of the Gulf crisis, it switched sides at the last minute to support the US-led coalition. In return, supporting the coalition served as a *quid pro quo* purpose as it brought economic dividends to Somalia. Qatar, for example, cancelled further repayment of all principal and interest payments on outstanding loans against Somalia, while Saudi Arabia followed suit and offered Somalia a US$70 million grant and promised to sell it oil below prevailing international market prices.[420]

Decades before these economic and financial supports, Somalia had been benefiting from Arab military assistance. From 1979 to 1983, the military government purchased about US$500 million in arms with the help of Arab petro-dollars; becoming the third most important client of the Italian arms industry.[421] Records reveal that it also benefited economically a great deal. For example, from 1975 to 1978, Somalia received US$361.1 million in OPEC development aid, which constituted about 14 percent of the total Sub-Saharan African outlay in the OPEC development programme.[422] The aid flow from OPEC, despite helping solve crucial domestic matters, had the great impact on Somalia's foreign policy because it assured the Arab League of Somalia's vote whenever required. The funds, likewise, facilitated the appeasement process with various clans and/or sub-clans whom the government needed pacification with.

## Somalia and the OAU

Upon assuming power, the military regime tasked itself to engage actors that would intervene in the regional issue regarding its borders. So, to set the stage, the military government's African policy initially focused on the OAU, where a mediation endeavour by presidents Gowon of Nigeria and Numeiri of Sudan to solve the issue of Somali irredentism failed to produce an agreement. Barre then concentrated on relations with north Afri-

---

[420] See A. Metz, *Somalia: A Country Study*, (Washington, D.C.: US Library of Congress, 1993).
[421] See A. Q. Ali, "The Foreign Factor in the Somali Tragedy," in Hussein M. Adam and Richard Ford, *Mending Rips in the Sky: Options for Somalia Communities in the 21ˢᵗ Century*, (Asmara: The Red Sea Press, Inc., 1997), pp.534-563:547.
[422] See D. D. Laitin and S. S. Samatar, *Somalia: Nation in Search of a State*, (Boulder, Colorado: Westview Press, 1987), p.145.

can states, and later joined the Arab League.[423] The main reason for Somalia's initial setback in the OAU was Haile Selassie's influence which ensured the OAU's support for Ethiopia as opposed to Somalia.

However, Somalia's hosting of the 12th OAU Summit in Mogadishu in 1974 and the deposition of Haile Selassie in 1975 changed the situation dramatically. During the Summit, Barre was elected as the OAU chairman and it is in this wider African context that his regime again considered the perennial issue of *pan-Somali* nationalism. Prior to this, the military government had shown moderation in the pursuit of that objective. Haile Selassie was prepared to symbolically concede a strip of territory to Somalia, as a border readjustment arrangement, without acknowledging further Somali claims. Haile Selassie offered this proposal tactically as it was dependent on the Somali government's agreement for a permanent boundary demarcation line along the still unmarked former Italian Somaliland border.[424] Barre, on the other hand, digested politically and socio-ideologically what Haile Selassie's tactical proposal entailed before vehemently rejecting it.

When talks on the issue finally failed, Somalia took the case to the OAU Summit held in Addis Ababa in 1973. To the credit of the then Somali Foreign Minister, Omar Arte Ghalib, and due to his popularity following the mediation efforts between Tanzania and Uganda in 1972, this was the first time that Somalia was able to secure consensus in the OAU for any discussion on the Somali-Ethiopian dispute.[425] Before that, Ethiopia, which dominated the OAU Secretariat, ensured the total exclusion of the issue from the agenda. This resulted in the appointment of a committee of eight member states to mediate between Ethiopia and Somalia and then report its findings back to the heads of state and government.

The opportunity which the OAU chairmanship provided and the constraints imposed suggested that if this nationalist issue were now to be rigorously revived, the anachronistic persistence of French rule in Djibouti should be the first target.[426] However, the military government's

---

[423] See P. Woodward, *The Horn of Africa: Politics and International Relations*, (London and New York: Tauris Academic Studies, 1996), p.126.
[424] Ibid.
[425] See J. M. Ghalib, *The Cost of Dictatorship: The Somali Experience*, (New York: Lilian Barber Press Inc., 1995), p.110.
[426] See I. M. Lewis, *A Modern History of the Somali Nation and State in the Horn of Africa*, 4th Ed., (Hargeisa: Btec Books, 2002), p.228.

ambitions to incorporate Djibouti into a 'Greater Somalia' were also shattered in 1977 after the Djiboutians overwhelmingly voted against the amalgamation of their territory into Somalia. Consequently, when Djibouti gained independence as a separate state, the military government relinquished its claims on Djibouti.[427] This occurrence prompted a more focused approach towards Ethiopia and, as a result, the Somali government adopted a policy of aggressiveness towards the country. On the Ethiopian side, not only had oil and natural gas deposits been discovered in the *Ogaden*, but Ethiopia was also facing domestic disarray and military turmoil (given the termination of US military aid).[428] A combination of these factors motivated the invasion of the *Ogaden* which both the Somalia-backed WSLF forces and the Somali army successfully penetrated deep into Ethiopian territory; although declared lost to Ethiopia due to an intervention of massive army manoeuvres by Cuba and the Soviet union.[429]

In the OAU, Somalia eventually received the wrath of members who viewed its invasion as an aggression against its neighbour. Undermining the OAU's perceptions and condemnation, Somalia's Minister of Foreign Affairs, Abdulrahman Jama Barre, walked out of the OAU good offices committee meeting held in Gabon from August 5-8, 1977. As a result, in one of its subsequent meetings at the foreign ministerial level held in Lagos, Nigeria, from August 18-20, 1977, the OAU good offices committee advised that the *Ogaden* region was an integral part of Ethiopia.[430] Similarly, in June 1981, the OAU Summit held in Nairobi adopted the ministerial report reaffirming Ethiopia's sovereignty over the *Ogaden*. Th reaffirmation, however, did neither go well with the Somali government nor with the Somali public. After so much blood was spilled with thousands of men losing their lives, staying empty-handed with no objective or goal

---

[427] Ibid, p.230; See also M. H. Mukhtar, *Historical Dictionary of Somalia: African Historical Dictionary*, (Maryland Oxford: Scarecrow Press, 2003), p.182.

[428] See M. Wubneh and Y. Abate, *Ethiopia: Transition and Development in the Horn of Africa*, (Colorado: Westview Press, 1988), p.166; See also M. H. Mukhtar, *Historical Dictionary of Somalia. African Historical Dictionary*, (Maryland Oxford: Scarecrow Press, 2003), p.180.

[429] H. A. Dualeh, *Search for a New Somali Identity* (Nairobi, 2002).

[430] See J. M. Ghalib, *The Cost of Dictatorship: The Somali Experience*, (New York: Lilian Barber Press Inc., 1995), p.112.

realized—it was indeed a painful moment for Somali history, socially, economically, politically and militarily.

However, perspectives on Somalia's loss of the *Ogaden* issue aside, some of the consequences of the *Ogaden* war included the shift of Somalia's clientelism to US patronage and a change in its foreign policy behaviour towards Kenya. Prior to this shift of policy, the relationship between the two countries was peaceful, although Kenya accused Somalia of attacking a border post in the NFD. On the other hand, Kenya also signed a treaty of friendship and cooperation with Ethiopia and, as a result, the two countries issued a joint *communiqué* during the *Ogaden* war condemning Somalia's action. Although Kenya's involvement was limited to denouncing acts of aggression, the actions of the two leaders of Kenya and Ethiopia were strongly attacked by Somalia as a threat to peace and security in the Horn of Africa.[431]

The initial rapprochement between Kenya and Somalia was initiated in 1979-80 by the government of the Kingdom of Saudi Arabia which offered to mediate over the latter's territorial claims.[432] Somalia's participation in this effort is mainly attributable [either] to the Somali government's fear of Ethiopia's military power[433] or the country's change of foreign policy as a strategy to handle the Ethiopian problem. As a result, following a 1981 summit meeting with Kenyan President Daniel Arap Moi in Nairobi, Barre publicly denounced any Somali territorial claims on Kenya, stating that:

> Somalia does not have any acute disputes with Kenya whatsoever, but all are images and reflections of the past European colonialism. Ethiopia tried many times to deteriorate the good friendly relations between Somalia and Kenya by false and cheap propaganda.[434]

Barre's public denouncement of Somali territorial claims in Kenya had the effect of reducing mistrust and improving relations between the two

---

[431] See K. G. Adar, *Kenya's Foreign Policy Behaviour towards Somalia, 1963 – 1983* (Lanham, New York and London: University Press of America, 1994), p.131.

[432] J. M. Ghalib, *The Cost of Dictatorship: The Somali Experience,* (New York: Lilian Barber Press Inc., 1995), p.112.

[433] *Somalia: Somalia's Arab, African and International Role* (Mogadishu: State Print Agency, 1980), p.17, quoted in K. G. Adar, *Kenyan Foreign Policy Behaviour towards Somalia, 1963 – 1983,* (Lanham, New York and London: University Press of America, 1994), p.132.

[434] Ibid.

# CHAPTER SIX

## Somali Foreign Policy: Emerging Issues

This chapter critically analyses the issues that have emerged in the previous five chapters and focuses on foreign policy and conflict in Somalia. The chapter is divided into two sections. The first section will give a critical review of Somalia's domestic environment, foreign policy orientation and foreign policy decision-making during the study period while the second section critically looks at the three critical issues that emerged from the study; namely colonial legacy, Somali nationalism, and Cold War politics and rivalry.

### Domestic Environment

The fact that the Somali Republic had pursued a foreign policy of 'Greater Somalia,' since its inception in 1960, makes it important to analyse the domestic environment, because it provides both constraints and opportunities in the pursuit of a country's foreign policy. The country has an area of some 640,000 km square with a 3,300 km coastline which runs from *Bab-al-Mandab* all the way to the border with Kenya.[440] Geographically, Somalia lies in the Horn of Africa where the African continent stretches towards the Arab world thus giving it strategic control over access to the Red Sea and close links with the Arabian Peninsula and the Gulf of Aden. Apart from this huge maritime territory, Somalia also claimed all Somali-populated territories in the Horn of Africa including the *Ogaden* region, NFD and pre-independent coastal Djibouti. In other words, the Somali nation stretches throughout the Horn of Africa sub-region.

In this context, the influence of geography on Somali foreign policy is necessarily linked to this strategic location and claims over 'lost' Somali territories. Similarly, the country's geostrategic location attracted foreign

---

[440] See S. M. Mousa, *Recolonization Beyond Somalia*, (Mogadishu: Somali Printing Agency, 1998), p.xiii.

interests. It also underlines its *rapprochement* with the west and the Soviet Union during the Cold War. The division of the Somali people, for example, due to territorial decisions taken by colonial powers, was an important geographical issue as Somalia pursued the return of these 'lost' territories as its principal foreign policy objective. It is these claims and counter-claims that led Somalia to conflict with its neighbours, notably Kenya and Ethiopia: for example, the 1963/64 conflict and the 1977-78 *Ogaden* war between Somalia and Ethiopia and the early 1960s *Shifta* war with Kenya. It is the consequence of these conflicts between Somalia and its neighbours regarding military support to armed opposition that led to the breakup of the Somali civil war—first in northern Somalia in 1988 and later on throughout the rest of the country in early 1991.

In line with this, apart from the social cohesiveness and national integration that informed Somali foreign policy, one other important element is the size of its population. In terms of population size, the Somali people make one of the biggest communities in the Horn of Africa region and have one considerable advantage: the large homogeneity of the Somali as they share a common language, religion, social structure and historical identity. Therefore, by reclaiming the territories held by neighbouring countries, the country would have been larger and hence would have played a dominant role in the Horn of Africa. This feeling of Somali nationalism, '*pan-Somalism*,' became infectious, making inroads throughout the Horn of Africa and beyond, and generating popular support for unity among all Somali areas in Ethiopia, Kenya and all of pre-independent coastal Djibouti. The same led to the formation of Northern Frontier District Liberation Front (NFDLF) in Kenya; the Western Somalia Liberation Front (WSLF) in the *Ogaden* and the Front de Liberation de la Conte des Somalis (FLCS) in Djibouti.

In terms of economic and military capabilities, Somalia's lack of physical and natural resources was a constraint on its foreign policy objectives. This explains the country's search for external aid to build both its economic and military capability. For example, Samatar argues that one "salient issue of Somali foreign policy was the designing of strategies for the retrieval of the three other Somali lands."[441] To Samatar, when such retrieval of missing parts of the Somali nation through peaceful

---

[441] See A. I. Samatar, *Socialist Somalia: Rhetoric and Reality*, (London: Zed Books Ltd., 1988), p.65.

means became impossible due to the intransigence of "...the elites in Kenya [and] Ethiopia,"[442] the Somali leadership began to forge close [military] ties with the Soviet Union which in turn:

> ... had an impact on the area in two ways: it set the stage for a close relationship between the embryonic Somali military forces and the Soviet Union; and it inaugurated an ominous arms race, replete with economic and social ramifications in the region... through acknowledging the working parliamentary democracy in Somalia, the United States reacted coldly to the Somali-Soviet agreement...underscoring the arrival of the Cold War politics in the Horn.[443]

Due to such external support, Somalia's military grew steadily despite the country's status as one of the poorest in sub-Saharan Africa at the time. This also led to Somalia's increased strength relative to its neighbours and increased arms race in the Horn of Africa. In particularly, Somalia was building its military might with the objective of battling with its main adversary, Ethiopia, so as to realize a balance of power that is in its favour. Somali analysts, for example, argue that this must have influenced the Somali government's decision to go to war over the *Ogaden* region.[444]

Political structures, on the other hand, provided opportunities while simultaneously imposing constraints on Somalia's decision-makers. Following independence, the country experienced a 9-year parliamentary democracy, an electoral system of government made up of three branches: the legislative, the executive and an independent judiciary. Despite clan politics and other anomalies, the vibrant democracy practiced in those formative years, for example, along with the remarkable cultural and economic cohesion of the Somali society, impressed critical observers, leading to the thinking that Somalia could become a model for democracy in Africa.[445] Siyad Barre, on the other hand, developed a central political organ made up of military officers to run the country. Although

---

[442] Ibid, p.66.
[443] Ibid.
[444] These include Ken Menkhaus, Matt Bryden, Abdulkadir Yahya, and Roland Marchal among others, interview with Ambassador Hussein Ali Dualeh, former Somali Ambassador to Kenya and Uganda, Nairobi, September 11, 2001.
[445] See for example, A. Y. Farah, "Somalia: Modern History and the End of the 1990s," in WSP International, *Rebuilding Somalia: Issues and Possibilities for Puntland*, (London: HAAN Associates, 2001).

there was corruption, nepotism and political and administrative inefficiencies throughout the Somali governments during the study period, the basic national objective—unity with other Somali territories, was never altered; instead, it was the means.

## Foreign Policy Orientation

Somalia's foreign policy orientation, in the period 1960-1990, can be discerned from its historical legacy, notably, *pan-Somalism* (Greater Somalia); Cold War clientelism; and the opposition between *pan-Africanism* and *pan-Arabism*. In Colonial Somalia, the Somali Youth League (SYL) had long advocated for the union of all Somalis in the Horn of Africa under one government.[446] Also, in the early 1960s, Somali foreign policy orientation was formed by what former Somali Prime Minister Sharma'arke called 'our misfortune.' This is a situation where he likens Somalia's neighbouring communities as "...Somali kinsmen whose citizenship has been falsified by indiscriminate boundary arrangements."[447]

Islam, on the other hand, played a major role in the *pan-Somali* movement in the Horn of Africa. Religious antagonism contributed to the national consciousness since alien non-Somali governments outside the Somali borders represented alien Christian infidel.[448] While the civilian governments in Somalia from 1960 to 1969 assumed the responsibility to pursue the goal of self-determination of all the Somali people in the Horn of Africa region through diplomatic challenges, Siyad Barre's military government initially chose selective military options as opposed to dialogue. As a result, the *Ogaden* war and the subsequent civil war broke, resulting in the collapse of the Somali state.

The Cold War clientelism policy orientation emanates from the earlier *pan-Somalist* philosophy since support from foreign powers was necessary in order to achieve the 'Greater Somalia' project. Initially after independence, the issue facing the civilian governments in Somalia was how to win both African and world opinion on the issue of *pan-Somalism*.

---

[446] See for example I. M. Lewis, *A Modern History of the Somali: Nation and State in the Horn of Africa*, 4th Ed., (Hargeisa: Btec Books, 2002).
[447] Ibid, p.197.
[448] See more on this in S. Touval, *Somali Nationalism: International Politics and the Drive for Unity in the Horn of Africa*, (Cambridge, Massachusetts: Harvard University Press, 1963), p.62.

First, the joining of the general Afro-Asian non-alignment movement within the UN was a major step forward. Somalia's turning to the west, first to Italy, then the UK and the United States was another good step. It was only after the west differed with Somalia's project that the country turned to the east: the Soviet Union and China. Military superiority by Ethiopia and the UK's counter-insurgency support for Kenya slowed any progress Somalia would have made in the early 1960s.

Soviet assistance was, according to Somalia's desire, not enough. Notably, when the Soviet Union differed with Somalia's adamance on its *pan-Somalism* project, it withdrew its loyalty from Somalia and supported its rival, Ethiopia in the late 1970s. The Cold War rivalry in the Horn of Africa had a number of effects: it sparked an arms race in the region and, specifically, between Somalia and Ethiopia. It was partly also the Cold War and its effects that pitted Somalia against Ethiopia in what seemed to be a proxy war between the Superpowers but was fought between the two Horn of Africa countries as a regional war.[449] This level and pattern of growth in military expenditure could not have taken place if the countries of the Horn of Africa had not been able to rely on superpower patrons who provided them with increasing levels of military assistance.

The third component of Somalia's foreign policy orientation was in the opposition between *pan-Africanism* and *pan-Arabism*. Somalia's orientation was initially towards black Africa[450] as the vital *pan-Somalism* project was not to block other interests, for example, development. Instead, the country developed its foreign policy towards *pan-Somalism* in terms of its desire for self-determination for all Somalis in the Horn of Africa.[451] The OAU's principles, on the other hand, also proved to be one of the greatest setbacks to the Somali cause. As a result, the country's diplomatic efforts aimed at bringing the complexities of their dilemma to world attention were drowned by the battles in the Horn of Africa region, leading to diplomatic isolation.

---

[449] See R. Lyob and E. J. Keller, "US Policy in the Horn," in D. A. Bekoe, *Grappling with a Difficult Legacy in East Africa and the Horn: Confronting Challenges to Good Governance* (Boulder and London: Lynne Reinner Publishers, 2006), pp.101-125:101.
[450] See C. Legum and B. Lee, *Conflict in the Horn of Africa*, (London: Rex Collings, 1977), p.31.
[451] See K. G. Adar, *Kenyan Foreign Policy Behavior towards Somalia: 1963-1983*, (Lanham, New York and London: University Press of America, 1994), p.98.

These occurrences were compounded by other factors which served to reorient Somalia's foreign policy towards the Arab world. The country's long history of cultural, religious and trade ties with the Arab world and their identification more with the Arabs than with black Africa, especially during the military government, was in opposition to the *pan-Africanist* thinking. This identity, fuelled more by the country's Arab-oriented *pan-Somalism*, was propelled by the *Nasserist pan-Arabism* movement. Egypt's leader, Gamal Abdel-Nasser, dreamed of the establishment of an Arab-Islamic empire whose power base would be Egypt,[452] a philosophy, which courted Somalia to be oriented towards the Muslim/Arab world. Since the two schools could not work hand in hand for Somalia, the country's leadership was left with a complex dilemma: choosing between the *pan-African* and *pan-Arab* movements in which it played its cards, but opted finally for the latter.[453] This, however, did not help with easing the tension but instead contributed to the continuation of war and strained and suspicious post-war relations with Somalia's neighbours.[454]

## Foreign Policy Decision-Making

Somali foreign policy decision-making processes from 1960-1969 were dominated by the ideals of the SYL and its elites, notably the old guard: Abdullahi Isse, Aden Adde and Sharma'arke. As a result, the National Assembly was equally influential, basically because it could elect the president through the assembly's secret voting system which could constrain the prime minister's actions. The executive, on the other hand, played a crucial role in foreign policy decision-making. For example, Mohammed Ibrahim Egal managed to assuage the deeply hostile anti-Somali sentiments of Ethiopian officials, on the one hand, and those of Jomo Ken-

---

[452] For more on *Nasserim* as a revolution, see Elie Podeh and Onn Winckler (Eds.) 2004. *Rethinking Nasserism: Revolution and Historical Memory in Modern Egypt*, Tampa: University Press of Florida).

[453] Interview with Yusuf Hassan Ibrahim (Dheg), former Somali Foreign Minister, Djibouti, February 21, 2007.

[454] Ibid.

yatta's government, on the other, hence bringing about *détente* with Somalia's neighbours and with Britain.[455]

The foreign policy decision-making process under the military government was one that placed primacy on the executive; decisions were, therefore, dominated by the president himself. For example, following the elections in the 'people's parliament' where all members belonged to one party, Siyad Barre reshuffled the cabinet, abolishing the positions of the three vice presidents. This was followed by another reshuffle in October 1980 in which the old Supreme Revolutionary Council (SRC) was revived. The reshuffle resulted in three parallel and overlapping bureaucratic structures within one administration: the party's *Politburo*, which exercised executive powers through its central committees; the council of ministers; and the SRC leaving decision-making solely in the president's hand.[456]

While party interest lines and clan, sub-clan and sub sub-clan affiliations were central to the inner workings of the Somali governments respectively, the decision-making process behind Somali foreign policy relied on the leaders' personalities and perceptions and the competition between various cronies and groups, which had an influence on the leaders and on each other. Despite the fact that the Somali leadership had the capacity to make authoritative decisions, all the three governments under study, maintained consistency with the 'Greater Somalia' issue, be it in their foreign policy orientation or decision-making processes. And, this is what led to conflict with the country's neighbours.

**Foreign Policy Behaviour**

*Salient Issues in Somalia's Foreign Policy Behaviour*

Somalia's foreign policy behaviour was a manifestation of its orientation towards the 'Greater Somalia' project. This section will analyse three key salient issues, which are also the key issues emerging from the study: a) Colonial legacy; b) Somali nationalism; and c) Cold war politics and rivalry.

---

[455] J. Drysdale, *Stoics Without Pillows: A way forward for the Somalilands* (London: HAAN Associates Publishing, 2000), p.81.
[456] Interview with Amb. Hussein Ali Dualeh, former Somali ambassador to Kenya and Uganda, Nairobi, September 11, 2001.

## (a) Colonial Legacy

Somalia's colonial legacy had fundamental implications for its foreign policy as well as for the conflict with its neighbours. The colonisation of Africa, which affected most countries on the continent, was initially institutionalised by the 1884 Treaty of Berlin. The heightened interest of colonial powers in the region brought about the creation of spheres of influence, either in the form of colonies or protectorates. At that time, and contrary to other African countries, Ethiopia took part in the imperial partition of the continent. As a result, the roots of the present turmoil in the Horn of Africa date back to this period when Menelik II took advantage of a number of propitious events and extended Ethiopian authority in Somali, Oromo and Afar land, thus quadrupling the Ethiopian empire by exploiting European imperial rivalry.[457]

As a result of the imperialistic expansion, Somalis lived under British, French, and Italian colonial administrations. In addition, the northern region of British colonial Kenya was mostly inhabited by Somalis, while Ethiopia claimed the traditional Somali grazing lands of the *Ogaden*, the Haud and the Reserve Area. Colonialism, therefore, had several implications for Somali foreign policy during independence. For example, Somalis' resistance to colonialism, which took the form of the *Dervish* rebellion, can strongly be argued to have laid the foundation of modern Somali nationalism. This rebellion indeed set the stage for the Somali consciousness against colonial rule and attracted large followers, especially due to Sayid Mohammed Abdulle Hassan's religious teachings which helped establish *pan-Somalism* by appealing to patriotic sentiments of Somalis as Muslims irrespective of their clan or lineage allegiance.[458] These efforts were taken over by the Somali political parties from the 1930s onwards.

Colonial legacy was also at the root of Somali foreign policy based on the 'Greater Somalia' concept. On this account, the constitution of independent Somalia explicitly challenged the borders with Ethiopia, Djibouti and Kenya, making these countries the main targets of Somali

---

[457] See D. D. Laitin and S. S. Samatar, *Somalia: Nation in Search of a State* (Boulder, Colorado: Westview Press, 1987), p.52.
[458] See for example, K. G. Adar, *Kenya's Foreign Policy Behavior towards Somalia, 1963–1983* (Lanham, New York and London: University Press of America, 1994), p.87.

foreign policy from 1960 onwards. For example, Article VI, Section 4, of the Somali Constitution (1960) reads:

> The Somali Republic shall promote, by legal and peaceful means, the Union of Somali territories and encourage solidarity among the peoples of the world, and in particular among African and Islamic peoples, i.e. the 'Greater Somalia' idea.[459]

Many of the problems faced by post-colonial Somali society were set in motion by the peculiar character of colonial occupation and by the nature of the resistance that it provoked.[460] European colonialism can, therefore, be said to have aroused Somali nationalism as one of the main reasons behind these territorial claims.

For example, prior to the advent of colonialism in the region, the Somali people were organized in encompassing national political and judicial systems comprising of a number of semi-independent political units.[461] Some parts of Somalia did at different points in history sustain Sultanates or quasi-state polities.[462] Therefore, it was not open to effective occupation. Somalia was, however, later divided into mini-lands which the people resisted as disintegration by colonial powers.

In view of this background, post-independent Somali governments argued for the adherence to the principle of self-determination for the disintegrated territories. In this case, the *Ogaden* region, the NFD, and coastal Djibouti were seen as units of self-determination as stipulated in Principal IV of the Annex to the UN General Assembly Resolution 1541 (XV).[463] To the Somali government, this criterion may be formulated as follows: nonself-governing person is the permanent population of a terri-

---

[459] See the 1960 Constitution of the Somali Republic.
[460] See D. D. Laitin and S. S. Samatar, *Somalia: Nation in Search of a State*, (Boulder, Colorado: Westview Press, 1987), p.53.
[461] See Ministry of Foreign Affairs, *Salient Aspects of Somalia's Foreign Policy: Selected Speeches of Dr. Abdurrahman Jama Barre, Minister of Foreign Affairs – Somali Democratic Republic, in 1978*, (Mogadishu: November 1978), p.6.
[462] See R. Marchal, "A Few Provocative Remarks on Governance in Somalia," Nairobi, UNDOS Discussion paper, November 1997; See also L. Cassanelli, *The Shaping of Somali Society* (Philadelphia: University of Philadelphia Press, 1982).
[463] See UN General Assembly Resolution 1541 (XV) of 15 December 1960.

tory which is geographically separate and is distinct ethnically and/or culturally from the country administrating it.[464]

With regard to the UN Charter, provisions in this respect were stipulated in the preamble, guaranteeing the right of peoples to self-determination. Consequently, it can be argued that colonialism laid the foundation for the struggle for self-determination by Somalis living in territories under non-Somali administrations. Similarly, it has been argued that the 'Greater Somalia' concept was never a Somali invention, but rather a British one,[465] invented to frustrate the Italians who were at the time at rivalry with the British. In 1941, the British army under the East African command defeated the Italian forces in both Italian Somaliland and in Ethiopia, bringing them the British military administration. Except for Djibouti, this was the first time in history that all Somali-speaking populations in the Horn of Africa became subject to one colonial power.[466]

The UK foreign secretary Ernest Bevin, giving a speech at the UN in 1946, requested from the Security Council that his country be allowed to administer all territories inhabited by the Somali-speaking people.[467] This request was immediately vetoed by the Soviet delegate who accused the UK of trying to expand their colonial territories. Bevin's speech and the proposal he made before the Security Council, however, culminated in the commission of the four-power commission comprising of the US, Britain, France and the Soviet Union, and their subsequent assignment to ascertain the wishes of the Somali people.[468] The Commission did not achieve the desired ends of the Somalis' ambitions, nor did it satisfy UK's desire for a 'Greater Somalia.' Consequently, it becomes evident that the UK's suggestion -- through Bevin -- sparked and extended the imagination of the Somali people, fuelling their sense of nationhood at a time when there was a lack of agreement among colonial powers which were jostling for continued influence in the Horn of Africa. These inter-

---

[464] See Ministry of Foreign Affairs, *Salient Aspects of Somalia's Foreign Policy: Selected Speeches of Dr. Abdurrahman Jama Barre, Minister of Foreign Affairs – Somali Democratic Republic, in 1978*, (Mogadishu: November 1978), p.7.

[465] See H. A. Dualeh, *Search for a New Somali Identity* (Nairobi, 2002), p.39.

[466] Ibid.

[467] See more discussions on the *Bevin Agreement in* G. Ware, *Somalia: From Trust Territory to Nation, 1950-1960*, Vol. 26, No. 2 (2nd Qtr., 1965), pp. 173-185..

[468] Ibid.

laced wrangles and rivalries left a dark legacy of unmet desires and ambitions that would lay the foundation for conflict in the Horn of Africa.[469]

Prior to this, in 1936, after the conquest of Ethiopia, Italy created a 'Greater Somalia' – the *Governo della Somalia* – that included the *Ogaden* and, briefly, British Somaliland. Italy thus also created the basis of *pan-Somali* nationalism; or, as the Italians called it, *le Grande Somalia*.[470] These together with the *Bevin Plan*, therefore, encouraged Somalis to fight for a *pan-Somali* state that transcended colonial borders,[471] and accommodated the idea of self-determination and unity of all disintegrated territories of the Somalis. The important role played by the colonial legacy in Somalia's subsequent foreign policy is hence evidenced by the development of Somali nationalism. The fact that Somalis generally regard themselves as members of a single nation, united by a common language, culture, and religion was not only a strong unifying influence, but allegedly posed challenges to the concepts of sovereignty, territorial integrity, and political independence in the Horn of Africa region. The idea became the root cause of conflicts and tensions between Somalia and its neighbours, mainly arising from the will to reunify the Somali people in one republic.

Furthermore, after Italian conquest and its expulsion by Britain, the Ethiopian emperor on reclaiming his throne "set about creating and supporting an irredentist movement for the incorporation of Eritrea and Italian Somaliland into the Ethiopian state."[472] In addition, Ethiopia was granted both the *Ogaden* and *Haud* regions. The *Ogaden* was annexed not only in the 1890s but also returned to Ethiopian administration in 1948. The area of *Haud* was returned to Ethiopia in February 1955 after negotiations led to the Anglo- Ethiopian Agreement in 1954.[473] Both of these incidents were accompanied by riots and inter-clan violence. This led to

---

[469] Ibid.
[470] See M. H. Mukhtar, *Historical Dictionary of Somalia: African Historical Dictionary*, (Maryland and Oxford: Scarecrow Press, 2003), p.4.
[471] See S. E. Prankhurst, *Ex-Italian Somaliland*, (New York: Philosophical Library, 1951), pp.218-260.
[472] See L. Lata, "Extra Regional Inputs in Promoting Regional Security in the Horn of Africa," *Amani Africa, The Journal of Africa Peace Forum*, Vol. 1, Issue 2, pp.7-33:15.
[473] See D. Ottaway and M. Ottaway, *Ethiopia: Empire in Revolution*, (New York and London: African Publishing Company, 1978), p.162; See also S. Touval, *Somalia Nationalism: International Policy and the Drive for Unity in the Horn of Africa*, (Cambridge, Massachusetts: Harvard University Press, 1963), p.157.

a foreign policy based on hostility between the two states as the Somalis were resentful for the occupation of these areas. Although Ethiopia was spared incurring the loss of *Ogaden* and *Haud*, it can be argued that the resentment which these actions arose played a crucial role in awakening political consciousness and interest in the protectorate and stimulating the growth of the nationalist movement. This legacy underlies the inevitability as well as intractability of conflict between Somalia and Ethiopia.

The impact of the colonial legacy is also evident in the relations between the two countries in terms of the question of boundary lines, which are not only a colonial construct but which can also be defined as arbitrary. Somalia's approach to the border problem is conditioned by its commitment to the principle that all Somali inhabited territories ought to be placed under one Somali republic. The Ethiopians, on the other hand, tended to view the disputes not as isolated cases of unfortunate misunderstanding but as manifestations of Somalia's expansionist ambitions. The boundary problem, however, seems to have been influenced more by the rivalries among the European powers than by local conditions in the Horn of Africa.[474]

The hostility between Somalia and Ethiopia was also exacerbated by Somali claims to the French territory of the Afars and Issas (TFAI) which was a direct source of conflict between them as the port of Djibouti was the terminus of the only rail link between Addis Ababa and the Red Sea. Similarly, Ethiopia claimed both Eritrea and Somaliland on historical, ethnic and geographical grounds.[475] In reality, however, and despite genuine Somali claims, Ethiopia's claim was strategic as it mainly wanted to prevent foreign control of the coastal areasdue to its desire to maintain direct access to the sea. The legacy of territorial claim and counter-claim brought about hatred towards the *Amhara* rule in Ethiopia and their historical expansionist policies that many in the region in general and in Ethiopia in particular saw as unacceptable and, therefore, legitimacy of defiance and aspiration for ethnic self-rule. Ethiopia's expansionist policies were evident in the late 1950s in the emperor's effort to fight irredentism with counter-irredentism, thus dismissing the viability

---

[474] Ibid, p.155.
[475] See M. Wubneh and Y. Abate, *Ethiopia: Transition and Development in the Horn of Africa*, (Colorado: Westview Press, 1988), p.164.

of a 'Greater Somalia', advising Somalis to emulate the Eritreans by "rejoining their mother country."[476]

The consequence of this legacy was that the two states not only sought to increase their preparedness for war, but also engaged in war, in 1963-64 and, again, in a more devastating encounter, in 1977-78. Furthermore, this also led the *Ogaden* dissidents to become attracted to the idea of an independent and united Somalia. This was also the case with the adjacent Oromos, whose struggle became intertwined with that of the *Ogaden*, leading early on to the creation of the WSLF movement. Moreover, and for the sake of creating unrest towards Ethiopia from several angles, independent Somalia became the most consistent supporter of the Eritrean movements which were determined to undo the annexation of their country by the Ethiopian empire. As an outcome of these hostilities, the two countries fought proxy wars by supporting insurgent groups against each other. The picture seen here shows how colonial legacy not only influenced the foreign policy orientation of both countries; but how it also made the Horn of Africa a cluster of dangerous conflicts that prolonged across generations.

## (b) Somali Nationalism

Somalia's proclamation to reclaim its 'unredeemed territories' became a major determinant to the country's foreign policy orientation, having a major impact on the type of relations it had with its neighbours as well as on the general course of events in the Somali republic. Presiding over a society where agro-pastoralists ignored fixed boundaries and whose traditional political economy depended on a dispersion of resources, Somali leaders became obsessed with changing the existing [colonial-made] boundaries of northeast Africa to concentrate Somalis under a single government.[477]

---

[476] See L. Lata, "Extra Regional Inputs in Promoting Regional Security in the Horn of Africa," *Amani Africa*, The Journal of Africa Peace Forum, Vol. 1, Issue 2, pp.7-33:18.

[477] See C. Geshekter, "The Death of Somalia in Historical Perspective," in H. M. Adam and R. Ford, (eds.), in *Mending the Rips in the Sky: Options for Somali Communities in the 21st Century*, (Asmara: The Red Sea Press, Inc., 1997), pp.65-98:74.

As a result, unification into a 'Greater Somalia' remained the central moral pillar of the country's national consciousness. To non-Somalis, however, the unification dream seemed unjustified, leading to the alienation of Somalia from the rest of the continent. Somalia's irredentist claims, to a large extent, informed its foreign policy of bonding with superpowers that Somalia could use – due to its leverage as a geostrategically important country in the Horn of Africa – to obtain the weaponry and political support it needed to achieve its aims.

In the context of the leverage as a geo-strategic location, alliances with the Soviet Union and later on with the US became a means to an end for Somalia, allowing it to gain a military advantage over its neighbours. It follows that Somalia's pre-eminently military position in the region allowed the country to sidestep the inhibitions of obeying the do's and don'ts of territorial integrity in pursuing its foreign policy and relations. To Somalia, establishing a long-lost territorial identity was more important than allowing part of her people to be incorporated into other non-Muslim countries.[478] Efforts in obtaining armaments were thus dictated by the theory that the realization of the destiny towards a 'Greater Somalia' lay in the leadership's hands. The implications of the ideology became increased militarization of the Somali state and the Horn of Africa region; and the subjugation of the country's undeveloped volatile economy to the attainment of this ultimate goal.

As more arms flowed senselessly into the country, the confidence of the Somali leadership was bolstered and the resolve to forge ahead meant that little would be spared in achieving this goal. Viewed from a different angle, Somalia became increasingly predisposed towards conflict-oriented foreign policy behaviour. It deviated from the normal pattern of behaviour to assume ambitions that did not go unnoticed in the Kenyan and Ethiopian capitals. In the eyes of Somalis, denial of the unification represented a belief of what the Somali leadership characterised as a colonial injustice to which the rest of the world showed little or no concern, though seen to be so fundamental to the country's own existence.[479]

---

[478] Ibid.
[479] See for example, A. Kinfe, *Somalia Calling: The Crisis of Statehood and the Quest for Peace*, (Addis Ababa: EIIPD, 2002), p.12.

## Pan-Somalism and Conflict in the Horn of Africa

Bolstered by overwhelming popular support, the Somali government achieved the 'legitimacy' it needed to forge ahead with its irredentist proclamations. The three-decade period 1960-1990 witnessed unwavering Somali nationalist support for the idea of *pan-Somalism* whose double-edged sword claimed two Somali governments that were eventually perceived as selling out to the ideals of a unified Somalia.[480] The rigidity of the Somali position and its subsequent militarization put the country on the path towards conflict with Kenya and Ethiopia. The possibilities of conflict became more likely as communication failures and mutually-felt fear and misperceptions combined to create a state of tension between Ethiopia and Kenya on the one hand and Somalia on the other.

As a result, what had initially been a Somali expression of its intention to reunite the Somali nation under one Somali flag turned out to be an agent of internationalization of conflict. It became increasingly difficult to isolate the internal Somali conflict from the wider conflict with its neighbours. Attempts to resolve the Kenya-Somalia and the Ethiopia-Somalia conflicts should have conclusively ended with the tackling of the causes of the economic decline and the diminishing reality of political accountability in Somalia. Instead, the interdependence of the Somali situation with the prevailing conditions in the international system [Cold War rivalry and race in geo-politics, for example] further contributed to the intensification of conflict in the Horn of Africa conflict system, whose epicentre was Somalia.[481]

Somali nationalism left few options for dialogue for the three conflicting countries, thereby preventing them from making concessions without jeopardizing their overall respective positions. The persistence of the conflict effectively attests to this as Somalia's policy of non-compromise on the issue dealt a blow to any OAU mediation efforts and the only real 'ripe moment' for negotiations came with the Ogaden defeat by Ethiopia in 1977.[482]

---

[480] Ibid, pp.15-27.

[481] See A. I. Samatar, "Under Siege: Blood, Power and the Somali State," in P. Anyang Nyong'o, *Arms and Daggers in the Heart of Africa: Studies on Internal Conflicts* (Nairobi: African Academy of Sciences, 1993), p.82-85.

[482] See J. M. Ghalib, *The Cost of Dictatorship: The Somali Experience* (New York: Lilian Barber Press Inc, 1995), p.112.

It has been observed that *pan-Somalism* impacted negatively on the conflict situation in the region. The country's foreign policy stance indeed won it little support across the region, dampening any efforts at seeking a solution to this attempted call for a re-ordering of the Horn of Africa regional political map. These reunification pronouncements also thrust onto the international stage the then delicate issue of self-determination at a time when many African states had just achieved independence and were intent on protecting it, along with the inherited vestige of colonialism that was the colonial boundaries. What had initially been a Somali pronouncement sucked in its neighbours and became the central issue in the conflict that pushed them to oppose Somalia.

Subsequently, this foreign policy of reunification triggered a response from Somalia's perceived enemies, notably Ethiopia and Kenya. The foreign policy processes in the Horn of Africa, particularly by Ethiopia and Kenya, had to react to this threat. There was a deliberate attempt both in Kenya and Ethiopia to isolate Somalia as the two not only united to sign a defence treaty but also sold their ideas to the OAU, NATO and even to the superpowers.[483] As a result, Somalia engaged in at least four 'wars of liberation,' in addition to numerous border clashes, which all failed and eventually caused the dissolution of the state itself so that there came to be no sense of Somalism, let alone *pan-Somalism*.[484]

## Pan-Somalism and the Internal Conflict Situation

In addition to creating external conflicts, the national preoccupation with Somali nationalism and the subsequent search for national reunification claimed an undue portion of the nation's attention, thereby draining energies and badly needed resources for internal development into fruitless external ventures. The *pan-Somali* sentiments eventually became the country's nemesis when attempts to hold the Somali state together failed as the different clans became absorbed into bitter rivalries which culminated in the collapse of the state.

---

[483] See I. M. Lewis, *A Modern History of Somalia: Nation and State in the Horn of Africa*, 4th Ed., (Hargeisa: Btec Books, 2002), pp.236-239.
[484] See M. H. Mukhtar, "Historical Dictionary of Somalia," *African Historical Dictionary Series*, (Maryland Oxford: Scarecrow Press, 2003), p.182.

Efforts allegedly aimed at uniting the Somali people under one territory were never complemented by a domestic policy that would seek to create a single Somali identity devoid of clan rivalries. For example, Siyad Barre's policy of *nomenklatura* politicized institutions that would have functioned best under the leadership of professionals.[485] Instead, like other previous governments, positions in public institutions were determined by clan allegiances, perpetuating corruption, economic mismanagement and nepotism. The mirage of a united Somalia that spoke one language, shared one history and professed one religion soon became, but, a shattered dream. The civilian administrations' nepotism, widespread corruption, and political and administrative inefficiencies and the military regime's manipulation of the clan divisions within Somali society negated the desire to unite the country under a 'Greater Somalia.'

*Pan-Somalism*, originally being the major determinant of foreign policy, was abused by Barre to clamp down on domestic detractors and hence prolong the stranglehold on state power. The chief foreign policy instrument of the military government was a state policy of premeditated repression to stifle any internal dissent.[486] Furthermore, the military government used pan-Somali pronouncements to direct Somali attention away from the internal demands and problems plaguing the country.[487] With the same master stroke, the government intended to regain the popularity and legitimacy which were declining as a result of the dismal performance of Somali forces on the warfront, the widespread belief that the last minute *détente* with Ethiopia and Kenya was betraying the *pan-Somalism* cause and the increasingly repressive nature of the government.

The Somali people were denied the chance to influence the decisions of the government and they generally became frustrated in their attempts to change this situation. Like all previous governments, the power to decide over the distribution of resources within Somalia solely lay with the government which manipulated this prerogative to further instigate

---

[485] See H. M. Adam, "Somalia: Personal Rule, Military Rule and Militarism," in E. Hutchful and A. Bathily, *Military and Militarism in Africa* (Dakar: CODESRIA, 1998), p.378.

[486] See for example, A. I. Samatar, "Under Siege: Blood, Power and the Somali State," in P. Anyang Nyong'o, *Arms and Daggers in the Heart of Africa: Studies on Internal Conflicts* (Nairobi: African Academy of Sciences, 1993), pp.67-100:86.

[487] See H. M. Adam, et al. *Removing Barricades in Somalia: Options for Peace and Rehabilitation* (Washington: USIP Press, 1998), p.3.

structural violence through selective appointments, not only in the public sector but also in the military.[488]

The military government's policy of instigating divisions among the people, and the employment of the military to instil fear and subjugate the populace, combined with indirect violence – insofar as decision making and resource distribution were concerned – brought the structural violence closer to the level of manifest violence. In effect, this led to direct violence becoming institutionalized. Also, the Somali government came up with brutal attempts to induce loyalty towards the military government, moving away from tackling the simmering discontent. Whether this was group-based or systematic was, however, not known.

Somalia's frontier disputes were, on the other hand, monopolising a huge chunk of the country's national wealth and foreign infusions of aid were not effectively devoted to improving the country's economic welfare.[489] Poverty bred further discontent, which was not tackled by the government as the *pan-Somalism* drive had become an obsession and a platform for winning collective support from all Somalis and an incitement towards war. But, contrary to Barre's perception of unison, the war devastated the country's meagre economy as production declined, currency devalued and donors started questioning his seriousness about amelioration of the government's human rights issues. The situation deteriorated as he reverted to a policy of clan favouritism and compromise of clan integrity and purchase of clan loyalty. As a result, conflict became widespread as clan divisions, coupled with poor economic conditions and the repressiveness of the government meant that few attempts were made to tackle these problems. Similarly, clan animosity intersected with class antagonisms to accentuate divisions within Somali society. They were also taken advantage of, by the military government in its campaigns, to pacify any opposition by both money and force. The lack of accountability and the expendability of military careers contributed, to a

---

[488] See A. Kinfe, *Somalia Calling: The Crisis of Statehood and the Quest for Peace*, (Addis Ababa: EIIPD, 2002), pp.15-27.

[489] See for example, H. M. Adam, "Somalia: Personal Rule, Military Rule and Militarism," in E. Hutchful and A. Bathily, *Military and Militarism in Africa* (Dakar: CODESERIA, 1998), p.376; See also C. Geshekter, "The Death of Somalia in Historical Perspective," in H. M. Adam and R. Ford, (eds.), in *Mending the Rips in the Sky: Options for Somali Communities in the 21st Century*, (Asmara: The Red Sea Press, Inc., 1997), pp.65-98:78.

certain extent, to the proliferation of arms and ammunition in the Somali state as well as in the hands of clan militias. The process of militarization had also instituted a culture of approaching internal problems and resolving state affairs through the use of force and threat, in disregard of peaceful and diplomatic solutions.

Eventually, and with the help of easily available weaponry, the militaristic style of operation eventually gave way to repression and to social dismay. The militarization was characterized by widespread violence meted out by the government and reciprocated by opposition movements that turned into rebel movements.[490] And as earlier observed, the Somali state, at its national level, was poorly grounded on the sentiments of the general public, except with regards to external threats. The militarization of the Somali Republic, combined with the government's crushing military attacks on opponents, over time turned the national psyche into one of violence. It became established that force was the only solution to problems ailing the country. The domestic political structure advanced the position of the Somali leadership, particularly the position of the top leadership as pre-eminent and unchallenged. As discontentment and demands on the government were met with hostility, the spiral of violence only added to the downward slide towards conflict and war.

## The Impact of the Ogaden War on the Internal Conflict in Somalia

The *Ogaden* war had far-reaching implications on Somalia's irredentist claims than many have analysts or members of the general public have anticipated. First of all, the military debacle of repressiveness and peace treaties with rivals shattered all hopes of achieving a 'Greater Somalia' and instead signalled the demise of *pan-Somalism*.[491] The defeat of the Somali armed forces in the *Ogaden* war, for instance, led to widespread disillusionment and discontent over the Somali government's failure to realize the Somali dream. The impact of the frustration after the defeat was two-fold: one was at the leadership level, the other at the public level. The

---

[490] See for example, I. M. Lewis, *A Modern History of the Somali: Nation and State in the Horn of Africa*, 4th Ed., (Hargeisa: Btec Books, 2002), p.252.

[491] See C. Geshekter, "The Death of Somalia in Historical Perspective," in H. M. Adam and R. Ford, (eds.), in *Mending the Rips in the Sky: Options for Somali Communities in the 21ˢᵗ Century*, (Asmara: The Red Sea Press, Inc., 1997), pp.65-98:75.

government's attempt to save face by signing last minute treaties with Kenya and Ethiopia, somehow effectively ending conflict with its neighbours, triggered the downfall of the military government. As was witnessed in the latter years of the military government, the disconnect between the government's foreign policy and the public mood was demonstrated in the intensification of armed opposition movements and the temptation and motivation to engage the regular national armed forced.

The colossal amount of money spent on the war effort and other internal military adventures indirectly led to the impoverishment of the people.[492] This conflict scenario of structural violence became complicated further by the new phenomenon of Somali refugees, mainly Ogadenis, from the *Ogaden* region. In northern Somalia, grazing disputes between the *Ogadeni* and the Isaaq herders boiled over into antagonisms over rural and urban lifestyle differences. There was also tension over the issue of loyalty vs. opposition to the government, which played favouritism as a tool to subjugate a group against the other. Inter-clan conflict was thus promoted by the government, in many cases deliberately and coercively. Throughout the 1980s, the government's base of support narrowed severely as Somalia's death spasms intensified.[493] The manipulation of clan differences and the repression of 'dissident' clans backfired with the rise of clan-based opposition movements created under the guise of 'self-protection.' Taking advantage of the general militarization of the Somali society by the government, these opposition movements became, in turn, increasingly armed and militarized, with support from neighboring rival states and clan businessmen who set the financial base of clan movements. Clan resistance fused with the popular warrior traditions of the Somali people, thus reducing the prospects of peace in Somalia.[494]

With the shrinking of Barre's financial power towards appeasement of certain clans and coercion of others, the weakening of the military government became conspicuous with the disappearance of Soviet economic aid and technical assistance. This led to a rethinking of the 'Greater Somalia'-based foreign policy. Confronted with the increasing number of insurgencies, coupled with the Somali government's weakening mili-

---

[492] Ibid.
[493] Ibid.
[494] See more in H. M. Adam, "Somalia: Personal Rule, Military Rule and Militarism," in E. Hutchful and A. Bathily, *Military and Militarism in Africa* (Dakar: CODESERIA, 1998), p.388.

tary capabilities *vis-à-vis* Ethiopia and the OAU's opposition to Somali reunification claims, the Somali government was finally forced to reconsider its territorial ambitions.[495] The general atmosphere of bellicosity rather than pacific, also had implications for the destructive and distracted conflict in the Horn of Africa. Indeed, the *détente* with Somalia's neighbours de-escalated the inter-state conflict, but opened and, at the same time, heightened the intra-state conflicts as the entire Somali leadership was branded but the general populace as 'traitors.' The economic squalor and filthy attitude towards lack of accountability and poor governance, brought about by the over-expenditure on military expeditions and the high levels of corruption, also heightened tensions within Somalia.

### (c) Cold War Politics and Rivalry

Somalia's foreign policy decision-making during the Cold War was to a large extent affected by developments of rivalry in the international system. The period 1960-1990 witnessed important milestones in the evolution of superpower rivalry that sucked in this nascent independent African state.[496] The events in the international arena had a major bearing on conflicts in Africa. During the Cold War, both the US and the Soviet Union vied for influence and control, mainly over Somalia and Ethiopia. Their actions, reactions and counter-actions were also influenced by the desire of these rivals to minimize each other's influence across the region and avoid any subsequent unchallenged marches into neighbouring countries.

In turn, the strategic concerns of the superpowers effectively determined Somalia's position as a subservient, client state; and, as a result, Somalia's foreign policy decision-making process was subsequently detrimentally affected by the geopolitics of the Cold War that centred on its strategic value.[497] To Somalia's long-term disadvantage, this was at the expense of her economic prosperity in terms of developing its civilian human capital rather than the military personnel. The country had, in

---

[495] Interview with Matt Bryden, ICG regional analyst, Nairobi, April 22, 2005.
[496] See R. W. Copson, *African Wars and Prospects for Peace* (New York and London: ME Sharpe, Inc., 1994), p.103.
[497] Ibid.

effect of all the three decades of quagmire and adventure of political *Siyadism* and ideology of militarism, gained independence against the backdrop of the Cold War rivalry. These untamed situations and the initial lukewarm relationship between Somalia and the superpowers would later change to one of symbiotic acquiescence,[498] indulgence in the use of military muscle and ignorance of the price of peaceful co-existence and national development. The philosophy of dictatorial adventurism as exercised by both rival regimes in Addis and in Mogadishu, and the financial and ideological and military backing by the Superpowers, signed, sealed and delivered the wrath of geopolitical rivalry in the Horn that spilled pools of precious human blood.

Somalia's absorption into senseless Cold War geopolitics had significant ramifications for its foreign policy decision-making. First of all, systemic variables became increasingly crucial in determining the country's foreign policy inclinations. For instance, Somalia's adoption of *'Scientific Socialism'* as its professed national ideology was out of sheer expediency meant to get Soviet endorsement and support and thus attract more armaments. In addition, Somalia's instruments of foreign policy became rank-ordered, with the military's position being accentuated in all levels of decision-making without consideration to the country's ailing economy and pathetic human development situation. The inflow of armaments was meant to prop up the ruling class and cushion it from any internal or external threats to its stability as well as ensure its continued subservience to the Superpowers. In addition to the Cold War rivalry and its politics, the Somali people in NFD, the *Ogaden* and in Djibouti, also had a bearing on Somalia's foreign policy as it considered them in the ideological context of 'Greater Somalia' frame of Somalia's external policy.

Somalia sought to upset the regional *status quo* by attempting to create a 'Greater Somalia' that would see it become arguably the largest country in Africa.[499] This quest was seen as a threat not only to Somalia's neighbours but also to the OAU principles of territorial integrity, sovereignty and political independence of its member states. It can, therefore, be surmised that Somali foreign policy was, as a result of the Cold War, belligerent, to say the least, and it is on this basis that it, therefore, be-

---

[498] See C. M. B. Utete, "Foreign Policy and the Developing State," in O. Ojo et al., *African International Relations* (Lagos: Longman Group, 1985), pp.43-51.

[499] See J. M. Ghalib, *The Cost of Dictatorship: The Somali Experience*, (New York: Lilian Barber Press Inc., 1995), p.126.

came imperative that Somalia builds a strong military in order to be successful in any military adventure; thus the importance of the Superpowers.[500] Public opinion, in turn, bolstered this drive for a 'Greater Somalia' and the whole nation was in unison in demanding a purposive and deliberate effort to bring all the Somali people under one independent state. For example, during the period leading up to independence, the SYL leadership galvanized the nation into supporting the drive for a territorially larger Somalia. Upon the attainment of independence, the civilian administrations pursued the same ideology of unification of all 5 Somali territories; while the political structure of the Somali Republic, especially after the 1969 military coup, also gave the executive immense powers in foreign policy decision-making.

The thirst for a 'Greater Somalia' would become subsumed in the clientele relationship between Somalia and her superpower allies—while yet every partner had specific interests to achieve. This period, the thirty-year period known as the independent Somalia era, therefore, saw the international system play an important role in determining Somalia's foreign policy by way of clientelism, appeasement, and economic and aid support of various spheres. It became necessary for Somalia to seek alliances with states from which it would expand its military and economic power in its desire for a new territorial identity. The Somali government, however, sought to diversify its diplomatic and foreign aid options by allying itself with the Arab League,[501] and other institutions that would serve it one purpose or the other, such as Organization of Islamic Cooperation (OIC), the non-aligned movement etc.

The resultant foreign policy during this thirty-year period had a profound effect on conflict within Somalia and with its neighbours. The scale of warfare experienced over this thirty-year period in Somalia and the Horn of Africa region would have been unsustainable without arms inflow measurable in millions of small arms, thousands of tanks and other heavy weapons and thousands of sophisticated aircraft.[502] The *Ogaden*

---

[500] See for example H. M. Adam, "Somalia: Personal Rule, Military Rule and Militarism," in E. Hutchful and A. Bathily, *Military and Militarism in Africa* (Dakar: CODESERIA, 1998), p.379.
[501] Ibid, p.368.
[502] See P. Heinze, *The Horn of Africa: From War to Peace*, (London: Macmillan, 1991).

war, for example, was fought between two poor states that were both, at different points in time, overwhelmingly armed by the Soviet Union.[503]

Somalia's constitution effectively transformed Somali nationalism from an expression of solidarity with the post-colonial independent state to a foreign policy of annexation that would only stoke the fire of conflict with its neighbours.[504] The desire to create a 'Greater Somalia' was devastating by extension and expression of the country's intent to challenge Ethiopia's hegemonic role and dwarf her neighbour on the western border.[505] This quest for 'Greater Somalia', the political elite and believers of the country's irredentist ideology thought, could be achieved through manipulating interested superpowers, an art that Ethiopia had perfected, to the extent of being on the ascendancy militarily in the region. This state of antagonism did little to promote good neighbourliness and eroded any willingness to co-operate in economic or social spheres between the two poor countries. For instance, Somalia's support for the *Shifta*, as mentioned above, placed the country in conflict with Kenya,[506] which received help from the UK rather than being involved in Cold War rivalry and politics.

## Conclusions

Despite the fact that the objective of a state's foreign policy is to advance its national interest – and by extension its domestic policy – in the case of Somalia, this policy was overtly belligerent and could not promote peaceful co-existence with its neighbours. Not only did this policy put Somalia at loggerheads with her neighbours, it also challenged the OAU and other international institutions that would have been useful in mediating and preventing the subsequent intra and inter-state conflicts that hampered the millions of needy people in the Horn of Africa area. So-

---

[503] See for example, R. G. Patman, *The Soviet Union in the Horn of Africa*, (Cambridge: Cambridge University Press, 1990), pp.573-579.

[504] See D. D. Laitin and S. S. Samatar, *Somalia: Nation in Search of a State*, (Boulder, Colorado: Westview Press, 1987), p.134.

[505] See C. Clapham, "The Horn of Africa: A Conflict Zone," in O. Furley, (ed.), *Conflict in Africa*, (New York: Taurius Academic Studies, 1995), pp.72-91:78.

[506] See for example, A. Simons, "Somalia: A Regional Security Dilemma," in E. J. Keller and D. Rothchild, (eds.), *Africa in the New International Order: Rethinking State Sovereignty and Regional Security*, (Boulder: Lynne Rienner Publishers, 1996), pp.71-84.

malia's irredentist claims, its support for rebel movements and active role in the militarization of the Horn of Africa region jeopardized the country's standing within the OAU. The failed efforts at mediating Somalia's conflict with Ethiopia, for example, were a result of the mistrust held of Somalia by other states and vice versa.

It took a catastrophic loss to Ethiopia in the *Ogaden* War before Somalia could gradually adopt a policy of rapprochement with her neighbours. The result was a thaw in relations between Somalia and its erstwhile enemies, Kenya and Ethiopia. This conciliatory policy of *détente* gave room for Somalia to engage in diplomatic exchanges that had been previously impossible since it had failed to acknowledge the positions of its neighbours. While the move contributed to minimising the tensions between states, this Somali overture and the resultant last-minute peace agreement with its two neighbours were rejected by the Somali people, especially armed groupings.

The disagreement between the masses and the government demonstrated the disconnect between the leadership of Somali governments, both civilian and military, and the public as far as foreign policy decision-making is concerned. Somalia's foreign policy – together with those of other key major players – can be judged to have promoted the simmering conflict situation between Somalia and its neighbours. These catastrophic foreign policies became drivers of conflict and added to the foundation laid by the historical legacy and other key factors such as Cold War rivalry and politics—without economic or territorial gain for the people.

# CHAPTER SEVEN

## Conclusions

The book has made a number of conclusions at the chapter level. At the most general level, the study has shown that foreign policy orientations are important influences on armed conflict. The 'Greater Somalia-'oriented foreign policy of Somalia led to preparations for war, primarily with Ethiopia but also with Kenya. One can claim that it indirectly contributed to militarization which also increased the likelihood that the militarized state would seek recourse to war as a means of achieving its objectives. The observation that foreign policy orientation can produce conflict is not only self-evident here and by the characteristic qualities engaged in by Somalia, but it is often overlooked in current research on the sources of armed conflict in the Horn of Africa and elsewhere.

Somalia's foreign policy orientation, as the guideline for its foreign relations, also led to a security dilemma in the Horn of Africa whose destructive legacy continues into the present. Somalia's claim to the NFD, the *Ogaden* and the whole of coastal Djibouti (before it became independent) sowed the seeds of suspicion between the country and its neighbours.[507] Consequently, it exacerbated a regional arms race and dependence on external actors to ensure their own security. For example, Djibouti depended heavily on France to protect itself from external aggression, especially from Somalia and Ethiopia.[508] As part of this, France has its largest overseas contingent of military forces positioned in Djibouti, by virtue of a cooperation agreement signed with Djiboutian authorities on the day it achieved independence in 1977. Close to three

---

[507] See for example I. M. Lewis, *A Modern History of Somalia: Nation and State in the Horn of Africa* (London and New York: Longman, 1980): See also I. M. Lewis, "The Dynamics of Nomadism: Prospects for Sedentarization and Social Change," in T. Monot (ed.), *Pastoralism in Tropical Africa* (London: 1975).

[508] Interview with Amb. Ismail Goulal, Djibouti's Special Envoy to the Somali peace process, Nairobi, September 11, 2003. See also the *Framework Partnership Document: France - Djibouti (2006-2010)*.

thousand troops, together with the Djiboutian armed forces ensure the security of the country.[509] Ethiopia, for its part, looked for help from the US and later from the Soviet Union; Kenya depended on Britain for military assistance; while Somalia depended first on the US, then on the Soviet Union before it later on, switched to the US again.[510]

Interestingly, Somali irredentism in the 1970s and 1980s did not produce armed conflict with Kenya and Djibouti, but only with Ethiopia.[511] Why Somali irredentism would have this selective impact, producing both warfare and subsequent skirmishes with one neighbour but relatively stable relations with two others, may be best answered with reference to domestic political calculations. For Kenya, one possible explanation lies in the failed *Shifta* war of the mid-1960s and the Egal administration's pursuit of *détente* with Kenya. Egal's pursuit of *détente* made the portion of the ethnic Somali-Kenyan population, which had supported the *Shifta* war and Somali irredentism, feel betrayed by the Somali government, believing they had borne all of the costs of an adventurist foreign policy which was abandoned when the mounting of pressure on Somalia grew.[512] Thereafter, Somali-Kenyans grew disenchanted with Somali irredentism and, without a strong local base, a continuation of the *Shifta* war was believed as pointless.

Likewise, in the micro-state of Djibouti, local enthusiasm for Somali irredentism among the portion of the Djiboutian population which is Somali (the Issa sub-clan) was likely muted. This is because they had more to gain by sharing or controlling power in their own state than in becoming a small fraction of the population in a 'Greater Somalia.' By contrast, the Somali government was, at the time, heavily populated by Somalis from the *Ogaden* region, most of whom fled to Somalia in search of education and jobs in the 1960s. This has also produced a much stronger internal constituency in Somalia for military incursion into the *Ogaden* region in 1977-78 when the local Somali resistance forces appeared poised to win liberation from a temporarily weakened Ethiopian

---

[509] Ibid.
[510] See M. Ottaway, *Soviet and American Influence in the Horn of Africa* (New York: Praeger, 1982), p.119.
[511] See J. Drysdale, *The Somalia Dispute* (New York: Praeger Publishers, 1964), p.122.
[512] Interview with Deqow Sanbul, former NFDLF leader, Garissa, October 21, 2004.

government.[513] Analysts argued that Somalia's hand in the Ogaden war was far more significant than only getting the Ogaden region back. As part of its incursion, the Somali government also facilitated the entry of armed Tigrean and Eritrean rebel groups into the Ethiopian conflict theatre. In the long run, it was these two-armed groups that led to Mengistu's downfall.

In the longer term, region-wide suspicion of the Somali state's ambitions—especially on the part of the Ethiopian government, led Ethiopia to embrace an ambivalent policy. The policy, which either undermines promising attempts at state revival (i.e. the former TNG of 2000-2002), or seeks to tightly control transitional, and other, governments which emerge (i.e. the former TFGs). Ethiopia's reluctance to allow a strong, autonomous Somali state to re-emerge, for about three decades, was in some measure due to its fear that a revived irredentist agenda would accompany the revived state. This is a significant finding. It also suggests that irredentist foreign policies can have a long-lasting impact on regional state behaviour, contributing to the perpetuation of a regional security dilemma even when the irredentist policy is dormant and the state making that claim is weak or ineffectual—Somalia, is in a condition of complete collapse; or it is haltingly trying to re-emerge.

For example, on September 2003, former Kenyan President Daniel arap Moi said one of the drawbacks in the Somali peace process was the regional suspicion that a united Somalia might pursue its 'expansionist dreams.' Speaking at the American National Defense University in Washington, D.C., the former Kenyan president said some of the countries neighbouring Somalia feared that a re-united and prosperous Somalia might resurrect its early claims.[514] In addition, the sensitive issue of unsettled border areas (particularly between Somalia and Ethiopia) and irredentist and counter-irredentism policies of neighbouring governments not only led to frequent clashes, but also to heavy policy of militarization in the Horn of Africa region.[515]

---

[513] See M. Ottaway, *Soviet and American Influence in the Horn of Africa* (New York: Praeger, 1982), p.119.
[514] Interview with Ambassador Bethwell Kiplagat, April 22, 2008, Nairobi.
[515] Ethiopia's security concerns in Somalia are spelt out well in its foreign policy and strategy towards Somalia. See "Ethiopia's Foreign Policy Towards Somalia," *Foreign Affairs and National Security Policy and Strategy*, the Federal Democratic Republic of Ethiopia, Addis Ababa at http://www.mfa.gov.et

Furthermore, the foreign policy of *pan-Arabism* that led Somalia to join the Arab League influenced conflict, especially with Ethiopia. This is due to the fact that Somalia benefited from Arab military aid, and because Somalia's pro-Arab policies aroused Ethiopia's historic fear of Islamic encirclement. Though this fear was misplaced--Somalia's principal Arab patron in the 1980s, Saudi Arabia, was more interested in weaning Somalia away from the Soviet camp than in pursuing an Islamist foreign policy[516]--it nonetheless heightened Ethiopian fears about the security threat Somalia might pose both at the time and in the future.

Islam, on the other hand, has had an important role in forging nationhood among Somalis who are Muslims.[517] The Cold War, on the other hand, also influenced regional conflict in several ways. It provided the hostile states with arms, weapons and military training; it provided an ideological justification and a geopolitical logic for war (with both superpowers concerned to prove to clients a worldwide that they were a reliable source of support); and, it led to proxy wars that also included foreign armed forces, for instance, the Soviet Union, Cuban, [eastern German], Yemeni and Libyan forces who came to the rescue of Ethiopia during the *Ogaden* War.[518]

The study demonstrates the impact of organisations such as the former OAU and the UN in deterring armed conflict. The former OAU's position safeguarding the sanctity of colonial borders and rejecting irredentist claims isolated Somalia diplomatically within the continent and greatly hampered its efforts to reclaim Somali-inhabited territories. The study also demonstrates that global geopolitics feature prominently in the shaping of Somali foreign policy—and those of other major players—as a result of Somalia's strategic position.[519] Somalia is placed at a geostrategically important position between the Horn of Africa and the Arab peninsula. Historically this needle eye, [or bottle-necked as is sometimes

---

[516] See M. Ottaway, *Soviet and American Influence in the Horn of Africa* (New York: Praeger, 1982), p.119.

[517] Interview with Aw Jama Omar Isse, Somali historian, Eldoret, December 12, 2002.

[518] See J. Drysdale, *The Somalia Dispute* (New York: Praeger Publishers, 1964), p.122.; See also A. I. Samatar, "Ethiopian Federalism: Autonomy versus Control in the Somali Region," *Third World Quarterly*, Vol. 25, No. 6, 2004., pp.1131-1154:1136.

[519] See A. Weber, "Islam and Symbolic Politics in Somalia," in M. Asseburg and D. Brumberg (eds.), *The Challenge of Islamists for EU and US Policies: Conflict, Stability and Reform*, (Berlin: SWP and USIP, 2007), pp.37-43:41; See also UNDP and UNESCO, *An Atlas for Somalis*, UNDP and UNESCO Somalia, First Edition, 2004.

put], meant good trade connections and relative prosperity.[520] It is also clear that Somalia's foreign policy was not shaped by ideology--its rhetorical commitment to *'Scientific Socialism'* should, in theory, have made it an ally of the revolutionary Marxist government in Ethiopia, a scenario that the Soviet Union sought in vain to promote among the two 'fraternal socialist brothers.' Instead, nationalist-inspired irredentism prevailed, even at the cost of Somalia's loss of Soviet patronage, a loss which eventually led to Somalia's devastating defeat in the 1977-1978 *Ogaden* war[521] and paved the way for the emergence of armed opposition groups radical to Barre's military rule.

Though this book focuses on pre-1991 foreign policy and conflict in Somalia, it is impossible not to consider the implications of these findings on the current, prolonged crisis that the country continues to undergo. Despite all the commonalities which bound the Somali people together – a shared national and ethnic identity, language, religion, and pastoralist culture—Somalia has been wrecked by civil war and division for almost three decades. The general findings from this study suggest that, in addition to foreign policy as a driver of conflict, some causes of previous conflicts, including colonial legacy, the legacy of the Cold War politics, regional rivalries and proxy wars and the politics of regime survival and personal rule of authoritarian leaders and warlords and *warlordism* in both Somalia and the region, may also all serve as useful points of departure for assessing the Somali crisis and its regional implications.

The fires of nationalism were constantly fuelled throughout the colonial period, not only by Somali nationalists but also by various colonial powers who, through words and deeds, came to legitimize the concept of 'Greater Somalia.' Colonial Italy's Mussolini, for example, saw *Le Grande Somalo* as the jewel of Italian East Africa, hence justifying Italy's invasion of Ethiopia and the liberation of Somalia.[522] The same applies with Colonial Britain as was clearly seen in the Bevin Agreement which advocated for the formation of a 'Greater Somalia.' Similarly, as the So-

---

[520] Ibid.
[521] See for example I. M. Lewis, *A Pastoral Democracy: A Study of Pastoralism and Politics among the Northern Somali of the Horn of Africa*, (London: James Curry, 1999).
[522] See E. J. Keller, *Revolutionary Ethiopia: From Empire to People's Republic*, (Bloomington: Indiana University Press, 1988). p.156.

mali diplomat-turned-scholar Mohamed Osman argued, Somalis, just like Germans, Vietnamese and Yemenis, have dreams of unification of the territories where their people reside in order to ensure integrated livelihood (pastures) of these people.[523] The current Somali conflict, therefore, presents a complex web of issues, interests and concerns that should inform a refocus of foreign policy priorities and preventive diplomatic measures in the Horn of Africa.[524]

Furthermore, current political developments in Somalia and in the Horn of Africa sub-region provide the best background to understand the complexity of the situation in Somalia and its effects on the region's stability and development. It is also best to explain the relationship between foreign policy and conflict in Somalia; and within the Horn of Africa context. Similarly, the present regional picture, even after almost thirty years of state collapse and complex peace-building and state-building processes in Somalia, is one that forces regional foreign policy and conflict concerns to continue to play themselves out—often violently within Somalia.[525] Such regional tensions have often been essentially replicated by political cleavages inside the country and the tendency of regional—and of late international powers to use local [strategic, but proxy] militias to advance their goals.[526]

While it can be tempting to portray some of these tensions as a 'clash of civilizations' between a highland, Christian Ethiopian leadership, backed by the Christian West, and a lowland Muslim bloc that combines Somalis, Arabs and other ethnic groups, the reality is more complex.[527] Somalia's relationship with the region – mainly Kenya and Ethiopia – is very uneven today, with some areas reviling their neighbours and others, beyond the region, looking to them for support. The same applies to the conduct of various post-1991 Somali governments. The roles of the Ar-

---

[523] See M. O. Omar, *Somalia: Nation Driven to Despair* (New Delhi: Somali Publications Ltd, 1990), p.26.

[524] For more on preventive diplomacy see B. Boutros-Ghali, *An Agenda for Peace*, (New York: United Nations, 1992).

[525] See "Somalia: Countering Terrorism in a Failed State," Nairobi/Brussels, *ICG Africa Report* No. 45, 23 May 2002., p.8.

[526] Ibid.

[527] Ibid; See also more about the Huntingtonian theory in S. P. Huntington, "The Clash of Civilizations?" *Foreign Affairs*, 1993.

ab states are diverse, while those of Djibouti, Uganda, and Eritrea do not fit easily into the African-Arab dispute over Somalia.

Despite the *Shifta* war and the 'Greater Somalia' notion, the *Ogaden* war has been the epicentre of the conflicts in the Horn of Africa during the study period. In this context, the study contends that the conflicts between Ethiopia and Somalia were perpetuated by the contradictory bases of the two countries' statehood. This is because Ethiopia is an ethnically mixed, multi-national state, while Somalia is largely a homogeneous nation-state.[528] The struggle (therefore) to achieve independence for, and potentially union with, the remaining Somali communities, especially those under Ethiopian [and Kenyan] rule, remains an abiding national interest for Somalia.[529]

While "the ineluctable decline of Somalia over the latter half of the 20$^{th}$ century, the failure of UN sanctioned interventions and the unsuccessful attempts at reconstituting a centralized state could have been written in stone,"[530] the foreign policies of the region, particularly those of Somalia, Ethiopia and Kenya, bear their share of the blame for what has happened in Somalia. And in line with this, in the long run, one of the main drivers of conflict in the pre-1990 period—Somali irredentism, may continue to fester as a region-wide source of tensions. Even as Somalia's efforts to gain control of Somali-inhabited zones of Kenya and Ethiopia failed entirely, the basic principle on which the OAU and the rest of the world objected to Somali irredentism is increasingly being eroded. More specifically, the colonially imposed boundaries are no longer sacrosanct, either in theory or practice. In theory, a growing number of policy-makers and academics are questioning whether the redrawing of certain colonial boundaries—either to break up unworkable states into smaller governments, or to absorb nonviable states into larger federal or confederal states—are justifiable.[531]

---

[528] See for example I. M. Lewis, *A Modern History of Somalia: Nation and State in the Horn of Africa* (London and New York: Longman, 1980).

[529] Ibid.

[530] To paraphrase Ahmed Ismael, "Understanding Conflict in Somalia and Somaliland" in A. Adedeji (ed.), *Comprehending and Mastering African Conflicts: The Search for Sustainable Peace & Good Governance* (London & New York: Zed Books, 1999), pp.236-256:251.

[531] See for instance M. Ottaway, J. Herbst, and G. Mills, "Africa's Big States: Toward a New Realism," *Policy Outlook*, Carnegie Endowment, Democracy and Rule of Law

In practice, colonial boundaries in Africa are already being challenged; for example, Eritrea, which earned independence from Ethiopia in 1993, and South Sudan, which in six (6) years' time following the signing of the Comprehensive Peace Agreement (CPA), decided to become an independent state through a referendum. In theory, the Ethiopian constitution in the new ethno-federal system of government allows regional states the right to secede as well. Though in practice this will be strongly resisted and blocked by the federal government, in the long run it may offer a peaceful, constitutional means for Somalis in the *Ogaden* region either to unite with Somalia or form their own state. And although, in that event, the very state boundaries which created so much conflict in the Horn of Africa in the first decades of independence could someday, ironically, be redrawn without a shot fired; it is, therefore, high time for Somalia and its neighbours to work out new ways that can contribute to the making and conduct of peaceful, constructive, and cooperative foreign policies that can and will provide the essential tools for peaceful co-existence, regional stability and development for the countries and the people of the Horn of Africa.

In conclusion, the central theme of this book is that Somali foreign policy, and those of regional states and other key external actors, during the study period, promoted armed conflict in Somalia by accident or design. The study also contends that while Somali foreign policy was a manifestation of its orientation towards a 'Greater Somalia,' other external factors like colonial legacy, Somali nationalism and Cold War politics and rivalry also contributed to the escalation of armed conflict. The study also finds that Somali irredentism had selective impact, producing both warfare and subsequent skirmishes with Ethiopia but relatively stable relations with Kenya and Djibouti.

---

Project (February 2004); See also L. Lawson and D. Rothchild, "Sovereignty Reconsidered," *Current History* (May 2005). Eminent Kenyan scholar Ali Mazrui has also voiced similar positions with regard to the selective redrawing of Africa's borders.

# Bibliography

Abdurahman Abdullahi (Baadiyow), *Making Sense of Somali History* Vol. I, (London: Adonis & Abbey Publishers Ltd (May 12, 2017).

Ali, A. Q., "The Foreign Factor in the Somali Tragedy," in Hussein M. Adam and Richard Ford, *Mending Rips in the Sky; Options for Somali Communities in the 21$^{st}$ Century*, (Asmara: The Red Sea Press, Inc., 1997), pp.534-563:542.

Abbink, J., "Dervishes, Moryaan and Freedom Fighters: Cycles of Rebellion and the Fragmentation of Somali Society 1900-2000," in Abbink, J., et al, (eds.) *Rethinking Resistances: Revolt and Violence in African History* (Brill, Leiden and Boston: TutaSudAegide Pallas, 2003), pp.328-365: 341.

Adam, H. A., et al, *Removing Barricades in Somalia: Options for Peace and Rehabilitation* (Washington United State Institute for Peace, 1998).

Adam, H. M., "Somalia: A Terrible Beauty being Born," in William W. Zartman (ed.) *Collapsed State: The Disintegration of Legitimate Authority* (Boulder and London: Lynne Rienner Publishers, 1994), p.70.

Adam, H. M., "Clan Conflicts and Democratization in Somalia," in Nnoli Okwudiba Nnoli. (ed.), *Government and Politics in Africa: A Reader*, (Harare: AAPS, 2000), p.860.

Adam, H. M., "Somalia: Personal Rule, Military Rule and Militarism," in Eboe Hutchful and Abdoulaye Bathily, *Military and Militarism in Africa* (Dakar: CODESERIA, 1998), p.377.

Adar, K. G., "Kenya-US Relations: A Recapitulation of the Patterns of Paradigmatic Conceptualization, 1960s-1990s," in Macharia, M., et al., (eds.), *The United States and Africa: From Independence to the End of the Cold War* (Nairobi: East African Educational Publishers Ltd., 1995), pp.89-104:98.

Adar, K. G., *Kenya's Foreign Policy Behaviour towards Somalia, 1963 – 1983* (Lanham, New York and London: University Press of America, 1994).

Adloff, R., and Thompson, V., *Djibouti and the Horn of Africa* (California: Stanford University press, 1968).

Africa Watch, *Somalia: A Government at War with its Own People* (New York: Africa Watch, 1990).

Ahmed, A. J., *Daybreak is Near: Literature, Clans and the Nation-State in Somalia* (Lawrenceville, NJ: The Red Sea Press, Inc., 1996).

Allison, G., *Essence of Decision: Explaining the Cuban Missile Crisis* (New York: HarperCollins, 1971).

Annan, K., "The Causes of Conflict and the Promotion of Durable Peace and Sustainable Development in Africa," Secretary General's Report to the UN Security Council, 16 April 1998.

Art, R. J., "America's Foreign Policy," in Roy C. Macridis, *Foreign Policy in World Politics* 6th Edition (New Jersey: Prentice Hall Inc, 1985), p.11.

Article III (3) of the OAU Charter.

Ayyitey, G. B. N., "The Somalia Crisis: Time for an African Solution," *Policy Analysis* No. 205, March 28, 1994, p.3-4.

Bezboruah, M., *US Strategy in the Indian Ocean: The International Response* (New York: Praeger Publishers, 1977).

Biennen, H. S., "The Role of the Military in Foreign Policy," in William J. Foltz and Henry H. Biennen (eds.), *Arms and Africa* (New haven and London: Yale University Press, 1985), p.157.

Botan, A. A., "Somalia; Regional State or Cantonization of Clans," in Hussein M. Adam and Richard Ford, *Mending Rips in the sky: Options for Somali Communities in the 21st Century*, (Asmara: The Red Sea Press, Inc., 1997), pp.255-270:254.

Brewer, T. L., *American Foreign Policy: A Contemporary Introduction* 3rd Ed (New Jersey: Prentice Hall, 1980).

Brown, C., *Understanding International Relations* (London: Macmillan Press Ltd, 1997).

Brown, M. E., "The Causes and Regional Dimensions of Internal Conflict," in Michael E. Brown, (ed.), *The International Dimensions of Internal Conflicts* (Cambridge and Massachusetts: MIT Press, 1996), pp.1-31; and pp.571-601.

Bouros-Ghali, B., *An Agenda for Peace*, (New York: United Nations, 1992).

Buerden, J. V., "Somalia in a State of Permanent Conflict" in Mekenkamp, M. et al, *Searching Peace in Africa: An Overview of Conflict Prevention and Management Activities* (Utrecht: European Platform for Conflict Prevention, 1999), p.157.

Cassanelli, L. V., *The Shaping of Somali Society* (Philadelphia: University of Philadelphia Press, 1982).

Clapham, C., "The Horn of Africa: A Conflict Zone," in Oliver Furley, (ed.), *Conflict in Africa*, (New York: Taurius Academic Studies, 1995), pp.72-91:78.

Compagnon, D., "Somalia Armed Movements," in Christopher Clapham, *African Guerillas* (Kampala: Fountain Publishers, 1998), p.75.

Copson, R. W., *African Wars and Prospects for Peace* (New York and London: ME Sharpe, Inc., 1994).

Cornell, R., *Somalia: fourteenth time lucky?* Institute for Security Studies, Occasional Paper No. 87, April 2004, p.2.

Couloumbis, T. A., and Wolf, J. H., *Introduction to International Relations: Powerand Justice* 4th Edition (Englewood Cliffs.: Prentice Hall, 1988).

Cox, M., "From the Cold War to the War on Terror," in John Baylis and Steve Smith, *The Globalization of World Politics: An Introduction to International Relations* 3rd Edition (Oxford: Oxford University Press, 2005), p.133.

Dessouki, A. E. H., and Korany, B., "A Literature Survey and a Framework for Analysis," in BahgatKorany and Ali E. H Dessouki, *The Foreign Policies of Arab States* (Boulder and London: Westview Press, 1984), pp.5-18:14.

Dos Santos, T., "The Structure of Dependence," in K. T. Fann and D. C. Hodges, (eds.), *Readings in U.S. Imperialism* (Boston: Porter Sargent, 1971), pp. 225-236:226.

Drysdale, J., *Stoics Without Pillows: A Way Forward for the Somaliland* (London: HAAN Associates Publishing, 2000).

Drysdale, J., *The Djibouti Dispute* (London and Dunmow: Pallmall Press, 1994).

Drysdale, J., *The Somalia Dispute* (New York: Praeger Publishers, 1964).

Dualeh, H. A., *Search for a New Somali Identity* (Nairobi, 2002).

East African Standard, "Somalia to Ignore OAU Frontiers," Nairobi, October 1964.

Elie Podeh and Onn Winckler (Eds.) 2004. *Rethinking Nasserism: Revolution and Historical Memory in Modern Egypt*, (Tampa: University Press of Florida).

Eno, M. A. *The Bantu-Jareer Somalis: Unearthing Apartheid in the Horn of Africa*. (London: Adonis & Abbey, 2008).

Ethiopia, "Ethiopia's Foreign Policy Towards Somalia," *Foreign Affairs and National Security Policy and Strategy*, the Federal Democratic Republic of Ethiopia, Addis Ababa at http://www.mfa.gov.et.

Farah, A. Y., "Somalia: Modern History and the End of 1990s" in WSP International, *Rebuilding Somalia: Issues and Possibilities for Puntland* (London: HAAN Associates, 2001), pp.6-29:7.

Farrell, R. B., (ed.), *Approaches to Comparative and International Politics* (Evanston: North Western University Press, 1966).

Fearon, J. D., "Domestic Policies, Foreign Policy, and The Theories of International Relations," *Annual Review of Political Science*, 1998, pp.289-313:302.

Foltz, W. J., "Africa in Great Power Strategy," in William J. Foltz and Henry H. Biennen (eds.) *Arms and Africa* (New haven and London: Yale University Press, 1985).

France, *Framework Partnership Document: France - Djibouti (2006-2010)*.

Gassim, Mariam Arif. *Somalia: Clan vs. Nation*. Printed in U.A.E. (2002).

Geshekter, C., "The Death of Somalia in Historical Perspective," in Hussein M. Adam and Richard Ford, (eds.), in *Mending the Rips in the Sky: Options for Somali Communities in the 21$^{st}$ Century*, (Asmara: The Red Sea Press, Inc., 1997), pp.65-98:74.

Ghalib, J. M., *The Cost of Dictatorship: The Somali Experience* (New York: Lilian Barber Press Inc, 1995).

Goldgeier, J. N., *Leadership Style and Soviet Foreign Policy: Stalin, Khrushchev, Gorbachev*, (Baltimore, John Hopkins University Press, 1994).

Goldstein, J. S., *International Relations*, 4$^{th}$ Ed., (New York: Priscilla McGeehan, 2001).

Gordon, D. L., "African Politics," in April A. Gordon and Donald L. Gordon, (eds.), *Understanding Contemporary Africa* 3$^{rd}$ Ed., (Boulder: Lynne Rienner Publishers, 2001), p.55-99:58.

Hashi, N. A., *Weapons and Clan Politics in Somalia* (Mogadishu: Horn of Africa Printing Press, 1999).

Heally, S., "The Changing Idiom of Self Determination in the Horn of Africa," in Lewis, I. M., (ed.) *Nationalism and Self Determination in the Horn of Africa*, (London; Ithaca Press,1983) pp.93-109.

Henze, P., *The Horn of Africa: From War to Peace*, (London: McMillan, 1991).

Hershberg, J. G., "Anatomy of Third World Crisis: New East Bloc Evidence on the Horn of Africa 1977-1978," *Cold War International History Project*, CWIHP Bulletin 8/9, Winter 1996.

Hershberg, J. G., "U.S.-Soviet Relations and the Turn toward Confrontation, 1977-1980: New Russian & East German Documents," *Cold War International History Project*, Bulletin 8/9, Winter 1996.

Hillal, A. E. and Korany, B., "A Literature Survey and a Framework for Analysis," in Korany, B. and Dessouki, A. (eds.), *The Foreign Policies of Arab States* (London: Westview Press, 1984), pp.5-18:5.

Hoskyns, C. (1969). *Case Studies in African Diplomacy 2: Ethiopia-Somalia-Kenya Dispute 1960-67.* Dar Es Salam: Oxford University Press.

Huntington, S. P., "The Clash of Civilizations?" *Foreign Affairs, 1993.*

Hussein, S., "Somalia: A Destroyed Country and a Defeated Nation," in Hussein M Adam and Richard Ford, (eds.) *Mending Rips in the Sky: Options for Somali Communities in the 21$^{st}$ Century* (Asmara: The Red Sea Press, inc, 1997), pp.165-192:170.

ICG, "Somalia: Countering Terrorism in a Failed State," Nairobi/Brussels, *ICG Africa Report* No. 45, 23 May 2002., p.8.

IRIN Reports, *Somalia: A Chronology of Events Leading to the Interim Government* (Nairobi: IRIN, 6 January 2005).

Ismael, A., "Understanding Conflict in Somalia and Somaliland," in A. Adedeji (ed.), *Comprehending and Mastering African Conflicts: The Search for Sustainable Peace & Good Governance* (London & New York: Zed Books, 1999), pp.236-256:251.

Jackson, R., and Sorensen, G., *Introduction to International Relations: Theories and Approaches* (Oxford: Oxford University Press, 2007), pp.222-224.

Jalata, A., *Oromia and Ethiopia: State Formation and Ethnonational Conflict, 1868-1992* (Boulder and London: Lynne Rienner Publishers, 1993).

Jalata, A., *Fighting Against the Injustice of the State and Globalization: Comparing the Africa America and Oromo Movements* (New York: Palgrave, 2001).

Jama, A. A., *Basis of the Conflict in the Horn of Africa,* (Mogadishu: NPA, 1978).

Jama, M. A., "The Destruction of the Somali State: Causes, Costs and Lessons," in Hussein M. Adam and Richard Ford (ed.), *Mending Rips in the Sky: Options for Somali Communities in the 21$^{st}$ Century,* (Asmara: Red Sea Press, 1997), pp.237-254.

Janis, I. L., *Victims of Groupthink: A Psychological Study of Foreign-Policy Decisions and Fiascos,* (Boston: Houghton Mifflin, 1972).

Jervis, R., *Perception and Misperception in International Politics,* (Princeton: Princeton University Press, 1976).

K. Menkhaus, (1989). Rural Transformation and the roots of Underdevelopment in Somalia's lower Jubba Valley. PhD Dissertation, University of South Carolina, Columbia.

Katambo, W. *Coup d etats: Revolutions and Power Struggles in Post Independence Africa* (Nairobi: Afriscript Publishers, 1985).

Kenya Statistics Division, *Kenya Population Census,* 1962.

Keller, E. J., *Revolutionary Ethiopia: From Empire to People's Republic,* (Bloomington: Indiana University Press, 1988).

Kinfe, A., *Somalia Calling: The Crisis of Statehood and the Quest for Peace*, (Addis Ababa: EIIPD, 2002).

Korany, B., and Dessouki, A. E. H. "The Global System and Arab Foreign Policies: The Primacy of Constraints," in BahgatKorany and Ali E. H Dessouki, *The Foreign Policies of Arab States*, 1984. pp.19-41:23.

Korany, B. and Dessouki, A. E. H., *The Foreign Policies of Arab States*, (Boulder & London: Westview Press, 1984).

Korany, B., "Foreign Policy Models and their Empirical Relevance to Third World Actors: A Critique and Alternative, "in *International Science Journal* No. 26, 1974, pp.70-94.

Kurgat, P. K., "Kenya's Foreign Policy and African Conflict Management," in Godfrey P. Okoth and Bethwell A. Ogot (eds.) *Conflict in Contemporary Africa* (Nairobi: Jomo Kenyatta Foundation, 2000), Pp.117-126:118.

Kusow, A. M. (ed,). *Putting the Cart before the Horse: Contested Nationalism and the Crisis of the Nation-State in Somalia*. (Lawrwnceville, NJ: The Res Sea Press, 2004).

Laakso, L., and Olukoshi, A. O., "The Crisis of the Post Colonial Nation State in Africa," in Adebayo O. Olukoshi and LiisaLaakso, *Challenges to the Nation State in Africa* (Uppsala: Nordiska Africa Institute, 1996), p.99.

Lata, L., "Extra Regional Inputs in Promoting Regional Security in the Horn of Africa," *AMANI afrika, The Journal of Africa Peace Forum*, Vol. 1, Issue 2, pp.7-33:15.

Laitin, David D., and Said S. Samatar, *Somalia: Nation in Search of a State*, (Boulder, Colorado: Westview Press, 1987).

Lawson, L., and Rothchild, D., "Sovereignty Reconsidered," *Current History* (May 2005).

Lederach, J. P., *Building Peace: Sustainable Reconciliation in Divided Societies* (Washington D.C.: USIP, 1997).

Lefevre, J., *Arms for the Horn* (Philadelphia: University of Pennsylvania Press, 1986).

Legg, K. R., and Morrisson, J. F., "The Formulation of Foreign Policy Objectives," in Richard Little, and Michael Smith, *Perspectives in World Politics* (eds.) 2nd Edition (London and New York: Routledge, 1991), p.62.

Legum, C., and Lee, B., *Conflict in the Horn of Africa* (London: Rex Collings, 1977).

Lewis, I. M., *A Modern History of Somalia: Nation and State in the Horn of Africa* (London and New York: Longman, 1980).

Lewis, I. M., *A Modern History of the Somali: Nation and State in the Horn of Africa* 4th Ed. (Hargeisa: Btec Books, 2002).

Lewis, I. M., *A Pastoral Democracy*, (London: Oxford University Press, 1961).

Lewis, I. M., *A Pastoral Democracy: A Study of Pastoralism and Politics among the Northern Somali of the Horn of Africa*, (London: James Curry, 1999).

Lewis, I., *Modern History of Somalia* (London: Zed, 1988).

Lewis, I. M. "Modern Political Movements in Somaliland: Part 1," Africa London, 28(3), July 1958, p.255.

Lewis, "The Dynamics of Nomadism: Prospects for Sedentarization and Social Change," in Theodore Monot (ed.), *Pastoralism in Tropical Africa* (London: 1975).

Lyob, R., and Keller, E. J., "US Policy in the Horn," in Dorina A. Bekoe, *Grappling with a Difficult Legacy in East Africa and the Horn: Confronting Challenges to Good Governance* (Boulder and London: Lynne Rienner Publishers, 2006), pp.101-125:101.

Makinda, S. M. *Superpower Diplomacy in the Horn of Africa* (London & Sydney: Croom Helm, 1987).

Marchal, R., "A Few Provocative Remarks on Governance in Somalia," Nairobi, UNDOS Discussion paper, November 1997.

Mazrui, A., "Crisis in Somalia: From Tyranny to Anarchy," in Hussein M. Adam and Richard Ford (eds.), *Mending Rips in the Sky: Option for Somali Communities in the 21st Century* (Asmara: The Red Sea Press, 1997), pp.5-11:8.

Menkhaus, K., and Creed, J., "The Rise of Saudi Regional Power and the Foreign Policies of Northeast African States," *Northeast African Studies*, vol. 8, nos. 2-3 (1987), pp. 1-22.

Menkhaus, K., and Kegley, C. W., Jr, "The Compliant Foreign Policy of the Dependent State Revisited: Empirical Linkages and Lessons from the Case of Somalia."*Comparative Political Studies*, vol. 21, no. 3 (October 1988), pp.315-46.

Menkhaus, K., "Somali: Civil War, Intervention and Withdrawal 1990-1995," in Writenet Country Papers, UNHCR Writenet project, 1995.

Menkhaus, K., "US Foreign Assistance to Somalia: Phoenix from the Ashes?" *Middle East Policy* vol. 5, no. 1 (January 1997), pp. 124-149.

Metz, A., (ed.), *Somalia: A Country Study* (Washington: Library of Congress, 1992

Modelski, G., *A Theory of Foreign Policy* (London: Pall Mall, 1962).

Morgenthau, H., *Politics Among Nations: Struggle for Power and Peace*, (New York: Knopf, 1973).

Mousa, S. M., *RecolonizationBeyond Somalia* (Mogadishu: Somali Printing Agency, 1998).

Mwagiru, M., *The Greater Horn of Africa Conflict System: Conflict Patterns, Strategies and Management Practices* (Paper prepared for the USAID project on Conflict and Conflict Management in the Greater Horn of Africa, April 1997, Revised September 1997).

Mwagiru, M., *Conflict: Theory, Processes and Institutions of Management* (Nairobi: Watermark Publishers, 2000).

Mwagiru, M., "The Elusive Quest: Conflict, Diplomacy and Foreign Policy in Kenya," in Godfrey P. Okoth and Bethwell A. Ogot, *Conflict in Contemporary Africa* (Nairobi: Jomo Kenyatta Foundation, 2000), pp.117-140.

Mwamba, Z., *Tanzania: Foreign Policy and International Politics* (Washington: University Press of America, 1978).

Mukhtar, M. H., *Historical Dictionary of Somalia: African Historical Dictionary Series*, No. 87 (Maryland Oxford: Scarecrow Press, 2003).

*New York Times*, June 17, 1961 quoted in S. Touval, *Somali Nationalism: International Politics and the Drive for Unity in the Horn of Africa*, (Cambridge, Massachusetts: Harvard University Press, 1963), p.176.

Nicholson, M., *Rationality and analysis of International Conflict*, (New York: Cambridge University Press, 1992).

Noble, P. C., "The Arab System Opportunities Constraints and Pressures," in Bahgat Korany, *The Foreign Policies of Arab States* (Boulder and London: West View Press, 1984), pp.41-78:41.

Nyinguro, P. O., "The Impact of the Cold War in Regional Security: The Case of Africa," in Munene et al., (eds.) *The United States and Africa: From Independence to the End of the Cold War*, (Nairobi: East African Educational Publishers, 1995), pp.65-83:66.

OAU, Resolutions and Recommendations of the Second Extra Ordinary Session of the Council of Ministers, Organization of African Unity, Dar e Salaam, 12-15 February 1964, OAU Mimeographed Texts, February 1964, OAU Doc Ecm/Res3(11).

Ofuho, C. H., "Security Concerns in the Horn of Africa," in MakumiMwagiru, (ed.), *African Regional Security in the Age of Globalisation* (Nairobi: HBF, 2004), pp.7-17:11.

Okoth, G. P. and Ogot, B. A. *Conflict in Cotemporary Africa*, (Nairobi: Jomo Kenyatta Foundation 2002).

Omar, M. O., *Somalia: Nation Driven to Despair* (New Delhi: Somali Publications Ltd, 1990).

Orwa, D. K., "Causes of Conflict in the Relations of African States," in O. Ojo, et al., *African International Relations*, (London: Longman, 1985), pp.129-141:135.

Ottaway, D., and Ottaway, M., *Ethiopia: Empire in Revolution* (New York and London: African Publishing Company, 1978).

Ottaway, M., Herbst, J., and Mills, G., "Africa's Big States: Toward a New Realism," *Policy Outlook*, (Carnegie Endowment, Democracy and Rule of Law Project: February 2004).

Ottaway, M., *Soviet and American Influence in the Horn of Africa* (New York: Praeger, 1982).

Patman, R. G., *The Soviet Union in the Horn of Africa*, (Cambridge: Cambridge University Press, 1990), pp.573-579.

Prankhurst, S. E., *Ex-Italian Somaliland* (New York: Philosophical Library, 1951), pp.218-260.

Rawson, D., *Somalia and Foreign Aid* (Washington: Foreign Service Institute, 1994).

Reynolds P. A, *An Introduction to International Relations* 3rd Edition (London and New York: Longman, 1993).

Robbins, M., "The Soviet-Cuban Relationship," in Kanet, R. R., (ed.) *Soviet Foreign Policy in the 1980s* (New York: Praegar, 1982 ), p.161.

Rosenau, J., "Pre-Theories and Theories of Foreign Policy," in Farrell, I. B., (ed.), *Approaches to Comparative and International Politics* (Evanston, Ill: Northwestern University Press, 1966), pp.27-93.

Rosenau, J., *The Scientific Study of Foreign Policy*, 2nd Ed., (London: Frances Printer, 1980).

Rothgeb, J. M., *Defining Power: Influence and Force in the Contemporary International System*, (New York, St. Martin's Press, 1992).

Rothstein, R. L., *The Weak in the World of the Strong: The Developing Countries in the International System* (New York: Columbia University Press, 1977).

Rourke, T. J., *International Politics on the World Stage*, (Englewood, Cliffs, NJ.:Prentice Hall, 1996).

Roy, C. M., *Foreign Policy in World Politics* 6th Ed., (New Jersey: Prentice-Hall, 1976).

Russet, B., and Starr, H., *World Politics: The Menu for Choice* (New York: W. H. Freeman and Company, 1989).

Samatar, A. I., *AFRICA's First Democrats: Somalia's Aden A. Osman and Abdirazak H. Hussen*, (Bloomington, Indiana: Indiana University Press, 2016).

Samatar, A. I., *Socialist Somalia: Rhetoric and Reality*, (London: Zed Books, 1986).

Samatar, A. I., "Under Siege: Blood, Power and the Somali State," in P. Anyang Nyong'o *Arms and Daggers in the Heart of Africa: Studies on Internal Conflicts* (Nairobi: African Academy of Sciences, 1993), pp.67-100: 85.

Scott, T. W., The Third World and the Conflict of Ideologies in Thomson W.

Scott, (ed) The Third World Premises of US Policy (San Francisco: ICS, 1978), p.13.

Shafat, A. "The Challenges the Youth of Northeastern Kenya Face: A Historical Analysis," *Journal of Somali Studies*, Vol. 1, No. 1, (2014), pp. 63-90.

Simons, A., "Somalia: A Regional Security Dilemma," in Edmond Keller J. and Donald Rothchild, (eds.), *Africa in the New International Order: Rethinking State Soereignty and Regional Security*, (Boulder: Lynne Rienner Publishers, 1996), pp.71-84.

Singer, M. R., "The Foreign Policies of Small Developing States," in James N. Rosenau, et al (eds.) *World Politics: An Introduction* (New York: The Free Press, 1972), p.289.

Singer, J. David, and Melvin Small, *Resort to Arms* (Beverly Hills, CA: Sage Publications, 1982).

Somalia, Ministry of Foreign Affairs, *Salient Aspects of Somalia's Foreign Policy: Selected Speeches of Dr. Abdurrahman JamaBarre, Minister of Foreign Affairs – Somali Democratic Republic, in 1978*, (Mogadishu: November 1978).

Somalia, *Somalia: Somalia's Arab, African and International Role* (Mogadishu: State Print Agency, 1980).

Spiegel, S. L., *World Politics in a New Era* (Los Angeles: Harcourt Brace College Publishers, 1994).

Touval, S., *Somali Nationalism: International Politics and the Drive for Unity in the Horn of Africa* (Cambridge, Massachusetts: Harvard University Press, 1963).

Touval, S., *The Boundary Politics of Independent Africa*, (Cambridge, Harvard University Press,1972).

UNDP and UNESCO, *An Atlas for Somalis*, UNDP and UNESCO Somalia, Fist Edition, 2004.

USAID, *Conducting a Conflict Assessment: A Framework for Strategy and Program Development* (Nairobi: April 2005).

US Department of the Army, December 1993, *Analysis of Somalia*, December 1993.

US Department of State, *Background Notes: Somalia*, (Washington, D.C.: Office of East African Affairs, Bureau of African Affairs, July 1998).

United Nations, 1237th Plenary Meeting, Eighteenth Session, *General Debates*, United Nations General Assembly, UN Doc APV.1237, 1963, p.6.

US Department of State, "Somalia: Background Note," *Bureau of African Affairs*, March 2006.

Utete, C. M. B., "Foreign Policy and the Developing State," inOlatunde, O., et al., *African International Relations* (Lagos: Longman Group, 1985), pp.43-51:43.

Ware, G., *Somalia: From Trust Territory to Nation, 1950-1960*, Vol. 26, No. 2 (2nd Qtr., 1965), pp. 173-185.

Weber, A., "Islam and Symbolic Politics in Somalia," in Muriel Asseburg and Daniel Brumberg 9eds.), *The Challenge of Islamists for EU and US Policies: Conflict, Stability and Reform*, (Berlin: SWP and USIP, 2007), pp.37-43:41

Weinstein F., *Indonesian Foreign Policy and the Dilemma of Dependence*, (Ithaca: Cornell University Press, 1976).

Welch, D. A., 'The Organisational Process and Bureaucratic Politics Paradigms: Retrospect and Prospect' in *International Security* 17 (2), 1992, pp.112-146.

Wolfgang, A., "The Italian Connection: How Rome Helped Ruin Somalia," *The Washington Post*, January 24, 1993, p.1.

World Bank, *Somalia Conflict Analysis: Synthesis Report*, (Nairobi: World Bank, 2004).

World Bank, *World Development Report*, (Washington: World Bank, 1991).

Woodward, P., *The Horn of Africa: State Politics and International Relations* (London and New York: Tauris Academic Publishers, 1996).

WSP International Somali Programme, *Rebuilding Somaliland: Issues and Possibilities*, (Asmara: Red Sea Press, 2005).

Wubneh, M., and Abate, Y., *Ethiopia: Transition and Development in the Horn* of Africa, (Colorado: Westview Press, 1988).

Yoh, J. G. N., "Peace Processes and Conflict Resolution in the Horn of Africa," *African Security Review,* 12 (3) 2003.

Zartman, I. W., *Ripe for Resolution: Conflict and Intervention in Africa,* (New York: Oxford University Press, 1989).

Zartman, W. I., and Kluge, A. G., "Heroic Politics: The Foreign Policy of Libya," in Korany, B. and Dessouki, A. E. H., *The Foreign Policies of Arab States,* (Boulder & London: Westview Press, 1984), pp.175-196.

Zewde, B., *A History of Modern Ethiopia 1855–1974* (Addis Ababa: Addis Ababa University Press, 1991).

## List of Interviewees:

Abdirahman Moallim Abdullahi, former colonel, Somali Army
Abdulkadir Yahya, former Co-Director & Founder, Centre for Research & Dialogue (CRD)
Amb. Abdullahi Ahmed Addou, Somali former Ambassador to the US
Amb. Bethwell Kiplagat, former Kenya Special Envoy to the Somali Peace Process
Amb. Hussein Ali Dualeh, former Somali Ambassador to Kenya and Uganda
Amb. Ismail Goulal, former Djibouti Special Envoy to the Somali Peace Process
Amb. Mohammed Abdi Affey, former Kenya Ambassador to Somalia
Amb. Mohammed Siyad Duale, former Djibouti Ambassador to the Somali Peace Process
Amb. Yusuf Hassan Ibrahim (Dheg), former Somali Foreign Minister
Aw Jama Omar Isse, Somali Historian
Deqow Sanbul, former NFDLF Leader
Mohammed Haji, former Assistant Minister, Somalia
Matt Bryden, ICG Analyst
Sheikh Ismail Moallim Hamud, Islamic Scholar
Malaaq Mukhtaar, Traditional Elder

# Index

## A

Abtidon, Hassan Guled, 63, 159
Addis Ababa, 61, 81, 89, 95, 125, 126, 127, 135, 156, 172, 174, 178, 189, 197, 206
Afar, 63, 168
African Union, 23, 28
Allison, Graham, xii, 34, 38, 48, 49, 50, 196
AMISOM, 28
Andom, Aman, 135
Angola, xv
Arab League, 41, 42, 65, 67, 138, 144, 145, 152, 153, 154, 155, 156, 183, 190
Arab nationalism, 62, 64, 86, 129
Arabian Peninsula, 99, 111, 140, 161

## B

Bab-Al-Mandab, 100
Barre, Siyad, xv, xvi, 26, 37, 41, 42, 43, 44, 46, 47, 55, 59, 65, 67, 74, 93, 94, 95, 96, 97, 126, 131, 132, 133, 135, 136, 137, 138, 139, 140, 142, 143, 144, 145, 146, 149, 150, 152, 153, 154, 155, 156, 158, 159, 160, 163, 164, 167, 177, 178, 180, 191
Bi-polar system, 52
Benadir Regional Administration, 28
Bevin Agreement, 191
British Consul-General, 82
British East India Company, 81
British Somali colonies, 25
British Somaliland, 25, 69, 71, 84, 116, 171

## C

Carter, Jimmy, 56, 93, 149, 150
Cassanelli, Lee, 47, 169, 196
Clannism, 137, 146
China, 54, 68, 108, 112, 165
Christian West, 192
Clash of Civilizations, 65, 192, 199
Cold War, xi, xii, xiii, xiv, 26, 30, 33, 36, 38, 40, 41, 42, 43, 44, 46, 53, 54, 55, 67, 72, 73, 90, 91, 92, 93, 103, 107, 108, 109, 115, 117, 138, 141, 142, 148, 150, 151, 160, 161, 162, 163, 164, 165, 175, 181, 182, 184, 185, 190, 191, 194, 195, 197, 198, 202
Cold War politics, xi, xii, 40, 43, 161, 163, 191, 194
Comprehensive Peace Agreement, 194
Council of Ministers, 128, 137, 143, 203
Council of the Secretaries of State, 137

## D

Department for International Development, 29
*Dervish* rebellion, 82, 107, 168
*Diya* system, 79
Djibouti, xiii, 25, 28, 30, 35, 38, 39, 40, 41, 57, 58, 59, 62, 63, 64, 65, 68, 72, 73, 74, 84, 87, 101, 102, 106, 122, 126, 133, 139, 140, 156, 159, 161, 162, 166, 168, 169, 170, 172, 182, 187, 188, 193, 194, 195, 197, 198, 206

201

## E

East Africa, 30, 69, 82, 117, 118, 135, 141, 165, 191, 201
East African Community, 23, 64, 126
Eastern Europe, 53, 63, 147
Egal, Mohammed Ibrahim, 64, 103, 113, 117, 124, 125, 126, 128, 131, 166, 188
Egypt, 42, 57, 68, 89, 91, 92, 112, 129, 166, 197
Ethiopia, xiii, xvi, 25, 26, 27, 28, 29, 35, 39, 40, 41, 42, 43, 44, 45, 46, 55, 56, 57, 58, 59, 60, 61, 62, 63, 64, 65, 68, 71, 73, 74, 75, 81, 83, 84, 85, 86, 87, 89, 91, 92, 93, 94, 95, 96, 97, 98, 101, 102, 105, 107, 108, 109, 110, 114, 115, 116, 118, 119, 121, 122, 124, 125, 126, 128, 129, 131, 133, 135, 136, 137, 139, 140, 141, 142, 146, 149, 150, 151, 156, 157, 158, 159, 162, 163, 165, 168, 170, 171, 172, 173, 175, 176, 177, 180, 181, 184, 185, 187, 188, 189, 190, 191, 192, 193, 194, 197, 199, 200, 203, 206
European scramble for Africa, 68, 72

## F

France, 39, 40, 58, 63, 66, 68, 81, 100, 146, 170, 187, 198
French Somaliland, 25, 83, 84, 101, 105

## G

Ghalib, Omar Arte, 56, 62, 64, 65, 125, 127, 132, 140, 144, 146, 156, 157, 158, 175, 182, 198
Gowon, Yakubu, 155
Greater Somalia policy, 25
Groupthink, 38, 199
Gulf, 28, 41, 43, 81, 92, 99, 111, 138, 150, 153, 155, 161
Gulf of Aden, 28, 81, 111, 161
Gulf States, 41

## H

Horn of Africa, vii, xi, xii, xiii, xiv, xv, xvi, 27, 28, 29, 30, 38, 39, 40, 41, 43, 44, 45, 46, 47, 48, 55, 56, 57, 61, 62, 63, 64, 65, 66, 67, 68, 69, 70, 72, 73, 74, 78, 80, 82, 83, 84, 85, 86, 87, 88, 89, 90, 91, 92, 93, 94, 97, 98, 99, 100, 101, 102, 106, 107, 108, 109, 110, 111, 113, 114, 115, 116, 117, 118, 119, 120, 121, 122, 123, 126, 127, 129, 133, 135, 139, 140, 141, 142, 144, 146, 148, 149, 150, 153, 154, 156, 157, 158, 159, 161, 162, 163, 164, 165, 168, 170, 171, 172, 173, 174, 175, 176, 179, 181, 183, 184, 187, 188, 189, 190, 191, 192, 193, 194, 195, 196, 197, 198, 199, 201, 202, 203, 205, 206

## I

Indian Ocean, 28, 55, 63, 90, 92, 138, 147, 196
Inter-Governmental Authority on Development, 23, 29
Italian Somaliland, 25, 69, 71, 156, 170, 171, 203
Italy, 68, 69, 71, 81, 85, 95, 100, 108, 114, 115, 116, 134, 145, 152, 165, 171, 191

## K

Kenya African National Union, 23, 60
Kenyatta, Jomo, 43, 60, 88, 89, 109, 113, 123, 167, 200, 202, 203
Kiamba, Anita, xv
Kuwait, 154

## L

Lancaster House, 123
League of Nations, 61

## M

Marxism-Leninism, 47, 154

Mazrui, Ali, 82, 149, 201
Mengistu, Haile Mariam, 46, 62, 74, 93, 97, 149, 159, 160, 189
Middle East, 41, 42, 91, 146, 150, 151
Mogadishu, 26, 28, 39, 55, 68, 70, 83, 88, 100, 115, 121, 122, 123, 125, 126, 133, 135, 136, 143, 147, 148, 151, 152, 153, 156, 158, 161, 169, 170, 182, 198, 199, 202, 204, 205
Moroccan Sahara, 58
Mozambique, xv
Muslim radicalism, 62
Mwagiru, Makumi, ix, xvii, 44, 56, 57, 60, 202

## N

National Security Service, 23, 147
Ngala, Ronald, 88, 123
Nile waters, 42
Nixon, Richard, 54
Northern Frontier District, 23, 25, 39, 58, 60, 68, 88, 101, 102, 162

## O

*Ogaden*, 25, 27, 28, 29, 39, 40, 41, 42, 43, 47, 55, 59, 60, 61, 62, 63, 64, 71, 72, 73, 75, 83, 84, 85, 89, 92, 93, 94, 95, 96, 98, 101, 105, 108, 115, 116, 124, 125, 133, 135, 136, 138, 140, 145, 149, 150, 151, 157, 158, 159, 161, 162, 163, 164, 168, 169, 171, 173, 175, 179, 180, 182, 183, 185, 187, 188, 190, 191, 193, 194
OPEC, 41, 155
Organisation of African Unity, 23, 39
Organization of Islamic Cooperation, 183
Oromo, 61, 62, 168, 199
Osman, Adan Abdulle, 26, 41, 72, 103, 111, 124, 125, 128, 192, 204

## P

Persia, 68
*Pan-Arabism*, 110, 112, 129, 164, 165, 166, 190
Port of Berbera, 147, 150
Puntland, 28, 72, 103, 104, 105, 113, 144, 163, 197

## Q

Qatar, 154

## R

Rapid Deployment Force, 23, 150
Ras Kiamboni, 100
Realism, 32, 193, 203
Red Sea, 26, 55, 71, 78, 79, 80, 81, 82, 89, 99, 100, 104, 111, 114, 118, 137, 138, 140, 147, 148, 149, 151, 152, 153, 155, 161, 172, 173, 178, 179, 195, 196, 198, 199, 201, 206
Republic of Somaliland, 25, 27
Rome, 66, 95, 123, 152, 205
Rosenau, James, 34, 35, 112, 203, 204

## S

Sandhurst, 104
Saudi Arabia, 41, 42, 92, 154, 158, 190
Security Council, 58, 94, 117, 170, 196
Selassie, Haile, 45, 61, 67, 93, 109, 119, 125, 149, 156
*Sharia* law, 26, 79
Sharmarke, Abdirashid Ali, 41, 55
*Shifta* wars, 25
Somali Democratic Movement, 23, 96
Somali National League, 23, 69, 70
Somali National Movement, 23, 26, 27, 95
Somali nationalism, xi, xii, 59, 70, 71, 83, 84, 87, 94, 98, 106, 120, 135, 138, 156, 161, 162, 167, 168, 169, 171, 175, 176, 184, 194

Somali Salvation Democratic Front (SSDF), 26, 94
Somali unification, 69, 126
Somali Youth League, 24, 70, 84, 106, 164
Soviet Union, 42, 53, 54, 55, 63, 91, 93, 100, 103, 108, 110, 112, 120, 121, 129, 133, 134, 138, 141, 146, 147, 148, 149, 150, 162, 163, 165, 170, 174, 181, 184, 188, 190, 191, 203
Standard Operating Procedures, 48
Sudan, xvi, 29, 43, 57, 58, 62, 82, 89, 128, 141, 155, 194
Supreme Revolutionary Council, 131, 136, 167
Swedish International Development Agency, 29

## T

Traore, Karim, v

## U

UN General Assembly, 71, 115, 123, 169
United States, xi, 24, 48, 53, 92, 103, 109, 117, 163, 165, 195, 202
University of Nairobi, ix, xv
US Agency for International Development, 24, 29
USSR, xiv, 24, 27, 40, 42, 46, 52, 53, 55, 67, 92, 115, 141

## V

Vance, Cyrus, 149

## W

Western Somalia Liberation Group, 125
Westphalian state system, 31
World Bank, 27, 29, 45, 206
World War II, 52, 53, 70, 71, 87, 90, 118
Warlordism, 29, 191

## Z

Zionist imperialism, 146

www.ingramcontent.com/pod-product-compliance
Lightning Source LLC
Chambersburg PA
CBHW011957090526
44590CB00023B/3763